FILM FESTIVAL YEARBOOK 1:
The Festival Circuit

Edited by

Dina Iordanova
with Ragan Rhyne

St Andrews Film Studies
St Andrews

First published in Great Britain in 2009 by
St Andrews Film Studies in collaboration with College Gate Press
99 North Street, St Andrews, KY16 9AD
http: www.st-andrews.ac.uk/worldcinema

British Library Cataloguing-in-Publication Data
A catalogue record for this book is available from the British Library.

ISBN 978-1906678043 (paperback)

Printed by Prontaprint Dundee, Scotland, UK

This book is published with the assistance of the
Centre for Film Studies at the University of St Andrews.
St Andrews Film Studies promotes greater understanding of,
and access to, international cinema and film culture worldwide.

University
of
St Andrews

The University of St Andrews is a charity
registered in Scotland, No SC013532

Cover design and pre-press: University of St Andrews Reprographics Unit

Front cover illustration: Screening in Piazza Grande, Locarno International Film
Festival, Switzerland – www.pardo.ch. © Fotofestival / Film Festival Locarno

Back cover illustration: Screen Machine 2. Photo by © Regional Screen Scotland

Inside images:
Part 1. Photo by © Serazer Pekerman
Part 2. Foyer in the Light House, Dublin. Photo by © Ron Inglis.
Part 3 Press Conference at Belgrade FEST 2009. © Fest Belgrade.
Part 4 Photo © Serazer Pekerman

Contents

Acknowledgements

This volume is not only the first in a series; it is also a first in the way it came together. We are grateful for the amazing discipline and responsiveness of all contributors, both academics and critics-practitioners, that we were able to generate timely scholarship in a field that we hope to see thriving very soon.

We are also grateful to colleagues, both academics and practitioners, who maintained unwavering interest in matters of festivals research and supported our work in various ways, like Stuart Cunningham and Adrian Martin in Australia, Thomas Elsaesser in the Netherlands, Irene Bignardi in Italy, Michael Curtin, Toby Miller, B. Ruby Rich, and John Trumpbour in the USA, and to Michael Gubbins, Aisla Hollinshead, Lucy Mazdon, Paul McDonald, and Julian Stringer in the UK, as well as to all colleagues who, by attending the Film Festivals Workshop in St Andrews in April 2009, helped us chart further the territory of film festival studies.

This publication is realised under the auspices of the *Dynamics of World Cinema* project sponsored by The Leverhulme Trust in the UK and hosted at the Centre for Film Studies at the University of St Andrews, one of the newest research centres at Scotland's 600-year old University.

This volume could not have materialised without the assistance of researchers Ruby Cheung and Thomas Gerstenmeyer, secretaries Karen Drysdale and Serazer Pekerman, production designer Duncan Stewart and accountant Eloise Campbell. A special thanks to *Cineaste*'s Richard Porton, editor of a related volume on festivals, for providing us with excellent feedback.

Thank you!

The Editors

Notes on Contributors

Kay Armatage is Professor at the University of Toronto, cross-appointed to the Women & Gender Studies Institute and Cinema Studies Institute. Author of *The Girl from God's Country: Nell Shipman and the Silent Cinema* (2003) & Co-Editor of *Gendering the Nation: Canadian Women's Cinema* (1999). Current research is on international film festivals.

William Brown is Lecturer in Film Studies at the University of St Andrews. He has published on a variety of topics in film. His interests include the use of digital technology in a range of national and transnational cinematic contexts and stars.

Ruby Cheung is Research Associate at the Centre for Film Studies at the University of St Andrews. She is working on The Leverhulme Trust-funded project *Dynamics of World Cinema: Transnational Channels of Global Film Distribution*. Her research interests include East Asian cinemas, Asian film industries, diasporic film distribution, regional and national film policy, Chinese diasporic online fandom and film promotion. She is the editor of *Cinemas, Identities and Beyond* (forthcoming), and is planning to work on an edited collection featuring diasporic festivals.

Mark Cousins is a Belfast-born and Edinburgh-based film writer, producer and director. As director of the Edinburgh International Film Festival in the 1990s, he pioneered the *Scene by Scene* discussion format, later adapting it into an acclaimed BBC television series. He is the co-editor, with documentarian Kevin MacDonald, of *Imagining Reality: The Faber Book of Documentary*, and author of the popular *The Story of Film*. His most recent book is *Widescreen: Watching Real People Elsewhere* (2008). Cousins co-founded the Nairn-based *Ballerina Ballroom Cinema of Dreams* film festival with award-winning actress Tilda Swinton; their next project is a new festival initiative in China.

Marijke de Valck is Assistant Professor in the Department of Media Studies at the University of Amsterdam. She is the author of *Film Festivals: From European Geopolitics to Global Cinephilia* (2007). With Skadi Loist she founded the Film Festival Research Network (FFRN), a lose connection of scholars working on issues related to film festivals that aims to make festival research more available and connect diverse aspects and interdisciplinary exchange between researchers. (Contact: m.devalck@uva.nl)

Rahul Hamid, Assistant Editor at *Cineaste* Magazine, teaches film at New York University.

Janet Harbord is Reader of Film and Screen Media at Goldsmiths, University of London. She is the author of *Film Cultures* (Sage, 2002), *The Evolution of Film* (Polity, 2007) and *Chris Marker: La Jetee* (Afterall/MIT Press, 2009).

Dina Iordanova is Professor of Film Studies and Director of the Centre of Film Studies at the University of St Andrews in Scotland. She is interested in the workings of the international film industry and leads The Leverhulme Trust-sponsored project of *Dynamics of World Cinema*. In 2008, she edited a special festivals issue for *Film International* (2008), where she also writes a special festival column. She organised the International Film Festivals Workshop (2009) and launched the Film Festival Yearbook series, which will explore various aspects of film festivals in dedicated volumes.

Dimitris Kerkinos, Balkan Survey programmer at the Thessaloniki IFF since 2002. Editor of numerous monographs for TIFF, writer of critical texts on cinema and ethnographic documentary. PhD, Social Anthropology, Professor of Visual Anthropology at the Panteion University, Athens (2004-2008).

Skadi Loist is Junior Researcher at the Institute for Media and Communications, University of Hamburg. Together with Marijke de Valck she founded the Film Festival Research Network as extension of the NECS Film Festival workgroup. Her current research project (PhD) analyses queer film festivals in the US and Germany/Austria. (Contact: skadi.loist@uni-hamburg.de)

Ma Ran is a third-year PhD student at the Department of Comparative Literature, University of Hong Kong. She was born in 1980, Kunming, Yunnan Province of southwest China, where she completed her undergraduate study in Chinese Language and Literature and got her B.A. in 2002. She then went to Amsterdam to pursue her M.A. study in Film Studies at the University of Amsterdam and graduated Cum Laude in 2005. She also received an M.A. degree in Comparative Literature at the University of Yunnan, China in 2006.

Ragan Rhyne is Research Associate at the Centre for Film Studies at the University of St Andrews on the *Dynamics of World Cinema* project. Her work has been published in *GLQ*, *Velvet Light Trap*, and the *Journal of Homosexuality*.

Nick Roddick taught film and theatre at universities in the UK, Ireland and the USA before becoming a journalist in the early eighties. After a stint with *Stills Magazine* in London he was editor of *Cinema Papers* in Australia from 1985-6, followed by a decade as a trade journalist as Editor of *Screen International*, then *Moving Pictures International*. He is the author of several books and currently runs Brighton-based Split Screen. He contributes regularly to *Sight & Sound* and the *Evening Standard*; is currently building Film File Europe, a pan-European database; and consults for a number of international film festivals.

Charles-Clemens Rüling is Associate Professor of Organization Theory at Grenoble Ecole de Management. His research is anchored in institutional theory and has looked at innovation and the legitimacy of innovative practices in organisations, organisational bricolage, and local practices in the production of movie special effects. His current work concentrates on field configuring events, ecological learning and careers in the animated film industry.

J. David Slocum is an historian and sociologist of film, media and the creative industries. After ten years at New York University, where he taught Cinema Studies and served as Associate Dean in the Graduate School of Arts and Science, he is now Professor and Special Adviser to the Academic Director at the Berlin School of Creative Leadership. Slocum's research interests include violence and visual culture, cinema and public life, especially in Africa, media and entertainment economies, and organisational management in the creative industries. He has published four books and is currently writing monographs on creative leadership (with Doug Guthrie) and film and terrorism.

Introduction

Dina Iordanova and Ragan Rhyne[1]

For more than three quarters of a century, film festivals have been a driving force behind the global circulation of cinema. But with the exception of a few key works, not enough attention has been paid to understanding the development of the festival circuit in a systematic way. Most festival scholarship has followed a model of case study research and there are significant reasons for the use of this methodology: the unique histories of festivals large and small have demanded consideration on the institutional level. This work has developed remarkably in sophistication over the last 15 years, as the case studies included in this volume will attest. But while this aspect of festival scholarship has continued to advance, too little work has sought to bring the diverse examples to bear on larger, structural models of the film festival circuit as a whole in a way that adequately takes into account their multiple institutional formations and identities. How is it, precisely, that these individual festivals create what we understand as constituting a circuit, a cohesive network, a singular phenomenon that has expanded at a dizzying pace? Why do they continue to proliferate?

This volume will address what we see as a lapse in festival scholarship, which we believe is due primarily to a dearth of spaces for productive debate and dialogue among those researching the festival institutions. It includes meta-commentary on the film festival phenomenon and the changes it has undergone over the last decade, as well as consideration of the field of festival studies itself. It also represents some of the most recent scholarship on festivals, covering specific nodes in the ever-expanding geography of the festival circuit – from Hong Kong to Annecy, Zanzibar to Toronto, New York to Thessaloniki. It is only through the continued development of both strands of festival studies – case studies and the theorisation of their broader relevance to our understanding of the festival as a circuit – that this research will continue to progress. Just as the study of museums and galleries has become crucial to our understanding of the institutionalisation of arts and heritage, so too must the study of festivals be central to understanding the socio-cultural dynamics of global cinema and international cultural exchanges at large.

The festival circuit seems to have grown nearly tenfold in the last three decades and festival research has struggled to keep pace. Only 30 years ago, *Variety* estimated the number of festivals at around 170 in total (Acheson 1996: 323). By 2001, the number of festivals had been set at over 500 (Stringer 2001), while in 2003 FIAPF (International Federation of Film Producers Association) counted about 700 festivals (Moullier 2003). In a

Introduction

conversation that took place in 2006, Amiens/Montpellier festival's Thierry Lenouvel estimated that France alone had about 350 festivals and only needed about 15 more to be able to match a festival to each day of the calendar year. A recent study revealed that Brazil now has 132 film festivals (*Diagnóstico Setorial* 2008). In the absence of a fully reliable count, opinions on the total number of film festivals still diverge. Yet there is consensus that since the 1980s, film festivals have proliferated at an exponential rate in every corner of the globe. More importantly, there is also consensus that the festival network has grown not only in terms of sheer numbers but also in influence.

But what are all these festivals for? Are they simply a celebration of cinematic art or more about extending the exhibition network for certain kinds of films? Is the festival circuit some sort of vernacular market place for the film industry? Do film festivals indeed have beneficial effect for local tourist and film production economies?

By launching the series of the *Film Festival Yearbook* with this inaugural volume, we aim to: 1) explore festivals in a systematic manner that, while relying on individual case studies, will foreground theoretical concerns at the intersection of arts management, cultural policy and film studies and 2) chart the complex structure of the international festival network, bringing along a better understanding of World Cinema. A level of abstraction is needed for the study of festivals to gain momentum and translate the currently scattered research environment of festival studies into a sufficiently structured context. Our hope is that the *Film Festival Yearbook* will serve this function.

In a programmatic essay, Thomas Elsaesser (2005) described the festival network as a specifically European industry response to Hollywood's distribution mechanisms and explored festivals in the context of actor-network theory. With respect to Europe, Elsaesser claimed, the festival circuit had become the key force and power grid in the film business, with wide-reaching consequences for the respective functioning of other elements of film culture, such as authorship, production, exhibition, cultural prestige and recognition. Julian Stringer (2001, 2008) and Janet Harbord (2002), who explored the spatial and temporal dimensions of festivals and theorised their role in fostering communities and urban discourses, consolidated the current thinking on these matters. Marijke de Valck's 2007 book on film festivals was the first monograph to address a range of historical and methodological issues and is still the most comprehensive study on the subject to date.

Despite these important works, the study of festivals remains largely anecdotal and is in need of more focused approach. Research on festivals has mostly taken place within the framework of singular case studies, many of which have remained confined within the context of national cinema and economies of distribution. A study of the Toronto IFF is perceived as a study on Canadian cinema, while a study on Cannes is regarded as contributing to the annals of French film culture. In our favoured methodology, by contrast, we would like to encourage festival researchers to build on existing case

Introduction

studies and focus on the dynamics of the festival circuit above and beyond specific socio-geographical dimensions. The *Film Festival Yearbook* brings these strands of research together, opening up a new space for the kind of systematic approach we think is necessary for the next phase of festival studies.

To this end, *The Festival Circuit* focuses primarily on the international dynamics of festivals, on defining the place of festivals in international film distribution, exhibition and production, and on identifying the underlying forces that drive the growth of the festival phenomenon within the system of global culture. In the context of this publication and in the volumes that will follow, we will also consider the specific temporal and spatial aspects of the festival circuit, the importance of concurrent film markets, the role of centralised festival regulation, and the impact of new digital technologies. Given the rapid proliferation of the festival network and the increasing attention being paid to it by scholars around the world, we have no doubt that during the course of the next decade the study of festivals will become central to film studies. The aim of the *Film Festival Yearbook* series is to put the study of film festivals onto a systematic footing, consolidate existing strands of work, and build bridges between the communities of scholars and festival practitioners through a single annual collection of the best festival research.

This volume is divided into four sections. The first section brings together essays that systematically explore the dynamics, economics and temporalities of the international film festival circuit, putting into practice the methodological considerations we have outlined in this introduction. Ragan Rhyne deploys some of the case studies in this volume, arguing that the various interests of festival stakeholders are negotiated through the administrative and economic structures of a newly globalised non-profit sector. Dina Iordanova challenges the standard line in festival studies that film festivals constitute an alternative system of distribution. Instead, her suggestion that it is better understood as an exhibition network sheds light on how the economy of the festival circuit actually functions. Janet Harbord takes a somewhat different approach to her conception of the festival circuit, calling for renewed attention to the temporality of the festival circuit, rather than a strict focus on festival geographies.

The second section compiles some of the most recent research on specific film festivals. These case studies span both the geography and the temporality of the festival circuit, ranging from archival histories to analyses of contemporary global trends. This research represents the work of scholars from various disciplines in the humanities and social sciences. Charles-Clemens Rüling approaches his history of the Annecy International Animated Film Festival and Market through the lens of organisational analysis. Rahul Hamid and Kay Armatage plumb the depths of the festival archive to narrate the establishment of two very different film festivals in North America: Hamid describes the institutionalisation and organisational politics of the first New York Film Festival, while Armatage examines the

3

Introduction

ephemeral history of women's film festivals through her own memory of programming the 1973 Toronto Women and Film International. Ruby Cheung and Ma Ran each examine the relationship between film, festivals and Chinese governments, though from distinct perspectives. Cheung narrates the transition of the Hong Kong International Film Festival from a government-run programme to a model influenced by corporate efficiency and sponsors. Ma examines how that policy and aesthetics collided as underground Chinese cinema found its way onto the international festival circuit, much to the chagrin of Mainland Chinese bureaucrats. Finally, David Slocum looks at the way that the discourse of cultural diversity has been deployed through two African film festivals: FESPACO and the Zanzibar International Film Festival.

The third section, *Dispatches from the Festival World*, presents perspectives on the festival circuit from the people on the ground, namely programmers and critics. Mark Cousins diagnoses what he calls 'the contemporary film festival problem' of unchecked proliferation and uninspired programming. Nick Roddick, commentator for *Sight & Sound*, shares with us some insights from his last few years covering the relationship between festival circuit and the film industry. Dimitris Kerkinos describes his experience of programming Balkan films at the Thessaloniki International Film Festival.

The concluding section of this volume takes the discourse on film festival studies a level higher and reflects on the field of festival studies itself. Its centrepiece is the ambitious and comprehensive overview of the current state of the film festival scholarship by Marijke de Valck and Skadi Loist. Their conceptualisations come along with an indispensible bibliography of festival research that has been compiled from a variety of sources and over a significant period of time. We are planning to run regular updates to this bibliography in the forthcoming volumes of the *Yearbook*. The bibliography is supplemented by William Brown's report highlighting key aspects of a discussion on the proposed conceptualisation of the field of film festival studies. Held in St. Andrews in April 2009, the discussion formed part of our film festival workshop and brought together a lively group of scholars, programmers and critics from around the world.

As this concluding report on the festival workshop indicates, there are challenges to putting the diverse research on film festivals into dialogue, as conflicts arise with any attempt to categorise its existing literature or to find common theoretical ground. For instance, the case studies presented in this volume represent film festivals from several nations, and as such they also represent different models of organisation and administration. In tracing the manifestations of film festivals around the globe in diverse political and economic contexts, different terminology is necessarily deployed. In this volume Rhyne uses the framework of the non-profit organisation, while Cheung refers to 'corporatisation' to describe the Hong Kong context. Similar inconsistencies in terminology and framework are pervasive throughout the field of festival research; it will take time and further dialogue to iron them out.

Introduction

It is our hope, however, that the *Film Festival Yearbook* will put different academic stakeholders – anthropologists, sociologists, film and media scholars, students of cultural policy and arts management, and others – into dialogue with one another and with festival practitioners in order to work through these kinds of terminological and methodological differences, if not toward consistency, then toward further interrogation of the theoretical models for film festival research.

Note

[1] Support for the *Film Festival Yearbook* was provided in part by The Leverhulme Trust, which funded the project *Dynamics of World Cinema* (2008-2011), and by the Centre for Film Studies at the University of St Andrews, which provided funding for the workshop on International Film Festivals (4 April 2009).

Works Cited

Acheson, Keith, Christopher J. Maule and Elizabet Filleul (1996) 'Cultural Entrepreneurship and the Banff Television Festival', *Journal of Cultural Economics*, 20, 4, 321-39.

de Valck, Marijke (2007) *Film Festivals: From European Geopolitics to Global Cinephilia*. Amsterdam: Amsterdam University Press.

Diagnóstico Setorial 2007 / Indicadores 2006 dos Festivais Audiovisuais (2008). On-line. Available HTTP: http://www.forumdosfestivais.com.br/diagnostico.pdf (1 February 2009).

Elsaesser, Thomas (2005) 'Film Festival Networks: The New Topographies of Cinema in Europe', in *European Cinema: Face to Face with Hollywood*. Amsterdam: Amsterdam University Press.

Harbord, Janet (2002) 'Film Festivals: Media Events and Spaces of Flow', in *Film Cultures*. London: Sage.

Kosslick, Dieter (2003) Personal interview, Berlin, 15 April.

Lenouvel, Thierry (2006) Personal interview, Paris, 7 February.

Stringer, Julian (2001) 'Global Cities and the International Film Festival Economy', in Mark Shiel and Tony Fitzmaurice (eds) *Cinema and the City: Film and Urban Societies in a Global Context*. London: Blackwell.

____ (2008) 'Genre Films and Festival Communities: Lessons from Nottingham, 1991-2000', *Film International*, 6, 47, 34, 53-60.

Part 1

The Festival Circuit

Chapter One

Film Festival Circuits and Stakeholders

Ragan Rhyne

The concept of an international film festival circuit has dominated discourse of both festival studies and festival practice. The models deployed in the most oft-cited scholarship have placed festivals within the sphere of international negotiation of culture and policy: festivals as cultural contact zones (Nichols 1994: 16), 'a kind of parliament of national cinemas' (Elsaesser 2005: 85), festivals as international 'symbols of socio-political ambition' (Rich 1999: 82) and as sites of competition among new global cities (Stringer 2001). This work has done a great deal to outline the political and cultural significance of the festival circuit, but the field of festival studies has, to my mind, yet to adequately present a viable and sustained theory of how it actually functions and why it has developed according to the economic model that it has.

Thousands of film festivals have come and gone since they began in the 1930s, but do those that remain in fact constitute a network or economic circuit that can be thought of as cohesive whole? The failure to theorise adequately the festival circuit has not been a consequence of poor scholarship, as the contribution of Marjike de Valck and Skadi Loist in this volume can attest; it is, I believe, a result of the inherent methodological challenges presented by the study of film festivals and the tenuous network they have created. The trouble is that materially, the film festival circuit is not nearly as connected as we have thought. In fact, we might abandon the structural idea of the festival circuit as a single entity altogether and instead understand it as an international cultural sector linked by a common economy of public and private subsidy.

The premise of this essay is that the integration of what we call the festival circuit is maintained through the discursive and economic articulation of a discrete and new cultural industry. It is upheld by the various stakeholders – filmmakers and studios, journalists and press agents, professionals and programmers, local cultural councils and supranational agencies, tourist boards, cinephiles and others – who have particular interests in seeing the network proliferate. This essay will first trace the ways in which the festival circuit as a cultural industry has come to be managed through a global non-profit sector. Second, it will argue that the festival circuit has adopted this model as a strategy for managing the often conflicting motivations of its stakeholders and channelling their diverse interests toward the goals of nation-states and global capital.

To that end, this essay will avoid conceptualising the film festival network as an organic global organism. The point here is not to undermine or fail to recognise the actual points of collaboration among film festivals around the world. But this vision of the festival as a cohesive circuit does not necessarily reflect the 'messy realities of practice' that take place within these organisations (O'Malley, Weir, and Shearing 1997). I hope not only to present a framework for understanding the institutional structures through which festivals do their work, but also to suggest a new direction in festival research that depends upon and respects case studies and puts this data to work in a broader context, advancing an understanding of the film festival circuit and its place within film studies and the study of cultural industries more generally. Indeed, film festivals are of relevance well beyond the study of the circulation and production of cinema and cinephile communities. They can tell us a great deal about new formations of cultural labour and policy in an increasingly globalised marketplace.

Film Festivals and the Global Third Sector

Contemporary festivals around the world are primarily administered and funded through public/private partnerships. Consequently, most have adopted the institutional structure of the non-profit organisation, a unique formation that may or may not receive funding from the state but participates in the kind of service provision and cultural management that has historically been the exclusive domain of governments. Some non-profits are funded primarily through national or local governmental support; most fund their activities through some combination of earned income, government funding, corporate sponsorship and private donations.

The non-profit organisation has been a mainstay of what has been called the third sector (the state and the market being the other two) in the United States for over a century. This third sector of private organisations and the corresponding systems of private financial support for them found a new form of professionalisation in the 1960s. After the Cold War, the model spread across much of the rest of the world, in both developed and developing nations to manage cultural, health, service, educational, human rights, and economic needs no longer being adequately addressed by governments. Since then, the non-profit has played a crucial role in establishing international cultural policy by institutionalising collaborations between nation-states, the corporate sector and private wealth toward the cultivation of citizens who make claims on none of these. While this model of cultural administration is one that is fairly new to festivals, which in Europe at least have historically been administered through national and local governments, its foundation in the collaboration between the state and the market was evident from the beginning.

Film Festival Circuits and Shareholders

Since the 1930s, when Benito Mussolini founded the world's first festival in Venice, international film festivals have been organised through public/private partnerships designed to support the interests of both the market and the state. Premiering in 1932, the festival was conceived as a tribute to fascism in Italy and Germany (Stone 1998). But from the very beginning, the festival was simultaneously a site of nationalist articulation, a forum for international relations, and a function of the commercial cinema market. Designed to extend the traditional tourist season (Bachman 1976), it also formed part of the local tourist economy. The festival was introduced as part of the 18th Venice Biennale, attracting more than 25,000 people to the city during its off-season.

From the outset, geopolitics and cultural politics have been co-articulated in the institutional structures and commercial affiliations of international film festivals. Cannes was founded shortly after the festival in Venice, when in 1938 Jean Renoir's fiercely anti-war *La Grande Illusion* (*The Grand Illusion*, 1938) was denied the top prize at the festival despite being favoured by both the jury and audiences. Instead, the 'Mussolini Cup' was jointly awarded to Riefenstahl's *Olympia* (1938) and *Luciano Serra Piolota* (*Luciano Serra, Pilot*, Goffredo Alessandrini, 1938), prompting the withdrawal of French, British, and American jury members. The inaugural festival at Cannes, though, was cut short after the opening night on 1 September 1939, as Germany launched its invasion of Poland and France and Britain prepared to go to war. When it reopened in 1947, the festival was moved from under the aegis of the French Ministry of Foreign Affairs and Education to the new Centre National de la Cinématographie. The festival became part of France's national post-war project of reframing European cultural identity in the wake of fascism and defending it from a burgeoning American cultural imperialism.

Despite these political and aesthetic conflicts with Venice, the festival at Cannes mimicked what Gideon Bachman (1976) calls the 'starlet-tourism-cinema' formula made so successful by its predecessor. Indeed, in his review of the inaugural festival, film critic Andre Bazin made reference to its role in cultivating markets, selling product, boosting tourism and peddling newspapers: 'An international if not a universal art thanks to its very technique, ... cinema is paradoxically the most national art when it comes to its commercial exploitation' (Quoted in Sklar 1996: 8).

Directly following WWII, there were hardly a dozen festivals around the world, but over the next 50 years the starlet-tourism-cinema model would be duplicated in nearly 500 different destinations and followed by a proliferation of festivals in major cities like Moscow, London and New York as part of a more wide-spread process of globalisation in the post-war period. Many of these festivals were funded directly out of subsidies from the United States government, military and private institutions as part of a broader campaign to stabilise the region following the war (Harbord 2002: 62). These sources of funding, the new models of management they required, and the new discourse of culture and democracy produced through the festivals reflected a significant shift of policy designed to help Western Europe resist the new

Chapter One

threat of Communism by shedding the socialist model of governmental arts management and adopting a structure more like the independent third sector of the United States.

In 1951, for example, the Berlin Film Festival was founded to reclaim the city's role in European arts and culture and to reiterate its participation in the global market of Hollywood and European film commodities. But this discourse was not restricted to Europe; in the early 1960s, the New York Film Festival was founded as part of a larger municipal project to challenge the traditional European model of the performing arts through a democratisation of architecture, medium and access. Indeed, as Rahul Hamid argues in this volume, the founding of the festival in New York represented a new institutionalisation of film connoisseurship that replaced the city's ad-hoc spaces of cine-clubs with the newly formed Lincoln Center performing arts complex. This placed film within the context of municipal support for opera, ballet, theatre, and the discourse of bourgeois arts patronage and consumption.

Stringer attributes the rise of the urban bourgeois model of festival proliferation to a number of changes in the landscape of international political and economic organisation: the process of decolonisation and the related rise of Third World nationalism, the spread of regionalism, the increasing transnational organisation of labour and capital, the widespread availability of air travel and tourist accommodations among the growing middle-class, and the 'de-territorialization of film production centers (especially Hollywood)'. Global cities replaced nations as the 'nodal points on this [festival] circuit', he writes, particularly as cities compete ever more vigorously for investment from transnational capital and the attentions of cosmopolitan tourists (Stringer 2003: 109).

Saskia Sassen puts this articulation of a new urban economy into a broader context (1991). Since the 1960s, cities like New York, London and Tokyo have become nodal points in global flows, facilitating the service provision and cultivation of markets required by a transnational economy of production. Taking the flow of corporate capital through these new global cities as the primary focus for her work, Sassen suggests that they might also be understood as loci for international cultural exchange and as centres for global culture industries that have risen around them. Like the specialised service economies of global cities that facilitate the organisation of transnational industries, their non-profit cultural sectors should also be understood as ancillary industries that rely upon and indeed support a globalised economy.

As these global cities grew in importance, they gave rise to secondary urban centres that used a variety of competitive strategies, both cultural and economic, to attract capital and the professional classes that follow it. Film festivals were one of these strategies, but a condition of their proliferation was an uneven investment of capital among them (Rushbrook 2002: 188). Stringer employs David Morley and Kevin Robins' work on what they call 'global media landscapes' when he argues that international film festivals, as

12

located in new cosmopolitan cities, operate beyond the boundaries of the nation through circuits of exchange that mirror the 'geographically uneven development that characterizes the world of international film culture' (2001: 106). The global organisation of media industries has replaced the political organisation of the nation-state, now seen as an impediment to the accumulation of capital, with new modes of affiliation tied to the values of international consumer culture (Morley and Robins 1995: 11). The circulation of film along the festival circuit constructs a hierarchy among cities as they compete for tourist revenue and industrial attention. Predictably, this hierarchy replicates the unequal power relations of a globalised economy.

The film festival phenomenon might be understood in much the same way as Morley and Robins position electronic broadcasting in post-Socialist Europe: as a play between the local and the global, mediated through supranational cultural policies and motivated through a complex negotiation between governmental bodies and corporations. The film festival, too, is profoundly located in cities, regions and nations, branded through their *local* tourism boards, promoted through their national cultural commissions and funded through *supranational* initiatives and private foundations, with the goal of establishing *international* networks of film distribution and exhibition, the efforts of which subsidise a *multinational* commercial entertainment industry that is often looking to find a way of exploiting untapped local markets.

Indeed, the political encouragement of competition among festivals for resources, patrons and prestige has been one of the most significant markers of the shift in their administration to the non-profit sector. In her history on the Karlovy Vary Film Festival in the Czech Republic, Dina Iordanova describes the transition that took place in the 1990s as many post-Socialist governments abandoned the state controlled and subsidised model of cultural management that had characterised Cold War regimes (2008). Some opted to replace it with what she calls a *laissez-faire* model of support that required cultural institutions to secure funding primarily through corporate sponsorship.

In the Czech Republic, government cultural funding had all but ceased as the new nation sought to shed the image of its former Communist government and ally itself with Western European politics and sensibilities. This shift sparked a cultural turf war between the established Karlovy Vary Festival and the new upstart in Prague as well as a subsequent re-articulation of the festivals as enterprises competing for international accreditation and the external revenue this would help secure. Without any funding or regulation from the Czech government to mediate their conflict, the Karlovy Vary Festival and the Prague Festival turned to a third, private regulatory body, the International Federation of Film Producers' Associations (FIAPF). This set out to coordinate festivals internationally and to mediate the distribution of resources among them based on criteria of artistic merit and market viability.

The Czech case, as Iordanova describes, was unusual in Europe, where models of cultural funding varied:

> ... from the federal socialist model (e.g. Germany) where public policy is in the hands of local and regional authorities, from the 'arms-length' model of Scandinavia and the United Kingdom where the central government is formally in control but policies and finance are independently arranged; and from the French one where the Ministry of Culture has a centralized control and actively manages local cultural matters. (34)

Many countries began to manage cultural institutions through some sort of non-profit model, exerting lesser or greater oversight primarily through governmental funding allocation. The Czech festivals, without either state funding or an established culture of private philanthropy to support them, had to turn to corporate sponsorship opportunities. The struggle between the two festivals was ultimately determined by which organisation was able to manoeuvre this new landscape of cultural funding by rebranding the institution through a discourse of European high-culture. 'Disguised as a triumph of art-house sophistication over insolent connives, Karlovy Vary's victory was, in fact, a conquest of a correspondingly mercantile nature... The real question was not *if* commercialism would prevail but *whose*' (Iordanova 2006: 32; italics in original).

But festivals as cultural institutions do more than mediate art and commerce. As the Karlovy Vary example suggests, they also mediate the interests of governments in managing their subjects and resources. The other narrative at play here is the establishment of a new post-Cold War structure of cultural management that is based upon public-private partnerships (the Czech government reinstated funding to the festival in later years) as well as a competition of resources among institutions themselves. The failed experiment to turn cultural management completely over to the market left a void that could only be filled by a private regulatory body which was tied to the market but effectively functioned in a nascent post-Socialist Eastern European third sector, mediating the interests of the film industry, the market and the festivals.

The establishment of the Karlovy Vary Festival as contemporary non-profit was less a compromise between the *laissez-faire* and the nationalised, but must be understood far more as an artefact of neoliberal, post-Socialist cultural policy in Europe which sought to channel the work of managing citizens through the private sector as well as the state toward the upward movement of capital. This goal was accomplished through the institutionalisation of the festival as a site of negotiation among various stakeholders, turning a competition for resources into an ethical virtue in the true tradition of capitalism. In fact, acknowledging the global third sector as a component of capitalism is a crucial element of this story.

Film Festival Circuits and Shareholders

The case of the Karlovy Vary Festival is indicative of what Toby Miller and George Yúdice identify as a shift in cultural policy. With the end of the Cold War national and international relations required a new narrative of culture's role which would articulate the new terms upon which national governments had an interest in funding the arts (2002). This shift evidenced a turn to what Foucault has called a structure of governmentality, in which the task of managing citizens is moved from the disciplinary arm of the state to bureaucrats and administrators, who ultimately outsource the job to citizens themselves (1991). This transition was not, of course, restricted to social service provision but extended to include the work of managing culture as well, creating a cultural sector that 'burgeoned into an enormous network of arts administrators who mediate between funding sources, on the one hand, and artists and communities, on the other. Like their counterparts in the university and the business world, they must produce and distribute the producers of art and culture' (Yúdice 2003: 2).

The play between the local and the global that is manifest in the film festival phenomenon demonstrates that these neoliberal policies have been enacted in various contexts around the world but with different goals and different effects. Recognising new formations in film festivals around the world is not to suggest that their development has been uniform, or that this neoliberalisation has been a monolithic force. Aihwa Ong has argued that while neoliberalism has in many ways become synonymous with American cultural imperialism, there are also instances – in the East Asian contexts she examines through her ethnographies, for example – in which these policies have been deployed as a technology of governance, often as an exception to other kinds of governance already in place (2006).

Ruby Cheung's contribution to this volume, in which she outlines the transition of the Hong Kong International Film Festival from a government-managed event to a private non-profit organisation in the midst of the handover of the city to the PRC no less, speaks of the complex ways in which these policies have been enacted unevenly. The effects of neoliberalism – the privatisation of services, the prioritisation of the market, and the cultivation of self-managing citizens – have materialised through diverse institutional solutions that address the specificities of local conditions. The cultural policies that structure the contemporary film festival circuit have not developed according to a single model, but the diverse strategies they have employed do address common pressures.

Indeed, the administrative structures of global non-profits have been deployed in the service of managing citizens precisely through multiple articulations of subjectivity manifest in the various institutions through which the work of culture is done. Film festivals are not just one example of the institutionalisation of cultural management through the non-profit model; far more they are the perfect example of the ways that these policies are enacted, though unevenly distributed, to link cultural labour, governance and commerce toward a common goal.

Non-Profits and the Management of Stakeholders

If the goal of neoliberal cultural policy has been to create subjects that uphold the circuits of global capital while simultaneously taking on the responsibility for securing their place within it, then understanding the ways in which the often conflicting interests of these subjects are negotiated through festival institutions is crucial. On the festival circuit, these negotiations range from debates over aesthetics, the politics of corporate sponsorship, cultural sovereignty and protectionism to the role of celebrity, the allocation of resources, and many other issues. The ethical and political weight that these conflicts carry with them is part and parcel of this process. We must recognise them as functions of a new kind of cultural sector that relies upon these debates in order to maintain its position in relation to global flows of capital. The non-profit organisation has become a nearly ubiquitous model of management for contemporary festivals precisely because of its effectiveness in managing conflicting stakeholder agendas.

The intersection of commercial, non-profit and aesthetic interests in film festival institutions makes the network indicative of a new breed of cultural industries that are shaped by global economic shifts in the transnational circulation of cultural products. Attention to the motivations of these stakeholders can help lay the groundwork for a methodology for festival studies that extends beyond the typical focus on filmmakers, programmers and audiences to account for other kinds of players in the intricate institutional dynamics that make up this cultural sector and the peripheral industries that have grown up around it. Understanding the festival as a space in which these interests are negotiated can tell us something about the relationship between film, cultural policy and globalisation in the new millennium.

In his foundational essay on film festival networks, Thomas Elsaesser deploys Bruno Latour's actor-network theory to describe these various interests at play in the festival circuit and its role in producing what he calls a post-national articulation of European cinema (2005). Elsaesser indicates a few reasons for this widespread expansion of the festival network, particularly in Europe, namely the growth and competition of secondary global cities in a new economy, as well as shifts in the commercial film industry and the production, distribution and reception of independent cinema. While these phenomena are indeed crucial to the shape of festivals as we know them today and, as he acknowledges, primary influences on them, their modern incarnation is indicative of far more fundamental changes in cultural policy. Around the world this new policy has structured a new economy of public/private subsidies for the arts toward the production of post-Cold War global citizens. Film festivals are not only significant for film studies but have become something of a bellwether for changes in global economic flows precisely because of the medium's unique commercial value on international markets including the ancillary distribution networks for non-Hollywood film that have proliferated during the last decade.

Film Festival Circuits and Shareholders

In fact, Elsaesser points to this new organisation of global creative industries and asks how the festival network fits into it:

> Given the degree of standardization in the overall feel of film festivals, and the organizational patterns that regulate how films enter this network, it is tempting to ask what general rules govern the system as a whole. Can one, for instance, understand the film festival circuit by comparing it to the mega art exhibitions that now tour the world's major museums? (2005: 92)

Elsaesser goes on to suggest that the various players in the festival circuit and the ways in which they exert power as intermediaries between the events themselves, the commercial film industry, and festival constituents have significant 'implications for how we come to understand what are called the creative industries' (2005: 93). The contemporary festival circuit is indicative of the same kind of changes in institutional, national and international cultural policy that have spawned things like the blockbuster museum show. Moreover, they must be understood as an even more dramatic example of this new, transnational organisation of cultural labour precisely because of film's commercial potential and geographic mobility. This is not to impose a kind of economic determinism upon the festival network but rather to suggest that the institutional negotiations of financial, professional and cultural stakeholder motivations on the festival circuit have ultimately manifested themselves as a unique institutional arrangement that straddles art, commerce and governance.

Janet Harbord identifies four distinct discourses that operate in the festival circuit: first, discourses of independent filmmakers and producers, second, discourses of media representation, third, business discourse of financing and legal transactions, and fourth, the discourse of tourism and the service economy of host cities (2002: 60). Harbord's delineation of these categories is extremely useful for what it tells us as much as what it obscures. While Harbord herself pays attention to the structures through which festivals are managed, her categories recognise that discursively the stakeholders that make up the festival cultural industry are to some extent written out of this international festival narrative. Thus I would add 'policy discourse' to her list to reflect an often hidden but equally as significant discourse that circulates through the festival circuit. In fact, we may deploy her categories in order to not only unpack the rhetorical articulation of the festival circuit as she does, but to outline the interests of stakeholders as well, rephrasing them for these purposes as 1) filmmakers and producers, 2) journalists, 3) the film industry of financiers, lawyers, distributors and studios, 4) tourist and ancillary industries, and 5) policymakers, funders and festival managers.

The first four categories that correspond to Harbord's discursive axes have received the most attention from festival researchers who have focused on the interplay between filmmakers, journalists, the film industry, and municipal tourist economies. Policy stakeholders, however, have received less consideration, if not in terms of the kinds of national cultural policy that influence the founding of film festivals, then certainly in terms of the material conditions of their management, the day-to-day practices of cultural administration, and the government and private bodies that fund them (corporate investment, on the other hand, has received a great deal of attention). This understanding of festivals as a culture industry is often lost in discussions about 'the circuit', which tends to imply a more organic model of organisation and hide the material practices of cultural policy that drive it. The proliferation of festivals over the last two decades has been largely in response to changes in policy and the increasing adoption of the non-profit model to manage festivals.

While the stakeholder categories I have outlined will undoubtedly blur, they can nonetheless provide a useful starting point for understanding how the festival circuit is constituted through the negotiation of several different kinds of investments. In his ethnography of Sundance, Daniel Dayan outlines the interests of filmmakers and producers, journalists, the film industry, and tourist economies and their roles in the construction of the festival event (2000). As an agonistic site of negotiation, he argues, festivals like Sundance depend upon a variety of conflicting interests and are structured to not only contain them but also to deploy them toward institutional goals through what he calls the collective performance of the festival – a performance that actually requires the negotiation of these conflicting interests. Ironically, these conflicts, he argues, are fundamental to the cohesion of the festival as an event.

Dayan considers the role of the players in this productive conflict, from audiences to filmmakers and distributors to festival professionals, but interestingly, it is his concluding remarks on the role of journalists that are the most provocative in relation to understanding the role of policymakers and the festival non-profit sector. With reference to Barthes, Dayan argues that the festival is constituted not only through the negotiation of these conflicts but also through journalistic chronicles of it – what he calls the 'written festival'. 'Like the physical event, but even more acutely so, the written festival turned out to be made of different versions, relaying different voices, relying on different sources of legitimacy. But it also provided its own common threads' (Dayan 2000: 52).

Through his concept of 'the written festival', Dayan suggests that film festivals – or at least Sundance in particular – are constituted not only through the negotiation of various stakeholders, but through the articulation of these conflicting positions in journalistic coverage of the festival. This negotiation, in other words, is not incidental to the festival institution itself, but crucial to both its function as an event and to the way that the festival is understood as a cultural phenomenon. We might understand this as suggesting that the constant public discussion of the battle of festivals for aesthetic autonomy from the varying pressures of Hollywood, audiences, critics and corporate sponsors is theoretically misleading. The festival cannot

18

solve these conflicts. Rather, it has an interest in playing them out in the cultural public sphere.

The regulatory function of non-profits – funding applications, grant reporting, tax regulations, policy administration, and other material practices of policy stakeholders – 'writes' this new breed of festival just as much as the journalistic coverage. The festival-as-non-profit functions to channel the tensions among our five categories of stakeholders into a common, if conflicted, quest for institutional independence. Each stakeholder has a different idea of from whom festivals should be independent, whether it be the interests of governments, the pull of the market, or the high-brow tastes of aesthetes. What the non-profit organisation does is to make the institution discursively independent while simultaneously making it financially dependent on the state, the public and the corporate sector for funding.

The festival-as-non-profit model also puts festivals in competition with one another. Each must have its own mission, its own agenda, and its regional or programmatic focus and prove that its activities and use of funds uphold this mission. In addition, each must convince funding bodies and regulatory commissions that its mission should be a financial priority. Out of this network grows a new class of professional festival programmers, directors and administrators – not to mention the ancillary journalistic professionals that grow in tandem – and these cultural administrators move from festival to festival and sometimes found their own as a means of furthering their chosen careers. Some are successful and some are not, but the end result has been what is increasingly being identified as a glut of film festivals and a crisis in the festival circuit.

While the explosion of film festivals around the world over the last decade has been heralded by some as a new dawn of independent and 'world cinema', others have been more sceptical about this proliferation of events. Sergi Mesonero Burgos, for one, identified a rash of festivals in Spain, asking whether this circuit has actually been effective in championing the cause of these films and peripheral film industries, or whether the glut of festivals has had deleterious effects (2008). Furthermore, he questions the wisdom of national funding bodies' willingness to support so many different local and niche festivals. The availability of funding for festivals '... has meant that some festivals started because they were *possible*, not because they were *necessary*, although "possible" does not mean that they are much above the line of subsistence' (2008: 34). What are all of these festivals for, he wonders, and do we really need them all?

In one sense, this proliferation is the logical result of this new model of festival administration and the negotiation of the five categories of stakeholders, as I have suggested. Their purposes are many and varied and include promoting commercial cinema, exhibiting peripheral films, cultivating local film production, etc. But more materially, they are also simply for the tautological purpose of sustaining and expanding the new cultural industry of the film festival in the interests of its various stakeholders. These interests, of course, reach well beyond the goals of supporting independent film production and exhibition. The festival-as-non-profit makes this kind of entrepreneurial expansion of the festival circuit possible in a way that no other model of cultural management could. But without understanding the non-profit festival as a laboratory for negotiating conflicting interests, including those of policymakers and cultural administrators themselves, the relevance of this rapid proliferation of festivals around the world cannot be properly understood.

Conclusion

My concerns in this essay are methodological as well as theoretical. While the field of festival studies has done significant work to analyse the micro-processes of festivals through case studies, it is time for those of us researching these institutions to begin to posit larger models for how the festival circuit actually functions beyond the traffic of films and the circulation of journalists and programmers. In doing so, we must begin to pay attention to the ways in which this network is constituted (materially and discursively), as well as to the distinct roles that festivals play in achieving the goals of various stakeholders.

To this end, I hope I have made two key points in this essay. First, the international film festival circuit cannot be understood as a cohesive network, but rather as a new cultural industry administered through the institutional model of the non-profit organisation and an economy of public and private subsidy. The development of the festival-as-non-profit should not be taken for granted; it is born of very specific changes in the new urban global economy and the post-Cold War cultural administration. This must be taken into account as we understand why the festival network has developed in this way since the 1980s.

Second, if we are to speak of a festival circuit at all, it must be understood as being materially and discursively constituted through the negotiation of varied, and sometimes conflicting, motivations of stakeholders, including filmmakers, financiers, journalists, ancillary industries and policymakers. The non-profit model of film festival administration has provided an ideal laboratory through which to manage the interests of these stakeholders precisely because of the unique position of the third sector as a mediator between the state and the market. It is an administrative structure that replaces direct governmental control with more subtle regulatory features and allows corporate interest to capitalise on festival events with a minimum of investment, all the while creating a network of organisations that manage themselves through a competition for resources and prestige.

The non-profit structure allows governments to retain some form of control over the agendas of festival institutions through funding allocations. It also allows corporations to exploit them for publicity and as a marketplace for product without bearing the burden of significant overhead costs. Finally there is the more abstract but equally important point that the non-profit structure encourages other kinds of stakeholders to redirect their claims linked to cultural management from the government and the market toward a voluntary and professional network of private organisations. Governments and markets thus reap the benefits of film festivals without shouldering the burden of their administration by shifting the responsibility instead to the film festival cultural industry itself and to its network of constituents.

Of course, not all film festivals have adopted the non-profit model; festivals in some national contexts are still primarily administered and funded through state support and remain under governmental control. But increasingly, festivals around the world have adopted the non-profit model as a global third sector of cultural management has grown up around the urban nodes of a transnational economy. Festivals are certainly not the only cultural industry to be increasingly administered through non-profit organisations but they are significant precisely because of the unique role of film as a profoundly mobile and increasingly accessible medium with commercial potential.

This essay is a call to those who manage or study film festivals to begin to think seriously about the ways that festivals as institutions fit into larger networks of cultural policy, governance and global capitalism. As we continue to debate the function of film festivals, the value of their unchecked proliferation, and the infiltration of corporate interest into their aesthetic and cultural agendas, we must begin to think about how the economic organisation of the film festival circuit and the internal and external politics of the events themselves create the conditions for these controversial clashes among stakeholders. Indeed, if the non-profit organisation is not the ideal model for certain stakeholders to achieve their goals, perhaps new models of administration and funding should enter into the circuit. The implications for research into film festivals that takes seriously the way that capital flows through them has importance well beyond film festival studies and even research into media industries more generally; it is of relevance to how we understand the function of culture and cultural administration in a new global economy.

Works Cited

Anderson, Benedict (2006) *Imagined Communities*. London: Verso.

Bachman, Gideon (1976) 'Confessions of a Festival Goer', *Film Quarterly*, 29, 4, 14-17.

Burgos, Sergi Mesonero (2008) 'A Festival Epidemic in Spain', *Film International*, 6, 47, 34, 9-14.

Cheung, Ruby (2009) 'Corporatising a Film Festival: Hong Kong', in Dina Iordanova with Ragan Rhyne (eds) *Film Festival Yearbook I: The Festival Circuit*. St Andrews: St Andrews Film Studies, 99-115.

Chapter One

Dayan, Daniel (2000) 'Looking for Sundance: The Social Construction of a Film Festival', in Ib Bondebjerg (ed.) *Moving Images, Culture, and the Mind*. Luton: University of Luton Press, 43-52.

de Valck, Marijke (2007) *Film Festivals: From European Geopolitics to Global Cinephilia*. Amsterdam: Amsterdam University Press.

de Valck, Marijke and Skadi Loist (2009) 'Film Festival Studies: An Overview of a Burgeoning Field', in Dina Iordanova with Ragan Rhyne (eds) *Film Festival Yearbook I: The Festival Circuit*. St Andrews: St Andrews Film Studies, 179-215.

Elsaesser, Thomas (2005) 'Film Festival Networks: The New Topographies of Cinema in Europe', in *European Cinema: Face to Face with Hollywood*. Amsterdam: Amsterdam University Press, 82-108.

Foucault, Michel (1991) 'Governmentality', in Graham Burchell, Colin Gordon and Peter Miller (eds) *The Foucault Effect: Studies in Governmentality*. Chicago: Chicago University Press, 87-104.

Harbord, Janet (2002) *Film Cultures*. London: Sage.

Iordanova, Dina (2008) 'Showdown of the Festivals: Clashing Entrepreneurships and Post-Communist Management of Culture', *Film International*, 4, 5, 23, 25-38.

Miller, Toby and George Yudice (2002) *Cultural Policy*. London: Sage.

Morley, David and Kevin Robins (1995) *Spaces of Identity: Global Media, Electronic Landscapes, and Cultural Boundaries*. London: Routledge.

Nichols, Bill (1994) 'Discovering Form, Inferring Meaning: New Cinemas and the Film Festival Circuit', *Film Quarterly*, 47, 3, 16-31.

O'Malley, Pat, Lorna Weir and Clifford Shearing (1997) 'Governmentality, Criticism, Politics', *Economy and Society*, 26, 4, 501-17.

Ong, Aihwa (2006) *Neoliberalism as Exception: Mutations in Citizenship and Sovereignty*. Durham: Duke University Press.

Rich, B. Ruby (1999) 'Collision, Catastrophe, Celebration: The Relationship between Gay and Lesbian Film Festivals and their Publics', *GLQ*, 5, 1, 79-84.

Rushbrook, Dereka (2002) 'Cities, Queer Space, and the Cosmopolitan Tourist', *GLQ*, 8, 1-2, 183-206.

Sassen, Saskia (1991) *The Global City: New York, London, Tokyo*. Princeton: Princeton University Press.

Sklar, Robert (1996) 'Beyond Hoopla', *Cineaste*, 22, 3, 18.

Stone, Marla Susan (1998) *The Patron State: Culture and Politics in Fascist Italy*. Princeton: Princeton University Press.

Stringer, Julian (2001) 'Global Cities and the International Film Festival Economy', Mark Shiel and Tony Fitzmaurice (eds) *Cinema and the City: Film and Urban Societies in a Global Context*. London: Blackwell, 134-44.

___ (2003) 'Regarding Film Festivals', unpublished PhD thesis, University of Indiana.

Yudice, George (2003) *The Expediency of Culture: Uses of Culture in the Global Era*. Durham: Duke University Press.

Chapter Two

The Film Festival Circuit

Dina Iordanova

There seems to be a growing consensus on festivals as an 'alternative distribution network' for world cinema beyond Hollywood. Toronto International Film Festival's Piers Handling claimed that 'a lot of foreign-language film that would get distribution ten years ago doesn't get seen anymore' (Turan 2002: 8). Nick Roddick, *Sight & Sound*'s industry commentator, remarked that 'with a greater number of cinemas showing an ever narrower range of films, festivals are often the only place where the work of a promising young director can be seen by enough people to enable the director to find the money to make his or her next film' (Mr Busy 2003: 10). Marco Müller, formerly of Rotterdam IFF, Locarno IFF and now Venice IFF director, observed that the role of festivals is 'to complement and answer what is lacking in the current cultural scene in films', and thus 'reveal what the markets normally hide' (Müller 2000). Thomas Elsaesser, the prominent film scholar, also saw the festival phenomenon as an autonomous and interconnected circuit with its own set of nodes, connections and tenets. He described them as 'points of contact and comparison between the increasingly globalized and interlocking "European" model of the festival circuit and the "Hollywood" model of world-wide marketing and distribution', a configuration that is branching out quite complexly as a 'highly porous and perforated' system, 'with nodes and nerve endings' and with 'capillary action and osmosis between the various layers' (Elsaesser 2005: 93, 87).

Thus, film festivals are talked up as an alternative distribution network that opens doors to 'real' distribution. Ultimately, however, a host of questions remain: Which function of film festivals proves more important: the marketing of new and alternative cinema (be it via an officially attached market or by providing opportunity for industry contacts)? Or the festivals' increasingly important role in fostering tourism? Is Europe's embrace of festivals not a confirmation of the tacit view that, unlike Hollywood, European cinema cannot turn a profit and should therefore be 'exempt' from performing in economic terms, that its distribution will always be hampered and subsidy-reliant?

Once festivals are accepted as vital elements of a distribution chain, all these questions seem to be pushed aside. Big festivals enjoy the reputation as sites of cultural celebration, yet this façade quickly fades away when one scrutinises their tense and competitive environment. Seemingly secondary concerns like the rank of celebrities on the red carpet and the numbers of accredited journalists take over the art of cinema.

In the framework of film festivals studies, however, questions of economic viability keep popping up again and again, making it essential to scrutinise the business logic of the 'festival-circuit-as-distribution' proposition. A closer inspection is likely to reveal that seeing festivals as an alternative distribution circuit is unlikely to withstand rigorous economic appraisal. It is worthwhile to open up such a critical investigation, even if purely for the sake of pointing out the incongruities in our current understanding of festivals. It is in this context that I plan to examine here issues related to festivals as a system of discrete exhibition sites that strive to commit to a set of connections while at the same time seeking to abstain from that commitment. In this essay I also pay close attention to the parallel workings of numerous circuits that function comparably and yet without much dialogue between them, as well as to the idiosyncratic linking of detached festivals to the 'festival treadmill'.

The Film Festival as Exhibition Site

Films need festivals. Sending a film to a festival, especially to a competitive one, is often thought of as a support mechanism that a film needs in order to get to its 'real' life and reach out to audiences beyond festival screenings in a red-carpet setting. Entering a film at a festival is seen as a way of opening doors to what lies beyond, to a string of showings at other festivals and, later on, to proper distribution via theatrical and DVD deals for a wide range of territories.

Film festivals lack clear governance or coordinating institutions, hence the difficult logistics of their supply chain management. Besides the official film markets that accompany some of the big festivals and remain the domain of film industry professionals and clear-cut distributors, there is the informal but increasingly networked and efficient system of flow through festival links, where a small film from an obscure source can be picked up by a succession of festivals and shown consecutively in various localities, thus getting truly global exposure. This is not 'distribution', and the exposure may not bring along measurable financial gains. Yet the value-added aspect of flow through the festival chain cannot be ignored. A randomly chosen example might be the work of Portuguese director Pedro Costa. Although not available in distribution, in recent years his films have received global exposure, having been shown and celebrated across the continents at festivals in Hong Kong, Buenos Aires, Belgrade, Toronto, Tokyo, Thessaloniki, Locarno and beyond.

In many cases, including Pedro Costa's, the string of showings on the festival circuit is where a film's exposure both begins and ends. 'Festivals effectively enclave a film', writes Janet Harbord, 'seal it off from general release and, further, restrict its circulation among and between festivals' (2001: 68). Many films which otherwise would not be seen beyond their immediate domestic environment stay solely within the festival track. In this respect, festivals are no substitute for something else. Screening the film at festivals is not a means of getting the film to real exhibition; it *is* the real exhibition. Increasingly, theatrical distribution potential is exhausted via festival showings, where international films get picked up and often play at over forty festivals around the world.

On the one hand, such festival showings give the film a wonderful subsidised exposure. For the same reason many Hollywood blockbusters premiere out of competition at key festivals. On the other, however, when the festival circuit comes to occupy such a critical role in the life of the film, it forms an added 'window of distribution' that almost certainly affects future revenues.[1]

Thus, various films have access to different types of exposure. Some are distributed via distribution networks, while others are exhibited through festivals. In that, there is a distinction to make: most festivals are not in the business of film distribution, either mainstream or alternative. They are in the business of showing films.

Hollywood and Bollywood films do not need the festival network to reach their audiences. Many play at festivals via prints provided by (or rented from) the distributor that has been attached to the project from inception. Most of the films made in independent contexts, however, depend on festival participation, as it secures circulation beyond their original environment.

Festivals need films. Usually taking place once a year in a fixed location, festivals create temporary exhibition venues that are meant to cater to a defined audience community. In committing to repeat the event on a regular basis, festivals create relatively steady (but not permanent) exhibition venues that require a regular supply chain which can adjust flexibly to a schedule that lacks in permanence. The specificity of festivals is that they need a supply chain that is ongoing yet disrupted. Festivals cannot function as active businesses with continuous operations in the way that traditional film distributors and exhibitors do.

The festival is thus an exhibition venue that needs films, but only at a certain time. By default, the very idea of the festival is in constant tension with the underlying logic of continuity as it cannot offer the all-important repeat business that is the premise of all distribution activity. Thus, from the point of view of the suppliers (producers and distributors), the festival does not offer on-going exhibition opportunities for the kind of product they work with, which is essentially 'perishable' and has only a limited shelf life. It therefore presupposes a disrupted supply chain, one that may not be fully practical in economic terms but that adds value to the product passing through it and could be effectively analysed through the management theory of the value chain (Porter 1985).

Indeed, festivals may be most productively understood if scrutinised more from point of view of exhibition.

Chapter Two

When we study the history of early Hollywood, we are often told that the growth in film production was triggered by the need to secure a steady supply of films for the exhibition venues that theatre owners had already set up (Bordwell et al. 1985; Gomery 1986). In other words, the initial growth in the film industry was a typical consumption-driven supply chain set-up. Like in early Hollywood, in the case of festivals, films are needed as content for existing venues.[2] And if we recognise the primacy of the venue in the study of festivals, we get a better chance of understanding and interpreting the various efforts festivals make in order to overcome the shortcomings of their idiosyncratic and limited supply chain. Marijke de Valck's description of festivals as 'the most prominent alternative exhibition context for film' (2006: 27) is particularly apt, as it recognises the primacy of exhibition but also the 'alternative' nature of the venue: it does not function on a regular basis but only comes about occasionally in the context of cinema's supply chain and in that it alternates with regular venues.

The global film festival phenomenon is not inherently networked. Most festivals come about as singular ventures, independently from each other as temporary entities and discrete exhibition sites. They mushroom autonomously from each other, copying each other's model and replicating it in their own locality. It is only after a festival is established locally that the issue of its relationship with other festivals in what constitutes a loose network comes about. In that, individual festivals are discrete phenomena that spring up independently rather than as part of an orchestrated move.

As festivals lack in permanence, their need for content flow is sporadic and limited in time. From the point of view of content suppliers, however, festivals ought to collaborate in a networked and coordinated manner; otherwise the product that is being supplied cannot move smoothly through the supply chain or receive the level of exposure that is sought for it. Thus, the main challenge for festivals is to establish a model that can function as (or at least resemble) a steady supply chain and simultaneously accommodate the reality of their discontinuity. It is the need to establish a fluid supply chain in a discrete milieu that makes festivals link in a loose network and seek to initiate some sort of sequence for product transmission.

It is not correct to think of festivals as a distribution network. Festivals are exhibition venues that need a sporadic supply of content. The network aspect only comes later and on an ad hoc basis. As temporary exhibition venues, festivals have difficulties maintaining steady relations with suppliers and cannot commit to working with distributors the way distributors would like. Most processes that evolve around festivals, then, are triggered by the need to seek solutions to this limitation.

Some leading festivals react by creating an ongoing supply relationship with *auteurs* whose films they showcase on an exclusive basis (indeed they sometimes compete fiercely amongst themselves for this exclusivity). If a celebrated director whose films have traditionally been showcased at Venice moves to Cannes, for example, this is usually regarded as 'defection'. In one context such a move may signal a change in the position of the filmmaker in the establishment of World Cinema, but in practical terms it is nothing more than a disruption in the supply chain.

Mark Peranson's (2008) discussion on the complex and secretive relations between distributors/agents and festivals reflects precisely on these issues. The lack of transparency he observes can be partially explained with the impossibility of setting up permanent supply chain arrangements between festivals and distributors. The fact that festivals' attempts to set up their own distribution operations do not seem to have succeeded so far is also suggestive: the very nature of the festival as a transitory exhibition venue precludes the idea of flow that is in the roots of distribution.[3]

It is notable that it is a producers' organisation, FIAPF (International Federation of Film Producers Associations, http://www.fiapf.org/intfilmfestivals.asp), which represents producers but not distributors, that has managed to make the most advanced inroads into correlating and controlling the chain of large festivals, thus suggesting that producers regard the festival circuit as a 'direct' showcase for their output, a unique set up that brackets out the powerful intermediaries of distribution.

The FIAPF has often been criticised for its supposedly heavy-handed arbitration on matters of geographical and temporal equilibrium. The controversies that evolve around its attempts to regulate are more than indicative. On the one hand, festivals that have managed to secure a relative permanence in their supply chain (Toronto, Sundance, Rotterdam) have routinely avoided seeking accreditation through FIAPF. Rotterdam's former director, Simon Field, summarised the stance most clearly: 'FIAPF would not deliver us any advantages that we could not negotiate for ourselves' (Timms and Seguin 2003: 2). Sundance, which has access to its own supply chain of indie cinema, has neither held nor sought FIAPF accreditation. Its director, Geoffrey Gilmore, proclaimed that FIAPF's designation of A festivals is 'an antiquated system' and 'has promoted a certain level of mediocrity' at that (Frater 2007). Montréal's director, Serge Losique, who at one point also had a showdown with FIAPF, renounced the A-category and declared it 'obsolete', pointing to the formidable reputation of the festival in Toronto which is not competitive and has only a third-category standing with FIAPF (Seguin 2005). No wonder these festivals do not feel beholden to FIAPF; they have all secured steady supply chains of their own. Sundance not only survives perfectly well without the FIAPF's alleged assistance; it also flourishes independently of any networks with other film festivals. Meanwhile, Rotterdam's programming is mostly done via scouting, and the only real 'network' link for it is Pusan in Korea the previous fall. Toronto relies on a network that it has set up itself with a select range of festivals; its non-competitive nature and its function to showcase a selection of new cinema for North American programmers gives it a unique function as a hub in its own region.

It is particularly noteworthy, however, that criticism levied against FIAPF efforts to arbitrate is simultaneously criticism against the only clearly articulated attempt to 'network' festivals officially according to certain criteria.[4] The 'alternative distribution network' FIAPF is attempting to instigate and regulate is overburdened by rigid screening rules and exclusivity stipulations. These effectively set the leading festivals in competition with each other while simultaneously claiming to guarantee them a special position within their assigned regions and thus facilitate the flow of quality cinema. Under the current FIAPF set up, twelve A-category festivals are scattered around the world, yet their content must not overlap; each of them should screen at least 14 brand new films as part of the official competition. Thus, the number of quality new titles needed to satisfy the A-festival circuit competition comes to a total of at least 168 films annually. It is a requirement which FIAPF, as an organisation of producers, needs in order to ensure that festivals function as a vertically integrated system guaranteeing exhibition to their product. In fact, however, critics have repeatedly remarked that no more than 20 to 40 films are artistically strong enough to merit screening them at major festivals. As the larger events vie to programme them, competition grows ever fiercer (Cousins 2006) – and all within a network that is supposed to link festivals rather than set them apart.

Parallel Circuits

In a recent conversation, Toronto's Kay Armatage (2008), who is researching women's film festivals around the world, made a crucial observation: she noted that the festivals that had burgeoned in the 1970s and 1980s had not come to create a network between themselves, and thus no 'calendar' or 'circuit' of such women's events at various locations in North America and around the world had ever come into existence. In addition, they had never become part of the general 'festival circuit' and were therefore outside the cycle of global film circulation, remaining alternative by default.

More importantly, Armatage remarked, even the best established and most visible of these festivals (such as the one in Créteil near Paris, which has now been in existence for 30 years) did not seem to have given much consideration to the matter of their positioning in relation to the so-called 'festival circuit'. Festival dates were determined usually by domestic considerations of convenience and coordination. Adjusting or correlating them to the dates of other festivals for which filmmakers or programmers may be travelling as well did not seem to have been a factor in deciding on the event's March dates.

Evidently, it comes down to the way the festival itself sees its mission and defines its identity. While Créteil is regarded as the veteran among women's festivals, it has neither been interested in spinning out nor in establishing itself as a network hub. Neither does it conceptualise itself as part of any other festival network. Indeed, Créteil may acknowledge that some correlation to the existing mainstream festival circuit could lead to growth and increase its profile, although these may not be among the festival's key objectives.

The Film Festival Circuit

The question is once again: how networked is the world of film festivals? Besides the fact that film festivals appear well coordinated to researchers approaching them as a system, do they really function as one? Can we imagine a situation where exchanges and interdependencies between festivals are not that significant, and, more importantly, not that vital?

Could it be that festivals are discrete phenomena that are only occasionally clustered in equally discrete circuits? That they replicate each other's models and function in parallel but are neither necessarily intrinsically linked nor inter-reliant on each other?[5]

Such an approach may be appropriate in the context of the growing concerns that festival practitioners have begun voicing over the incessant proliferation in the number of festivals.

For the time being, in defiance of all prophesies of saturation, festivals continue multiplying. But for how much longer can this growth be sustained? Scholars' and practitioners' views seem to differ on this matter. While practitioners are nervous over the conveyor-belt approach that they claim reigns over the festival circuit, scholars see further possibilities for growth.

Let's look at the practitioners first:

More and more festival professionals seem to share the view that some sort of crush is imminent. Mikel Olaciregui, director of San Sebastian IFF, said: 'On an international level the presence of so many festivals is insane … there simply cannot be a festival every week' (Green 2006). Former Edinburgh IFF director Mark Cousins insisted that even if 'masked by glamour and ubiquity, the world of film festivals is, in fact, in crisis. There are too many of them, they are too political, and too colluding' (2006). Barcelona-based programmer Sergi Mesonero Burgos spoke of a 'festival epidemic in Spain' and quoted distributor Pedro Zaratiegui, who had stated: 'We are experiencing a scandalously overwhelming and stupid emergence of festivals throughout the entire country' (Mesonero Burgos 2008: 9). Journalist Geoffrey Macnab predicted that many of the film festivals 'are bound to be buffeted eventually' in the context of deepening recession (2008).

Yet scholars who investigate festivals do not seem to share these concerns. de Valck believes that festivals can continue proliferating without much serious repercussion because of specialisation: 'Despite the proliferation of festivals, the network/system has not collapsed', she writes. 'The reason for this is that there is a strict task division between festivals; a small number of major festivals have leading positions as marketplace and media event and the remaining majority may perform a variety of tasks ranging from launching young talent to supporting identity groups such as women or ethnic communities' (2006: 45). Elsaesser also believes that the system of festivals can bear even further expansion because, in his expression, it has 'capillary action and osmosis between the various layers' and is 'highly porous and perforated' (Elsaesser 2005: 87).

An interesting example related to the functioning of parallel circuits is revealed in the case of the large festivals in Toronto and Montréal.

Chapter Two

Montréal's World Film Festival, until recently the only A-category status festival in North America, traditionally took place in high summer. Occasionally its dates came extremely close to the dates of the big festival in Toronto (in early September), a festival with no FIAPF accreditation but nonetheless a real magnet for industry professionals. Yet as Turan has claimed, the two festivals never really had much to do with each other as they occupied different niche positions within the international circuit. While Toronto functioned as showcase for films hopeful to find a North American distributor, Montréal was respected as a non-commercial celebration of cinematic art (Turan 2002: 172-80). It appears that the two events never came into particularly fierce competition, even though there are plenty of anecdotes in circulation about the special measures taken by the Montréal fest's leadership to undermine film professionals trying to benefit from the geographical and temporal proximity and attend both events. Clearly, Toronto and Montréal never functioned in a networked manner, but they never openly fought either; it was more of a parallel co-existence of nodes belonging to different circuits.

More recently, however, in the period 2003–05, the attempt to set a newly established fest (*Festival International du Film de Montréal*) as a direct local, temporal and, most importantly, conceptual competitor to the embattled *Montréal World Film Festival* (MWFF) ended in a serious and highly publicised row (Danielsen 2007).

The fact that the festivals in Toronto and Montréal maintained a parallel co-existence without much interaction and managed to stick to their own agendas over the years without colliding in spite of their proximity in space and time is revealing. A clash only comes about when two festivals are made to engage in a turf war over the same audience. The showdown provided a vivid illustration of the disastrous effects of trying to pursue analogous cultural agendas within a limited time and space while drawing on the same consumer pool. The highly publicised outcry over the arrival of the new high profile festival in Rome in 2006 was of similar nature; the newcomer was accused of impinging on the all-important cultural mission of the veteran IFF in Venice.

The festivals at Rotterdam and Berlin are relatively close in both geography and scheduling, with only ten days or so in late January to early February separating the two. At a first glance it may seem that the two events would annihilate each other. Yet the relationship between these key players on the global circuit has been more like rubbing shoulders; the scheduling seems to have worked well over the years as many of the important attendees who go to Rotterdam also go to Berlin (after having attended Sundance, if they come from America).

How is such amicable co-existence possible? Isn't it all down to clever positioning on the calendar that would secure avoidance of calendar clashes?

Apparently, there are other factors at play here, not least the fact that the main supply chains of these festivals overlap very little: Sundance showcases American indies, Rotterdam relies mostly on premiering Asian fare, while the FIAPF-accredited A-category Berlinale is one of the winter 'heavy-weights' (the other two being Cannes and Venice). Bringing in an exclusive and healthy supply of quality films for the programme appears to be of paramount importance. However, securing good films is down to the approach of the individual festivals. It is not determined by their position on the calendar but much more by the strategic work of artistic directors (hence issues of succession planning at the key festivals attract close scrutiny).

It is noteworthy that lead programmers may regularly attend other festivals, but they do not depend on such attendance as they have other ways to source the material for their events. Programmers are much more dependent on personal networking, targeted visits, and solicitation of direct submissions. In fact, they see films mostly from the DVD screeners that are submitted as part of the entry procedure, and as a rule their viewings take place after the host of submitted DVDs have been seen and filtered by a group of scout-screeners. These eliminate a significant proportion of the submissions and then prepare a 'short list' for the attention of the selection committee. Attending other festivals in person is not of decisive importance for festival programmers, as it is not here that they make their choices. Yet they still go to festivals, mostly to show they are part of the community but also to keep up with industry developments and exchange views on who is 'in' in the world of current cinema. Trade magazines, such as *Screen International*, regularly publish information about which festival directors go to which festivals, so that one can figure out which festivals are considered to provide an influential forum for international film.[6]

If some key festivals were to fail entirely or in part, such a collapse may indeed have dismal consequences for the industry itself, including people and businesses. But it would not really affect the other festivals very strongly because their *modus operandi* is not part of a structured network. Similarly, the current proliferation of festivals does not seem to crowd the festival calendar in any troublesome way. It is more about escalation in festivals of parallel type, mostly taking place outside the group of large competitive festivals and not within it. The events that constitute these parallel circuits form pronounced networks between themselves. Thus, while highly 'porous and perforated' (Elsaesser), their structure is such that some parts can exist easily without the others. There is a clear division between the different circuits, and they follow parallel, overlapping cycles across the globe and around the year.

These parallel circuits are so numerous that it is difficult to even to begin listing them. For example, the global circuit of festivals of the Soviet sphere during the Cold War (Moscow, Karlovy Vary, Tashkent, Havana, etc.) existed for decades without much interface or interference with the system of festivals in the West. A list of various parallel circuits could include networks of type (short film, ethnographic film, animation, documentary), genre (comedy, mountain films), target audience (children, seniors), or social concern film festivals (human rights, women's issues, gay and lesbian issues). Then there are festivals of local survey (Brazilian film in Paris), regional survey (East Asian, Eastern European, Mediterranean), diasporic festivals (Bosnian film in Chicago, the network of Jewish Film Festivals around the world), and even events following their own idiosyncratic agenda, like my favourite one in the tiny sardine-factory town of Douarnenez in Brittany, France, which has persisted over more than three decades with its interest in minority cultures from around the world. There are festivals with significant commercial activity (Cannes, Berlinale, Sundance), festivals of festivals (Toronto, London), commercial showcase festivals (Deauville's American Film Festival), thematic festivals (slow food, fashion), tourism-enhancing festivals (Bahamas, St. Barth, Marrakech), festivals promoting cinephilia (Pordenone, Telluride) and festivals promoting film professionalism (cinematography in Bitolja, Macedonia; screenwriting in Cheltenham, England). Wherever there are networks, they are formed around specific agendas that focus on fostering and showcasing (and not distributing) a certain type of cinematic product.

Conveyor Belt or Treadmill?

'The big festivals have become like a bumpy conveyor belt, waiting for the films that are ready'
– Moritz de Hadeln, professional festival director (Rodier 2003: 1)

Every time I go to a film festival, I witness a variation of the following exchange. It usually takes place between two men, usually bespectacled and with longish grey hair. Other props include trainers and a bag full of promotional materials over the shoulder. The scene is somewhere near the press office, around the festival pigeonholes assigned at the time of accreditation. The protagonists bump into each other, and each time an almost identical dialogue occurs:

A. Did you manage to do the X Fest this year?
B. No, I couldn't. There was a bad overlap with the Y Fest and I could only do one or the other as I was headed for the Z Fest immediately after returning from the Y Fest. But I hear it was nothing special this time. Did you go? How was it?
A. Well, the X Fest was certainly interesting, especially some contacts I made there, but they had to leave early in order to catch the last day of the Y Fest.
B. Yes, very busy indeed. And I've got to go even now. Maybe you're going to the XX Fest, though? I'm set to go and whatever I missed at the X Fest, I'll probably still manage to see there ...
A. Yes, sure. I'll be there, but only if I manage to coordinate it with the trip to the YY Fest. I've got commitments there, you know.

The Film Festival Circuit

B.   Well, see you at the XX Fest! Let's try to catch up there finally. Would be great!

The same scene takes place again the next time around at the XX fest, as they discuss plans for attending the XXX Fest, the YYY Fest and the ZZZ Fest and, later on, the next cycle of the X Fest, the Y Fest, and the Z Fest.

Moritz de Hadeln, who certainly knows the ins and outs of the film festival circuit, has compared it to a 'conveyor belt'. Still, given the typical festival episode I have just described, I wonder if it is not more appropriate to speak of the circuit as a 'treadmill'. The conveyor belt metaphor implies a set-up that functions independently from the people who service it. When, in *Modern Times*, Charlie Chaplin turns away from the conveyor belt, it does not stop; instead it goes on and on and on. In contrast, the treadmill is in motion only for as long as there is the living person to 'service' it, only as long as there is someone to keep it in motion. Like the treadmill, the festival circuit sustains itself only for as long as people like the two gentlemen A and B keep going to X, Y, and Z Fests to have their little exchanges about the XX, YY and ZZ Fests in the context of what critics like Jonathan Rosenbaum have called 'festival-hopping' (2002: 143). If these men stop returning, there will be no festival *circuit* any more. It is through the incessant movements of these 'sole traders' between festivals that the appearance of a 'networked nature' is created. They are usually engaged in agreeing to small-scale projects of a self-employed nature (organising a panel discussion, programming a sidebar). Their goings-on can be likened to the activities of door-to-door salesmen, a way of selling that is regarded as uneconomical and survives only in a handful of areas. Yet the 'networked nature' of festivals proves to be truly dependent on the existence of this class of cinephile freelancers who keep the festival treadmill going.

As festivals have come about independently from each other, there is no central body to organise what is happening on the 'circuit' and the events work without elaborate coordination between them. Wherever there is coordination, it is usually a matter of goodwill of individual arrangements and not a matter of principle. As a matter of fact, more anecdotes are told about steps taken by festival organisers to stand in the way of other events rather than collaborate with them. Sooner or later, it becomes clear that festivals do not really work in a properly networked manner. From the point of view of suppliers (film producer, distributor, agent), however, they ought to function in some networked way. Otherwise the product that is being sent in on a regular basis would not reach the level of exposure that it needs in order for the whole operation to break even. Sending a film to a single festival cannot possibly make economic sense. There must be a string of festivals for the effort to pay off, and there must be a distribution network beyond the festival for it to make real sense (and maybe even turn in a profit). In most cases the suppliers of film content are satisfied with ensuring that the product is showcased at a string of festivals, and it is the sole traders of the festival treadmill that are crucial in securing the transmission links between festivals.

Chapter Two

One such person, for example, is the Frenchman Pierre Rissient, a key 'sole trader' who is credited with being one of the most influential film industry and festival circuit operators (see the discussion of his role in Corless and Darke 2007). He is also specifically responsible for creating a 'network' between European and North American cinephile culture by linking the Cannes and Telluride Film Festivals.[7] So important is the role of Rissient as a 'go-between' that a film was even made about him; *Man of Cinema: Pierre Rissient* (Todd McCarthy, USA, 2007) was partially shot by festival superstar Abbas Kiarostami. Other similar figures are Briton Tony Rayns, who has played a vital role in securing the triumph of East Asian cinema at festivals across Europe and North America, or the tireless Berlin-based American Ronald Holloway, who has been instrumental in bringing obscure East European cinema to the attention of the West for over 40 years.

Some of the sole traders on the festival-hopping treadmill have tried to rationalise the linking of festivals. There was an attempt several years ago, for example, by publicist Sandy Mandelberger to create package programmes of current cinema. These packages would be put together in the context of big film festivals and showcased as travelling sidebars at a circuit of secondary festivals. This way one programming effort would lead to multiple exposures, a situation that would resemble more a distribution chain than a mere act of singular exhibition. I have no information on what happened to this idea, but as nothing much has been heard of it since it was first covered in the trade media, I assume it has not taken off. On the other hand, there are some examples of successful coordinated programming of sidebar features between festivals based in different geographical areas as well as between cinematheques. If there is a Catherine Breillat sidebar at some of the big European festivals, for example, there is likely to be a variation of it scheduled at several of the smaller European festivals within the next year and a few months later at some of the American, Asian and Latin American festivals. Programming at leading cinematheques around the world is often networked. If the Munich cinematheque, for example, puts together a Fassbinder retrospective, for the next two years cinematheques at London, Paris, New York, Los Angeles, Mexico City, Toronto, Hong Kong and Tokyo will feature it.

The discrete and disjointed nature of festivals is rooted in an awkward management issue related to the festivals' human resources: high turnover of staff. Festivals rely on volunteers and internships. In order to secure regular access to this vital free labour, they are compelled to maintain the hype around what they are doing. Most of the people involved with festival work are self-employed with low incomes reported on tax-returns. They are largely reliant on the vernacular economy of piece-meal payment for small-scale projects and on the freebies that they get for being on the festival treadmill (flights, accommodation, meals, drinks and movies). Normally, festivals cannot afford to employ staff on a full-time basis; even the biggest festivals operate with a small permanent staff of fewer than 20. While the staff of Cannes has been quoted at 300 'during the height of the festival'

(Beauchamp and Béhar 1992: 46), out of season there is only core full-time staff and a network of casual scouts and screeners who supplement their income by freelancing for a range of other events (thus 'networking' them). A visit to the Berlinale headquarters outside of season, in April 2003, took me to their nearly empty large edifice on Potsdamer Platz, where the small group of full-time festival employees had clustered in one of the top level corners of the building, occupying no more than five to six rooms. All the rest was empty prime office space guarded by a concierge downstairs.

The human resources reality of festivals — keeping only essential core staff on a full-time basis while simultaneously maintaining an active recruitment pool of large numbers of reliable cheap or free labour around the time of the event — creates an intrinsic need for all those events that are not entirely run on a part-time basis to establish activities that keep them going beyond the dates of the festival and create extra jobs. It is in this context of pursuing regular business that festivals have sought to cultivate audience communities, to set up markets where executives come to meet (even if not to see any films),[8] to involve arthouse cinemas and cinematheques (Munich, Paris), to link up with TV channels (Sundance), use Internet–enabled distribution (Palm Springs via Jaman.com), set up associated production arms (MonteCinemaVerite Foundation, Hubert Bals Fund, or similar enterprises at Thessaloniki, Yerevan, Vienna, and many other festivals), distribution operations (Rotterdam's distribution initiative), special screening tours (London IFF's travelling shows), cinematheque-type activities (Douarnenez festival's association), Institutes (Sundance),[9] consortia (Toronto Film Festival Group), archival libraries (Toronto IFF), initiated by festivals come about.

Conclusion

Historically, de Valck has noted (2007: 14-16), festivals sprang up to compensate for the poor system of film distribution in Europe.

European film distribution has many shortcomings indeed; some would even say it is beyond repair. Undoubtedly festivals compensate for some of its ills, but our investigation seems to cast doubt over the view that festivals may have formed a meaningful distribution network that can stand up to or rival Hollywood's tightly-coordinated distribution operation. If festivals operated as a well-coordinated network, they probably would have overcome the inconsistencies of the disrupted supply chain that still prevent them from operating as a smooth set of connections. For the time being, however, most of the evidence points in the direction of their frail economic logic.

'With respect to Europe', Elsaesser has written, 'the festival circuit has become the key force and power grid in the film business' (2005: 83). As Cousins has argued, however, even if some festivals seem to diversify into production and distribution and, with their affiliated markets, play an increasingly important role as power-brokers in the world of industry, their position of 'visible and glamorous' shop windows remains reactive and responsive and they do not really have much clout of their own (2006).

Yet in spite of the variety of interpretations, festivals continue to thrive and proliferate. This very fact defies, at least for the time being, any scepticism that may surge in the context of closer scrutiny of the festival circuit. In a context of decreasing importance of theatrical distribution, with the introduction of further technological developments and the ongoing shift of cultural consumption into the 'Long Tail' domain (Anderson 2006), it is possible that festivals as well will be reinvented in some new viable alternative forms.

Notes

[1] With data generally unavailable on the details of how deals between sales agents and festivals are being worked out (Peranson 2008), it is difficult to estimate the danger festival exposure poses to diminishing the commercial prospects of a film by festival exposure.

[2] Certain examples illustrate this very clearly: For instance, Serge Losique, the unsinkable director of the Montréal World Film Festival, owns the festival's principal venue, the Imperial Theatre (Danielsen 2007). Retaining control over the exhibition venue is probably the key factor that explains the survival of the festival even after the massive, well-funded, authorities-supported and organised onslaught it sustained in the 2003-05 period.

[3] Or, as Marijke de Valck aptly observes: 'The temporary structure of the festivals, in fact, harked back to the pre-distribution era ... Film festivals bypassed distribution ...' (2007: 93).

[4] For further discussion of FIAPF's difficulties see my article on the accreditation controversies related to the Karlovy Vary Festival (Iordanova 2006).

[5] It is a model that compares to Higher Education Institutions. Some universities have entered networks, as seen in the case of looser or more formal groupings such as *Ivy League* in the USA, *Russell Group* in the UK, or *Universitas 21* internationally, where individual members have agreed to join forces around certain principles, like a shared target audience or level/model of service offered. The interaction between the networks, however, is a different matter and in many cases it is non-existent. As with film and other festivals, the same geographical location can be home to several universities that do not interact with each other as they target different demographies.

It is noteworthy that even the proponent of Latour's Actor-Network Theory (ATN), Marijke de Valck, remarks that ATN 'offers a less appropriate perspective when it comes to the point of where local festivals connect to the international film festival circuit. The festival circuit is not like a Latourian network ...' (2007: 35).

[6] In a recent interview with *Screen International* (May 2008), Cannes Film Festival's Thierry Frémaux listed the festivals he attends. In the past, before taking over the helm at Cannes, he preferred some of the reputed American cinephile festivals, like Telluride and San Francisco. But these days he goes to Berlinale (February), Venice IFF (late August) and Pusan IFF, Korea (October). See Iordanova (2008).

[7] Within days of writing these lines on Rissient in February 2009, I happened to sit in Belgrade in the company of veteran director Dusan Makavejev, who, completely out of the blue, told an anecdote from the 1971 edition of Cannes that involved Rissient and director John Ford. With that he once again asserted the importance of the 'sole trader' who in this case had been instrumental in introducing aspiring Makavejev to the American veteran.

[8] It is particularly noteworthy that dedicated market events in Europe (like the veteran October film market in Milan, Italy) did not seem to withstand the booming competition of festival-affiliated markets (like Berlinale's ever-growing European Film Market). Yet the success of the recently launched Paris and London screenings of local productions suggests that there may be new marketing forms that are likely to be instrumental in countering the festivals' efforts in dubbing as marketplace.

[9] In a recent article John Hazelton (2008) reported on the evolution Sundance Institute's *Arthouse* project in which the festival enters ongoing interactions with arthouse cinemas across the US. According to Russ Collins who runs the initiative, the purpose is mostly geared to fostering growth in 'community-based, mission-driven' speciality theatres and cultivating steady audiences for the indie product the supply of which Sundance regulates ('to support independent artists and audiences for independent artists', 'to build institutions in local communities that will build audiences for independent art product').

Works Cited

Anderson, Chris (2006) *The Long Tail: How Endless Choice is Creating Unlimited Demand.* London: Random House.

Armatage, Kay (2008) Personal interview. Paris, June.

Beauchamp, Cari and Henri Béhar (1992) *Hollywood on the Riviera: The Inside Story of the Cannes Film Festival.* New York: William Morrow and Co.

Chapter Two

Bordwell, David, Janet Staiger and Kristin Thompson (1995) *The Classical Hollywood Cinema: Film Style & Mode of Production to 1960*. New York: Columbia University Press.

Corless, Kieron and Chris Darke (2007) *Cannes: Inside the World's Premier Film Festival*. London: Faber and Faber.

Cousins, Mark (2006) 'Widescreen: Film Festivals', *Prospect*, 129, December.

Danielsen, Shane (2007) 'Serge Losique Conquers Montréal Scene: Festival's Middle-of-the-road Maverick', *Variety*, 24 August. On-line. Available
HTTP: http://www.variety.com/index.asp?layout=cannes2007&jump=features&id=2656&articleid=VR1117970812 (1February 2009).

De Hadeln, Moritz (2000) 'In the Year 2000, and Beyond...', in W. Jacobsen (ed.), *50 Years Berlinale: Internationale Filmfestspiele Berlin*. Berlin: Nicolai, 535–41.

de Valck, Marijke (2006) 'Film Festivals: History and Theory of a European Phenomenon that Became a Global Network', unpublished PhD thesis, University of Amsterdam.

____ (2007) *Film Festivals: From European Geopolitics to Global Cinephilia*. Amsterdam: Amsterdam University Press.

Elsaesser, Thomas (2005) 'Film Festival Networks: The New Topographies of Cinema in Europe', *European Cinema: Face to Face with Hollywood*. Amsterdam: Amsterdam University Press, 82-108.

Frater, Patrick (2007) 'Gilmore Launches Scathing Attack on FIAPF,' *Variety*, 18 June. On-line. Available
HTTP: http://www.varietyasiaonline.com/content/view/1545/53/ (1 February 2009).

Gomery, Douglas (1986) *The Hollywood Studio System*. New York: St. Martin's Press.

Green, Jennifer (2006) 'San Sebastian Chief Warns of Festival Overcrowding', *Screen Daily*, 25 September.

Harbord, Janet (2002) 'Film Festivals: Media Events and Spaces of Flow', in *Film Cultures*. London: Sage, 59-76.

Hazelton, John (2008) 'In the Arthouse', *Screen International*, 5 December, 10.

Iordanova, Dina (2006) 'Showdown of the Festivals: Clashing Entrepreneurships and Post-Communist Management of Culture', *Film International*, 4, 5, 25–37.

____ (2008) 'Film Festivals: Cannes Director's Calendar.' *DinaView*, 14 May. On-line. Available
HTTP: http://www.dinaview.com/?p=40 (1 February 2009).

Macnab, Geoffrey (2008) 'Film Festivals Brace for the Recession', *Business Week*, 12 December.

Mesonero Burgos, Sergi (2008) 'A Festival Epidemics in Spain', *Film International*, July, 34, 9-14.

Mr. Busy (2003) 'Accountability at Cannes', *Sight & Sound*, September, 10.

Müller, Marco (2000) On the Role of Festivals', *Kerala International Film Festival*. On-line. Available HTTP: http://www.keralafilm.com/iffk5/chatmuller.html (2 October 2005).

Peranson, Mark (2008) 'First You Get the Power, Then You Get the Money: Two Models of Film Festivals', *Cineaste*, 33, 3, 37-43.

Porter, Michael (1985) *Competitive Advantage: Creating and Sustaining Superior Performance*. New York: Free Press.

Rae Hark, Ina (ed.) (2002) *Exhibition: The Film Reader*. London and New York: Routledge.

Rodier, Melanie (2003) 'Venice: Next Stop on "Conveyor Belt"', *Screen International*, 1415, 8–14 August, 1–2.

Rosenbaum, Jonathan (2002) 'Trafficking in Movies: Festival-Hopping in the Nineties,' in *Movie Wars: How Hollywood & the Media Conspire to Limit What Films We Can See*. Chicago: Capella Books, 143-75.

Seguin, Denis (2005) 'Distinguishing Marks', *Screen International*, 1511, 19-25 August, 14.

Timms, Daniel and Denis Seguin (2003) 'Credit Where it is Due', *Screen International*, 1408, 6–12 June, 1–2.

Turan, Kenneth (2002) *Sundance to Sarajevo: Film Festivals and the World They Made*. Berkeley: University of California Press.

Chapter Three

Film Festivals-Time-Event

Janet Harbord

The desire to understand the specific nature of the film festival circuit has focused on the spatial dimensions of the event, the many facets that connect festivals to the specificity of sites, and the relation of those sites to one another. When attempting to think of a film festival, its meaning is inseparable from its particular location. And if it is not possible to make sense of a film festival without its emplacement, it is increasingly difficult to imagine certain cities apart from their film festivals. Film festivals both utilise and re-inflect the meaning of a particular site in an endless feedback loop to the extent that the topography of a place is changed to suit the needs of a festival; consider the new infrastructure for the Berlin Film Festival in 2000 and, more recently, the relocation of the Pusan Film Festival across the city. Given the brevity of their duration in the calendar year, this impact on the physical design of a place reveals the cultural and economic import of film festivals. And if a festival appears once annually on the cyclical wheel of civic life, it plays its own part in another kind of rotation: the distribution of films. Festivals act as turnstiles in the largely invisible flow of trade in cultural goods, throwing into relief border crossings and, less visibly, marking out certain blockages and omissions in trade routes.

Given the richness of thinking spatially about film festivals, it is unsurprising that the significance of time in the meaning and structuring of these events has received less consideration. The fact that festivals just seem to happen one after the other, like a series of dominoes falling onto each other throughout the year, is testament to the naturalisation of these curiously intense yet hybrid events. It is my aim here to unravel some of the temporal aspects of film festivals that reveal, beyond this seemingly banal notion of events happening, the complex ways in which time manufactures the event of the festival. Critical to this is the production of a film culture that requires and is played out in a set time. In the context of a proliferating range of viewing practices, themselves multiplying the concept of film culture, the film festival asserts a uniform, unfolding time of film viewing. In this respect it harks back to the institution of cinema as a programmed series of events located in time and space. Yet the festival programme, always offering more films than we can make time for, binds films into a limited structure where the giving of our time is unquestioned. The limited schedule of screenings and ticket sales, the last-minute release of the full programme, and the connected events surrounding screenings all contribute to an obfuscation that time, our time, is a limited resource. It is the fleeting spectre of the festival as event that positions itself as the scarce resource.

There is another way through which the time of film festivals is seen to be significant. If time manufactures the event, the film festival conversely manufactures time, producing an experience of temporality that is in dialogue with the contemporary fragmentation and de-structuring of time. If the time of labour and the time of leisure are less clearly defined at this historical moment than they were a hundred years or so ago, the festival provides the event, an occurrence unfolding in the 'now', which offers both structured and disrupted time. Before approaching the question of how to understand the festival as event, I want to explore how an experience of time is manufactured. This question is made all the more complex and critical in relation to film, a medium known as 'time-based', which is a recording and a document on the one hand and an unfolding series of occurrences on the other. I hope to make the case that cinema is a critical component in the manufacture of time at various historical junctures and that, in the contemporary, the film festival provides a particular experience of temporality.

In Mary Ann Doane's account of cinema at the turn of the twentieth century, the emergence of what she names cinematic time is embedded in the dynamic forces of modernity. Far from an abstract concept, 'Time was indeed *felt* – as a weight, as a source of anxiety, and as an acutely pressing problem of representation' (2002: 4). She continues, 'Modernity was perceived as a temporal demand', a demand for a consensual measure of time operating across space and necessitated by railway timetables and telegraphy, a demand for bodies to be regulated by a centralised time scale in industrial labour practices (the factory). The measure of time is ideologically part of a rationalisation of behaviour, a measure of energy expended in a given period that can be calculated as an economic outcome (wages). Pocket watches were the accessory of the late nineteenth century, adorning the body with its own regulatory device that connected the individual to the clock time of capitalist production. Watches, for Doane, are not simply an accessory but a visualisation of time as a series of units amenable to calculation and a sense of veracity: 'Time becomes uniform, homogenous, irreversible, and divisible into verifiable units' (2002: 6).

Cinema appears, at the outset, to conform and comply with this new experience of temporality in its visualisation of time, its archiving capacity, and its ability to render time as a unit of leisure organised in advance. Yet for Doane, cinema in its earliest and most popular manifestation performs a resistance to the oppressive rationalisation of experience as knowable, linear and recordable. The most popular genre of early cinema was the actuality film, the recording of events that happened to occur before the camera and outside of the control of the operator. In so doing, cinema attested to the limits of the control of time and events, upending or even complementing rationalisation with the spectre of chance. Contingency exploded onto the cinematic screen to reveal happenings, curiosities of accidents and hazards. In another version of the genre, it presented within the frame details that the observing subject may have missed: the eye of the camera undercut the security of human vision. The appeal of contingency as a comic form did not disappear but continued as a manufactured contingency in the capers of silent film where the slapstick gesture became the *accidental performed*.

There is a well-rehearsed argument that the loose experimental forms of early cinema gave way to the structuring devices of narrative and that cinema was quietly sculpted (not least by distributors keen to standardise product) into the dramatic sequence that became synonymous with the Hollywood studio system. Film, the argument runs, was made servile to the Taylorised labour practices of the production line. But this moment of early cinema remains a significant moment historically for its illumination of a paradox at the heart of modern life: the demand for routine on the one hand, as a working rhythm of daily life in which leisure and labour time are clearly distinguished, and the need for manoeuvre, differentiation and diversity on the other. Cinema provided both, deploying the appeal and threat of contingency contained within the temporal parameters of the cinema programme: film viewing as an anticipation of the unexpected and hazardous, but safe within the knowledge that the event has already happened (and is therefore contained) in a time prior to screening. In Doane's reading, cinema afforded a type of safety valve for the pressures of modern temporality, a release from the demands of an increasingly rationalised experience of time always already measured, calculated and given value in advance.

There are, although perhaps not obviously so, correspondences between the institutionalisation of cinema and film festivals a century later. Where an early form of cinema sought to embed film as a pre-recorded medium into a live theatrical context, the film festival approaches the same task, although moving from the direction of an established cinematic programme towards a live event. The film festival re-appropriates the time of contingency but does so within a rigid temporal structure, the short duration of the festival programme. Contingency is rooted in a ritual practice that is both known in advance and open to the forces of chance, a contingency produced by the act of staging. Each city or town hosting the event is required to invent theatre. On the website of the coming Locarno Film Festival (2009) there is a notable celebration of the staging of the festival, a short film that shows the dressing of the location. *The Piazza Getting Ready* is a two minute time-lapse film that compresses the week of preparation for the festival: the vast piazza screen is built as a skeletal framework, the pieces attached one by one, and projection tested in a series of images flashed up.[1] The site is suddenly clear of traffic, the chairs begin to appear row upon row in the manner of Vertov's opening sequence to *Chelovek s Kino-apparatom* (*Man With a Movie Camera*, Dziga Vertov, Soviet Union, 1929). In the construction of this theatre, surrounded by the historical buildings of the main square, the time of human labour is minimised. The effect of this time-lapse is that the scene builds whilst the human figures disappear, smudged or rubbed out by the mechanism of ellipsis. At moments, figures appear fleetingly at the edges of the construction, but the main effect is to bring the event magically into existence. The festival comes to life by an animation that is removed from, and removes, the labour of human hands.

The contingency of early cinema, of the magic of anticipation, has become the contingency of the event itself. In this short film, which shows what is to come through the lens of what has been, the twin forces of planning and chance are made evident: whatever is planned may become undone. The appeal of the event is not evident simply in the ritual practice of viewing a showcase of films, in the case of Locarno, open-air screenings. It is also evident in the fact that the event may be interrupted, that its liveness may spill over into the unexpected, a performance witnessed but not reproducible. The time of the film festival reworks the contingency of early actuality films and the thrill of the accidental, placing it in the unfolding structure of the event. Immediacy is often associated with the televisual, with the live relay of an event as an anticipation of a radical loss of control. But the televisual is mediated, framed, at a distance. The liveness of the film festival is a curious choreography between various performers acting now and a recorded medium. The strictly controlled access to the event ensures that the festival creates what might be taken for the present, a time of now, paradoxically working with the recorded medium of film.

The accidental in film festivals may appropriate the capering form of slapstick. Two jury members at Cannes 2008 (Iranian director Marjane Satrapi and French actress Jeanne Balibar), who smoked their way through a press conference despite the ban on smoking in public places, appeared Chaplinesque as unwitting victims of circumstance. Of a different genre, and more widely reported, were Sharon Stone's comments (at the same festival) dismissing the Sichuan earthquake as 'karma' for the Chinese government's treatment of Tibet. Each of these spectacles produced not only controversy but, more significantly, a sense of the event running live, and of a temporal liveness that is guaranteed by speech and actions misfiring. 'The accident always happens in the present', Sylvere Lotringer says, 'but is *untimely*' (Lotringer and Virilio 2005: 100), suggesting that it is a happening that appears to have no 'place' in the event, that it throws time out of joint. Yet, on the contrary, the accidental secures the time of the festival event. And there is a further reversal if one considers the standard reportage of the 'glamour' brought by actors and directors to the event. Their inability to 'perform reliably' (or their reliable unreliability) would appear to be their service to the festival as guarantors of the contingent.

What emerges from this line of questioning of the role of the 'accidental' is the inseparability of structure from contingency. Structure takes shape from the inchoate stream of life, but the inchoate threatens to return, to erupt within the festival. The structuring agency of a festival requires, even demands, the accidental: the festival would cease to be a live event if its

Chapter Three

mechanical smoothness were not disrupted. A critical factor in the manufacture of live time is the role of reporting, the witness statements of journalists and bloggers sent out to the wider public to describe the event that has already happened. If the gate-keeping functions of film festivals are most evident in spatial terms, the barriers and ropes that demarcate internal worlds, the temporal also has a function in this practice of demarcating the event from everyday life, from the outside. Written reportage, which is the main form of festival journalism, is a delayed experience, a postcard as it were emitted from the place of happening. The newspaper report helps to seal the time of the event as a live happening that can only be recounted *afterwards* to those outside of its boundary.

The time of film festivals however is not simply the immediacy of occurrence. It is unlike a sporting or dance event in that its central proposition is a mixing of temporalities, the recorded time of the film and the present time of projection. If this was the paradoxical appeal of film in early cinema, which released its audience from the over-determined clock-time of labour, the time of the festival works a different paradox, one related to the temporalities of digital technologies and decentralised labour. As many have noted, the computer brings with it the blurring of the distinction between the time of work and the time of leisure. In front of a laptop, both labour and leisure are simultaneously available and, perhaps with the current fetishisation of 'creativity', increasingly indistinguishable. The activity of film viewing may be broken up, distributed across the time of days, inserted between a host of other activities. The pre-given unit of film as a product bought or hired is made pliable, available as segments to be downloaded, and tailored to service the temporal needs of the viewer. With the de-institutionalisation of film viewing, the time of the running film is less assured as a unit, open to dispersal across differently textured times and places in a renewed definition of modernity's trope of distraction. A film festival, on the contrary, gathers together the time of the film and the time of viewing. In so doing, it re-institutionalises the collective attention of film viewing and re-centres the time of projection as a live event. This choreography of a dance between the live event on one hand and the recorded, pre-fixed film on the other is the manufactured time of the festival. The alchemy resulting from these different temporalities, the now and the then, characterises the potency of the film festival as event.

The task of the film festival is to make time matter, to give urgency to the viewing of film in an historical context in which the public release of film is no longer a necessarily compelling event of itself. The condensed structure of the festival makes the here and the now of viewing critically important. Contingency, which marks the festival as an unfolding event whose details are unknowable in advance, affords a singularity to the experience: to see a film here and now will be unlike any other time of viewing. This moment of viewing will attach itself to the film in many cases, bringing a film notoriety or award that then becomes part of its circulation, a moment 'carried over'. The past as a disquieting force that animates the present came into focus in a particular way at the Rome Film Festival in the autumn of 2008. The film *Il Sangue dei Vinti* (*Blood of the Losers*, Michele Soavi, Italy, 2008), based on a book by Giampaolo Pansa, fictionalises the period 1943-5 in Northern Italy, a period of intense fighting between proponents of fascism and the resistance, brought the past into the present forcefully. The evocation of this period had many layers of mediation starting with a non-fiction book that was subsequently fictionalised and adapted as a script, and finally constructed, performed and recorded as a film. Following the screening in Rome, a controversy arose: the film had created characters that did not exist in the book. The question of what the past was and how we access it is made more complex by process of filmmaking and the medium of film. The time of the screening event gives that complexity one more twist in another temporal dimension to account for.

There is a way of thinking of film as an assurance of the temporal, a confirmation that time is archive-able, a record of events fixed in the moment of recording. And yet the time of the festival appears to demonstrate the opposite: the present (viewing) is permeated by the past (the recorded film), and the recorded film is changed by every projection. The time of the film and the time of the festival event are inextricable. 'Time doesn't flow', argues Michel Serres, 'it percolates' (1990: 58), and the compressed event of the festival strengthens that percolation process. The work of contingency here is not, as it was in the period of modernism, a mechanism to release the pressure of standardised time. The contingent has additional significance in performing the unknowable outcome of events as a productive force. 'The French language in its wisdom uses the same word for weather and time, *le temps*', says Serres. 'At a profound level they are the same thing ... predictable and unpredictable' (ibid.). This is also the case for film festivals.

Note

[1] *The Piazza Getting Ready two-minute trailer*, 62nd Locarno Film Festival official website: http://www.pardo.ch/jahia/Jahia/home/lang/en/pid/830

Works Cited

Barber, Stephen (2002) *Projected Cities: Cinema and Urban Space*. London: Reaktion Books.

Doane, Mary Ann (2002) *The Emergence of Cinematic Time: Modernity, Contingency, the Archive*. Cambridge, Massachusetts and London, England: Harvard University Press.

Lotringer, Sylvere and Paul Virilio (2005) *The Accident of Art*, trans. Michael Taormina. New York: Semiotext(e).

Chapter Three

Serres, Michel with Bruno Latour (1990) *Conversations on Science, Culture and Time*, trans. Roxanne Lapidus. Ann Arbor: University of Michigan Press.

Part 2

Festival Case Studies

Chapter Four

Festivals as Field-configuring Events: The Annecy International Animated Film Festival and Market[1]

Charles-Clemens Rüling

Introduction

Events play an important role in the emergence and evolution of organisational fields. Festivals create spaces, in which industry actors meet, construct reputation, and constitute and contest shared frames of reference. This study analyses the historical development of an important international film festival and market event, the Annecy International Animated Film Festival and the International Animation Film Market. It examines its growth from the vantage point of recent literature on field-configuring events.

Since its creation in 1960, the Annecy event has established itself as a major international competitive venue and marketplace in the animated film industry. The 2008 festival attracted 6,700 accredited professionals. Five hundred films were screened, with 219 films (selected by an independent jury from over 2,200 festival submissions) competing in five categories: feature films, short films, commissioned films, TV films and graduation films. In addition to the competitive screenings, the festival featured retrospectives, exhibitions, and free public evening screenings on a giant screen by the lake. A total of 115,000 tickets were issued. The festival's three-day International Animated Film Market (*Marché International du Film d'Animation —Mifa*, established in 1985) attracted 1,900 industry professionals from 63 countries including 330 exhibitors and 180 programme buyers. Next to the festival and the market, a 'Creative Focus' has hosted project competitions and recruitment sessions with global firms including Disney, Sony, DreamWorks, Pixar, Marathon and Ubisoft as well as a large number of smaller firms seeking to recruit creative talent. Creatives, film directors and decision makers gathered at various round-table meetings, and a series of high level conferences addressed key issues related to the development of the animation industry.

The current Annecy Festival and Market is the product of a long period of institutional and organisational co-evolution with the animated film environment. Since its beginnings in the late 1950s, the festival has played an important role in creating possibilities of exchange between international animation artists. It has also created mutual awareness of an artistically oriented animation community and both a physical and an institutional space dedicated to this emerging community. Throughout its development and growth, the Annecy event has been regularly confronted with the question of how to respond to changes in its environment. From its initial role of contributing to the institutionalisation and recognition of artistically oriented animation, it has subsequently opened up to actors and contributions from other geographic regions (for example, Japanese animation studios in the early 1970s). It has also welcomed new forms of distribution (for example, the development of private TV channels in the early 1980s), and new technologies and business models (for example, the arrival of digital technologies for animation production, and the recent convergence of animated film, computer games and mobile telecommunication).

Looking at the festival from an organisation theory perspective, this paper seeks to discuss what factors have contributed to the development of the Annecy festival and to its ability to maintain a field-configuring role. Based on the case study data I argue that the Annecy festival has created and maintained its global dominance in the field of animation in a number of different ways: as well as developing a strong symbolic role, it has contributed to the configuration of the field of animation and been able to recognise major industry changes. More recently it has also developed an active role for itself as broker and repository of knowledge within a strongly growing industry and made a conscious effort to position itself on the industry's event circuit.

The remainder of this paper comprises five sections. The next section gives a brief overview over recent research on 'field-configuring events', and the following section presents the historical development of the Annecy festival and market. The subsequent two sections discuss co-evolution and a set of issues related to the management of a field-configuring event. The conclusion finally summarises the main contributions of this study.

Studying Film Festivals as Field-configuring Events

Published research on film festivals from an organisational perspective is scarce. Despite high public and media attention, only few studies seek to understand film festivals from an organisational perspective (see, for example, Benghozi & Nénert 1995; Gamson 1996). For the purpose of this paper, I will adopt a perspective on film festivals as field-configuring events. In order to do so, I will first introduce briefly the notion of field and the field-configuring event and then highlight some implications for this study. The recent concept of 'field-configuring events' (Lampel et al. 2005) provides an interesting avenue for conceptualising the role of film festivals. It sheds light on how particular events (such as major film festivals) consolidate and change organisational fields by providing a setting for the emergence, reproduction and challenging of field-level identities, norms and standards.

From the perspective of institutional theory, organisational fields and field-level processes are crucial to understanding firm level action. Organisational fields include 'those organisations that, in the aggregate, constitute a recognised area of institutional life: key suppliers, resource and product consumers, regulatory agencies and other organizations that produce similar services or products' (DiMaggio & Powell 1983: 148). Fields are characterised by a common meaning system, the field's 'institutional logic', which provides field participants with organising principles and practice guidelines (Scott et al. 2000). Institutional logics evolve through a process in which 'members of an evolving professional group need to seek opportunities to capture their diversity into a set of joint cognitions and shared sense-making that will reduce the cognitive distance between each member' (Oliver & Montgomery 2008: 1049).

Field-configuring events are 'temporary social organizations such as tradeshows, professional gatherings, technology contests and business ceremonies that encapsulate and shape the development of professions, technologies, markets, and industries ... They are settings in which people from diverse organizations and with diverse purposes assemble periodically, or on a one-time basis, to announce new products, develop industry standards, construct social networks, recognize accomplishments, share and interpret information, and transact business' (Lampel & Meyer 2008: 1026). They provide time-spaces for discontinuous and localised processes in the structural and cognitive evolution of organisational fields. By assembling various actors in a limited setting, they create opportunities for social interaction including the construction of reputation and status. In their analysis of the annual Grammy award ceremonies, for example, Anand and Watson (1994) show how this event simultaneously attributes reputation, sets priorities and standards via collective sense-making and identity building, allows the (re)production (or contestation) of power and hierarchies, and creates a space in which normal boundaries temporarily disappear and make room for new forms of exchange and interlocking.

Lampel and Meyer (2008) argue that field-configuring events play different roles within different phases of field development. During field emergence, they contribute to the creation of a common meaning system by defining standards, practices and vocabularies and by positioning the field in relation to entities outside it. Garud (2008), for example, shows how conferences shape technological fields not only through information exchange but also by serving as an arena in which various propositions for technological solutions and standards compete with each other. McInerney (2008) provides evidence of the role of events in the transformation of relatively loose networks into a cohesive field with an established institutional identity. In more mature fields, field-configuring events contribute to the replication of dominant field norms and logics, and to the protection and reinforcement of field identity.

Chapter Four

Historical Development of the Annecy Festival and Market

The historic reconstruction of the Annecy Festival development presented here is based on research interviews with key actors in the festival organisation as well as documents from the festival archive, trade journal articles, and a one-week period of participant observation during the event in June 2008. Following Langley's (1999) suggestion of 'temporal bracketing', I distinguish three main development phases in the historical development of the festival: antecedents and early development (1956 to 1982), growth, market creation and annualisation (1983 to 2003), and Mifa renewal, CITIA, and the feature film challenge (2003 to today). Each phase corresponds to a particular logic of development and a particular kind of role the event plays within the animation field. The end of each of the phases is marked by a crisis in the festival organisation, which is overcome by a change in the event orientation and/or organisation.

Antecedents and early development (1956-82)

The foundations of the Annecy festival were laid in the 1950s, when Pierre Barbin, from the *Association Française Pour la Diffusion du Cinéma*, and the Annecy Ciné-Club, one of the biggest local film societies in France (with several thousand members), met in the context of a cinema week organised by the French National Centre of Cinematography (CNC). After this experience, both parties teamed up to present a non-competitive animated film programme, the *Journées Internationales du Cinéma d'Animation (JICA)*, at the 1956 Cannes Film Festival. This first programme included more than 100 films from all over the word. The second Cannes JICA took place in 1958 and brought together some of the most famous names in animation at that time: Jiri Trnka, Norman McLaren, Alexandre Alexeieff and John Hubley, among others.

For the third biannual JICA in 1960, the organisers decided to transfer the meeting to the city of Annecy. The research interviews and other retrospective sources concur in their suggestion that the organisers and participants did not feel comfortable in the 'glittery world' of the Cannes event, nor did animation receive the expected exposure there (Teninge 2000: 74). Politically, the transfer of JICA to Annecy was underlined by the presence of French president Charles de Gaulle in the context of the centenary celebration of the Savoie region joining France. Economically, the creation of the Annecy festival was welcomed by local authorities and by the festival's historical venue, the Casino Theatre. For the latter, the festival allowed dealing with a regulatory obligation to programme cultural events.

The 1960 Annecy meeting constituted the first ever international animation festival. It led to the creation of ASIFA (*Association Internationale*

52

The Annecy International Animated Film Festival and Market

du Film d'Animation), a professional association of animation artists from all around the world constituting a 'group of enthusiastic animation filmmakers gathering together to share experiences, exchange information and try to come up with the formula that would promote the art of animation around the world' (Teninge 2000: 75). ASIFA put a strong emphasis on East-West exchanges and developed a patronage system enabling the worldwide accreditation of animation film festivals. The permanent office of ASIFA was located in Annecy, and the Annecy festival rapidly became *the* official ASIFA event at which, for example, the general assemblies were held. This can be illustrated with one of the many veteran filmmakers' statements reprinted in a brochure edited for the occasion marking the 25th anniversary of the Annecy Festival:

> Annecy and the festival – I can't imagine anyone in the animated film circles for whom these words do not mean anything. Even those who unfortunately have been unable to attend know of this festival. Is it not the cradle of ASIFA? The first important festivals of our special type of cinema have taken place in this mountainous town and they have made film directors aware of what is important. Thanks to their friendly, merry but nevertheless studious atmosphere, they have created our close community. I have been invited several times by the festival, and those days in Annecy are among the most interesting and the most beautiful in my filmmaker's life. (East German film maker Katja Georgi in *Journées Internationales du Cinéma d'Animation* 1985: 30)

All ASIFA accredited festivals followed a biannual schedule in which Annecy took place in odd-numbered years and most other international animation festivals in even-numbered years (Mamaia, 1966-70; Cambridge/Cardiff, since 1968; Zagreb, since 1972; Ottawa, since 1976).

In the 1970s, the festival was running smoothly. Its organisational structure had remained almost unchanged since the beginning. Film selection and programming were in the hands of a permanent festival office in Paris, headed by Raymond Maillet (who had succeeded the festival's founder Pierre Barbin in 1971), and the local organisation of the festival was the responsibility of the Annecy Ciné-Club. Every other year the festival attracted 300 to 400 film professionals, and the festival programme put a particular emphasis on personal animation (*films d'auteurs*), typically in form of short films:

> Veteran festival goers concur; of course, it was a fantastic experience to be able to see all these films and, sometimes, meet the great masters. But the diversity of techniques and styles was also an eye-opener, and the festival was an unprecedented opportunity to share experiences with other filmmakers. For every artist, Annecy was a barometer. (Teninge 2000: 75)

Chapter Four

In the late 1970s and early 1980s, some stakeholders felt that the artistically oriented festival neglected new developments in the animated film industry, especially the growing importance of didactic and commercial animated film in the context of deregulation and privatisation of television channels together with the emergence of a growing number of thematic channels. Tensions started to develop between Raymond Maillet and ASIFA, and selection and admission criteria used in the Paris festival office were increasingly criticised by excluded participants, namely the CNC and some of the local Annecy stakeholders who blamed Raymond Maillet for his autocratic and patronising management of the festival. In the words of 1983 festival board president Pierre Jacquier:

> The Film Society and its members were still working as hard as they had always done and the organizers in Paris were still doing their job as well as ever. Yet it was the environment that was changing. I'm talking about audience expectations, the whole scale of production and distribution. The festival was running very smoothly but we were going round in circles. It was becoming a kind of stopgap or refuge for personal animation films and rather academic. It was missing out on the new developments in animation and new types of cinematography. New technology and the new economic situation were passing it by. (Pierre Jacquier, quoted by J.-L. Xiberras in Teninge 1997)

With the support of ASIFA and CNC, the festival board decided to move the festival headquarters from Paris to Annecy. This move created strong resentment in parts of the French animation community, which accused the city of Annecy of being a 'reactionary small town trying to appropriate the festival' (Teninge 2000: 77). As a consequence, Raymond Maillet left the festival organisation, and a significant number of professionals temporarily cut their communication with the festival. A new festival director, Jean-Luc Xiberras, was appointed in late 1982. Significant support from ASIFA and especially the Zagreb festival was mobilised in the organisation of the 1983 festival in order to help the new festival management and to compensate for the loss of data and contact information that had been compiled over the years in the Paris office to which the new festival management had no access.

Growth, market creation and annualisation (1983-2003)

Eventually, the 1983 event proved a milestone in the festival history and the beginning of a new era for the festival. It featured a new festival director, a new management team, and also a new Annecy festival venue, the newly inaugurated Bonlieu Culture Centre. The new festival director increased the number of movie theatres from one to six, allowing for a threefold increase in competition screenings together with a large number of tributes, retrospectives and exhibitions. Participation reached a new high of 1,300 accredited professionals. In a 1997 interview, Jean-Luc Xiberras recalled the ideas he held at this time for the future development of the festival:

> The idea ... was to integrate all animation techniques, including the much maligned new technologies, into the competition segment. We also began to work on the idea of a film market for an industry that didn't even exist at the time ... What happened at the time was that filmmakers would come to Annecy and show their films, but everything stopped there. (Jean-Luc Xiberras in Teninge 1997: 17)

In the years following the management change, competition categories multiplied to reflect the development of the economic environment: TV series, advertising and commissioned film categories entered the general competition in 1983. A specific feature film competition was created in 1985, and a special graduation film prize was created in 1995. Since 1989, the festival has awarded distinct prizes for each of the categories.

Jean-Luc Xiberra's overall strategy was to create a highly diverse and buoyant 'animation fiesta': 'He felt that Annecy's public was as diverse as animation itself and needed as wide a range of film programming as possible. He believed, rightly or wrongly, that there should be an abundance of films and that frustration was part of the "game"' (Teninge 2000: 77).

One of the most far reaching changes in the new festival constellation was the creation in 1983 of a 'prototype film market' next to the movie theatre, which provided the foundations for the first official instance of the Mifa *(Marché International du Film d'Animation)* in 1985. The creation of the market was initiated by the festival board and backed by the French government, who had issued a *Plan image* in order to promote the animation industry.[2] From its initial 500 square meters, the Mifa gradually expanded to 3,000 square meters in 1995 'to reach the growing demand from the US majors' (Teninge 1997: 18).

The second major change during this stage of development was the 1998 annualisation of the festival and market. In a 1997 interview, festival director Jean-Luc Xiberras outlined the rationale underlying the creation of an annual event:

> It is exactly what I have been trying to do since 1989! Animation has changed so radically since the festival was set up in the early 1960s that it is simply inevitable. Thirty years ago it took months, even years to make a short film lasting a few minutes. Nowadays, you can put out a new 13 x 13 minute TV series in just six months. The animation industry needs an annual gathering in Annecy, with an annual competition which can act as a showcase for the latest and greatest in this branch of seventh art. The festival and the market, like animated filmmaking and the economics of the industry, are

inextricably linked. And the rendezvous is in Annecy. (Jean-Luc Xiberras in Teninge 1997: 19)

Other official arguments for becoming annual included the need to hold the film market Mifa in an annual rhythm as well as the emergence of American and Asian competitors, the very high number of festival submissions (and thus high number of rejections), the need to develop sponsorship loyalty and the need to further professionalise the festival by ensuring the continuous work of a larger permanent staff − 15 after the annualisation instead of four before.

The decision itself was highly controversial within the animation community. Animation festivals that were held in odd years in accordance with the old ASIFA scheme, namely Zagreb and Cardiff, suffered heavily from the annualisation of the Annecy festival and market. ASIFA harshly criticised the unilateral decision of the Annecy board and argued that 'Annecy was breaking rules that it had asked ASIFA to set, at a time when Annecy feared competition from other mushrooming festivals, and without regard for the other festivals which had been partners for many years' (Teninge 2000).

When Jean-Luc Xiberras, architect of the annualisation and artistic director of the festival since 1983, surprisingly passed away in late 1998, Serge Bromberg was appointed as Xiberras' successor. The new artistic director's main challenge was to define a convincing programme for the new annual festival and market. Critical comments at this time point to the much shorter festival preparation period, the growing weight of the commercial aspects of the festival, and a weakening of the artistic side as well as to the quality of retrospectives and other festival content (see, for example, Ciment 1999). The 40th anniversary festival in 2000 was particularly criticised by more artistically orientated critics:

This new edition will have sadly given wrong to the indulgence of the past: this year, the world's largest animation film festival has completely disappointed, without being able to blame the economic situation. Even though the Mifa has found its marks and proven its legitimacy and the overall organization of the event is of excellent quality, the artistic dimension of the festival left a lot to be desired, so much that, accustomed to return from Haute-Savoie the head full of images, we have a hard time this year remembering any that has deeply marked us. (Let us simply express our irritation with the repeated projection at each session of an interminable and annoying clip presenting partners and sponsors). (Ciment 2000; translated by the author)

The overall animation industry crisis in the aftermath of the burst of the internet bubble and the September 2001 events contributed to falling festival and Mifa attendance in 2001 to 2003, which created a sense of crisis among both the festival organisers and major stakeholders, including the CNC.

Mifa renewal, CITIA, and the feature film challenge (2003-today)

The annualisation of the festival since 1998 put a stronger emphasis on the Mifa film market, but at the same time it paradoxically revealed the imperfections of the existing market format. Since its informal beginnings in 1983, Mifa had been mainly oriented towards informal encounters and the exchange of ideas rather than towards economic transaction of finished films and series (as was the case in established 'pure' film and communication markets like MIP-COM). Turnaround or discontinuation of the Annecy animation film market were the two alternatives discussed in 2004. Notably the CNC questioned the setup and the organisation of the Mifa. In summer 2004, after three years of declining participation and growing pressure from both CNC and the festival board, the manager of Mifa resigned.

An external audit commissioned by CNC concurred with a survey among animation professionals conducted by the new managers of Mifa. It revealed that a large number of market participants felt that the market was lacking business opportunities, and that too few buyers attended Mifa due to a lack of emphasis on sales and concrete transactions. Historically, the market had had a strong focus on content, providing a space where participants could discuss projects, but selling and buying finished productions had not been among the priorities of the Mifa.

The changes implemented by the new Mifa managers since 2005 reinforced the market's transaction orientation by increasing the number of film buyers attending the event, and by attracting participants from traditionally under-represented geographic regions. Initial measures included the invitation of 40 film buyers in order to signal the importance of economic transaction at the Mifa. Feedback from buyers was positive, and many returned in the following years. Other measures included the development of an online video library including all films in the official festival selection as well as Mifa participants' projects. The online library and all professional participants' contact details are available before the festival, thus allowing contacts between potential partners and the planning of meetings ahead of the event. According to the Mifa managers interviewed, the overall number of Mifa participants has developed in close correlation to the number of buyers attending since 2005.

The new emphasis on economic transaction is complemented by a strong emphasis on the Annecy event as a unique learning opportunity for all actors within the global animation field:

A one-week stay at the festival exposes to all major traditions in contemporary animation and enables encounters with all actors playing a role in the animation field: filmmakers, studios, producers,

Chapter Four

distributors, TV channels, technology providers. (Interview with Mifa managers, 25 March 2008; translated by the author)

A further important change was the creation in 2006 of CITIA, the *Cité de l'image en mouvement* (City of moving images), which provided the festival and the market with a new governance structure and embedded the event into a broader strategy of regional economic and cultural policy. CITIA is sponsored by the Annecy agglomeration, the Haute-Savoie department, the region Rhône-Alpes and the French state. Its aim is to develop cultural, economic, and training and research activities related to all aspects of moving images. One of the goals underlying the creation of CITIA was to leverage the festival organisation's experience and reputation in order to favour economic development in the Annecy region. CITIA combines its different activities to complete the festival and market *events* with the idea of becoming a *permanent* actor in regional economic development.

This new orientation seeks to leverage the experience and strong industry expertise of the Annecy organisation and to clearly position the annual Annecy event and its underlying organisation in the animation industry. The Annecy festival and market are embedded in a well-defined industry event circuit (for the idea of a film festival event circuit, see Elsaesser 2005):

The first meeting [for an international co-production] might have taken place in Annecy in June, the partners see each other again at the MIP-COM Junior in October, and eventually sign their project at another event ... We position ourselves on the international event agenda: Forum Cartoon, a European TV meeting, in September, MIP-COM Junior and MIP-COM in Cannes in October, Kidscreen Summit to meet the Americans in New York in February, Cartoonmovie for European feature film pitches in March in Germany, and MIP-TV in Cannes in April. Then there are some regional markets, for example in Hong Kong, to meet the Asian studios that do not come to Cannes. You have to be on the agenda. (Interview with Mifa managers, 25 March 2008; translated by the author)

Maintaining Annecy's place on the industry agenda is a key issue for the festival organisers. The strong link between the festival and the market in bringing together art, technology and commerce plays an important role in singling out the Annecy event within the animation industry. The managers of Mifa spend most of the year visiting other festivals and markets, and meeting studios, buyers, distributors, regional film organisations, etc. This enables them not only to present the Annecy Mifa but also to sense how the industry is developing and to understand new trends as well as the evolution of potential Mifa participants' needs and expectations.

The Annecy International Animated Film Festival and Market

There is a need to remain constantly in contact with the industry. For example, in September, we go to the Cartoon Forum. We do not at all negotiate for the Mifa, we just go there and exchange. We listen carefully to understand the ongoing projects – who does what; we shake hands and build relationships. We do not sign any contract, but it is important to be present in order to be part of the landscape. Those who consider coming to Annecy, they now have contacts. This is part of the change: being available to optimally respond to their needs. They now have someone to talk to. About the logistics in Annecy, but also beyond – you guys have been to Japan, we are looking for a studio there, do you have an idea whom we could contact? ... By meeting all the players, we know who can be interesting for someone else, and we know who is serious and trustworthy in the industry. (Interview with Mifa managers, 25 March 2008; translated by the author)

The festival and market currently face two principal challenges. The first concerns the aim of moving from a 'showcase' event to playing a more pro-active role in the animation field, notably by selecting promising project ideas and by playing an active brokerage role beyond the festival and market in order to ensure project support and accompany project development over time. The second challenge for the Annecy festival and market concerns the event's attractiveness for animated feature films, the animated film genre enjoys both the highest public visibility and the strongest economic development. With its historic image as an artistically oriented festival, its emphasis on short films and its idea of catering primarily to the animation field, Annecy has repeatedly encountered problems in attracting a high quality selection of international feature films into competition. According to the festival management, it is easier to receive international productions for preview screenings than as competition entries. A possible explanation is that producers and distributors refrain from seeing an extremely costly project 'losing' in a competitive setting. Other aspects are related to the growing involvement of more generalist production and distribution companies that do not belong to the traditional Annecy 'animation family'. For the Mifa, which has traditionally strongly focused on TV productions, the new emphasis on feature films implies a stronger orientation towards the movie sector.

In the context of growing public and economic interest in animated feature films, and with the new economic actors involved, new direct competitors for the Annecy festival and market emerge: a growing number of animated feature productions is screened at large generalist festivals like Cannes, Berlin or Venice. In order to meet this challenge and to avoid losing the animated features altogether, the festival has set up a deliberate feature film strategy for the years to come.

Co-Evolution of the Annecy Event and its Environment

Field-configuration assumes a mutual influence between fields and events. Events depend on fields, and the development of a given field will be influenced by events that are related to it. A key argument underlying the idea of co-evolution is that the persistence of an event is related to its adaptability in a situation of environmental change. A field-configuring event's contributions must be in line with the demands of its environment. Table 1 (see overleaf) presents a synopsis of festival development in order to illustrate the co-evolution of the event and its environment.

In the early 1960s, Annecy had a strong influence on the constitution of a group of formerly unrelated, artistically oriented animation filmmakers. Emphasis was on community building through networking and exchange (with the idea of creating regular animation festivals in North America, Western and Eastern Europe, and Asia) and the setting of common rules and standards mainly through ASIFA and its various national sections. Historically the festival organisation depended very much on the personalities of the first festival directors, who had the sole responsibility for selection and maintained important personal networks in the growing animation field.

The emergence of an economically strong market for animated film in the context of structural changes in the television environment together with the willingness of a group of festival stakeholders to open up the festival for more commercial productions created a new form of event during the second phase of co-evolution. The 'community event' was supplanted by a 'showcase event' or 'animation fiesta'. In its new form, the event did not seek to strengthen the identity and recognition of one particular model of animated film; it sought instead to confer legitimacy to various forms of animation, as represented by the growing number of categories in the competition. The creation of a market event reflects the growing diversity of participants. Instead of relying mainly on a network of personal relations with creative and artistic filmmakers, the organisation now emphasised the event and its ability to create a showcase featuring the 'best of animation' in all of its forms.

The third phase identified above is characterised by the movement from a passive 'showcase event' to a more active 'industry event' and beyond towards a new role as an 'industry actor'.

The Annecy International Animated Film Festival and Market

Table 1: Synoptic View of the Development of the Annecy Festival and Market

	Phase 1: 1956-82	Phase 2: 1983-2003	Phase 3: 2004-today
Environment	**'Art driven'** Initially: No recognised field for artistic animation, absence of a venue to learn and exchange about artistic animation. Later: Artistic animation as a recognised art form without economic interest. Since the 1970s: Beginning globalisation of the animation industry (subcontractors in Asia).	**'Market driven'** Strong market growth for short films and series related to development of TV channels; further globalisation of the animation value chain; changing technologies (IT) and shortening production cycles.	**'Business driven'** Global value chains and markets; emergence of new markets, technologies, economic actors and business models; growing interest in 'creative industries' in economic and cultural policies (regional, national, EU levels).
Event characteristics	**'Community event'** Artistically oriented animation (as opposed to commercial production); political agenda: East-West exchange; participants = filmmakers.	**'Showcase event'** New competitive categories, 'animation fiesta', development of film market; participants = filmmakers, producers, distributors.	**'Industry event and industry actor'** New market format, growing creative focus, strongly growing participation of animation students.
Event organisation	**'Person-oriented'** Move from Cannes to Annecy in 1960, biannual event managed from the Paris festival office, 300-400 filmmakers.	**'Event-oriented'** Creation of the Annecy permanent festival office, professionalisation of the organisation, new venue; annualisation and further professionalisation since 1998.	**'Project-oriented'** Consolidation and professionalisation of permanent organisation; creation of CITIA, moving from an event logic to a logic of ongoing industry activity.
Contribution to field configuration	**'Field creation'** Contribution to the emergence of an animation community centred around Annecy and ASIFA.	**'Field consolidation'** Legitimacy conferred to various forms of animation; market creation, knowledge transfer through programmed round tables and conferences; competition categories define different legitimate types of animation.	**'Field transformation'** Leveraging industry experience and legitimacy of the Annecy organisation in order to act as a broker for projects, ideas and innovation.

While the emphasis in the second phase was mainly on presenting finished work and on providing spaces in which industry actors could meet, the new orientation seeks to leverage industry knowledge gathered over the past four decades in order to play an active brokerage role among field participants. Project competitions provide a good example of this approach. Here, the Annecy organisation selects highly promising projects in early stages and actively puts these projects in contact with other important industry actors. This more active role is in line with a field that is marked by rapid technological development, economic changes and the convergence of various industries (animated film, special effects, computer games, mobile telecommunication, etc.). All these tendencies bring new actors with them who need to rely to some extent on brokers and knowledge hubs in order to find their way through the animation field.

Managing a Field-configuring Event

In their historical study on the Paris Salon of art, Delacour and Leca (2007) suggest that in order to maintain their position over time, field-configuring events must constantly embrace innovation within their fields and manage their relationships with associated and potentially competing events. Three areas in which the management of the event itself plays a role in maintaining its strong role within the field to prevent de-institutionalisation are (1) balancing innovation and identity, (2) balancing competing logics, and (3) positioning the event within the field and in relation to other events.

Innovation and identity

The festival and market organisers' ability to sense innovations and to adapt the festival and market while maintaining the specific identity of the event and meeting the expectations of long-time festival participants is a recurring theme in the research interviews. The Annecy organisers have been able to break away from routines that were no longer in phase with the environment. In doing so, they have managed to balance innovation with identity. On the other hand, the festival history conveys a strong sense of continuity. Many images that are used by the organisers today (e.g. the 'animation family') originated in the early festival days. Annecy cultivates the specific image of an event that unites the various members of the 'animation family' and claims a unique relationship between art and business.

Competing logics

Since its beginnings, the festival has been characterised first by a latent and then an open tension between the competing logics of art versus commerce.

The Annecy International Animated Film Festival and Market

The most contested and controversial decisions in the festival history – relocating the festival office to Annecy, opening the festival to TV productions in 1983, and the creation of an annual event in 1998 – are all related to the festival makers' attempts to define an event that would balance competing logics. For a festival that had positioned itself as an artistic venue in opposition to the dominant public association of animated film with the Disney tradition, it was difficult to reposition the festival in line with important industry level economic and technological developments. In the Annecy case, these 'adjustments' systematically involved the departure and replacement of key individuals. The festival organisation relies on multiple stakeholders with their particular interests and agendas and has to find ways to create an event that responds to different groups' interests. In this context, the 'animation family' metaphor has been playing an important role since the early festival days. As one of my interview partners suggested: 'It is like a family meeting, where family members with different characters and personalities meet'.

Positioning, relational work and network building

Two aspects of positioning concern the uniqueness of an event and its relation to other competing events within a field. The way in which an event is positioned in order to remain on field participants' agendas is a further key issue in the management of a field-configuring event. When their event is compared to *pure market* or *pure festival* events, the Annecy organisers tend to highlight the unique, complementary constellation of festival *and* market (for the case of the Cannes Festival and market, compare Benghozi & Nénert 1995). According to the Annecy organisers, both sides of the event reinforce each other, and the strong presence of well-known artists as well as young talents plays an important role in producing a particular 'Annecy feeling'. Especially the festival's positioning as a worldwide showcase for creative and artistic animation differentiates the event for market participants. Artistic and aesthetic innovations often originate in short films and graduation work, and even well established animators seek inspiration from the work of their colleagues. In this context, an important role of the Annecy event is to contribute to the discovery of interesting new films and projects, technologies and regions. Unlike in a large generalist market event like MIP in Cannes, a company coming to Annecy is able to act in different domains: the producer can find a director, the technical directors can find software solutions and hardware, and the company can recruit and discuss with the buyers the development of a new project or the acquisition of a programme. The Annecy market is an actively managed environment in which encounters are programmed. The market managers see their role as 'market creators' who have a strong influence on the type of encounters that will take place, and who are committed to helping Mifa participants they meet regularly during the year at different moments in the event circuit to find the right people in the Annecy market.

Relational work and network building, together with a strategy of leveraging industry knowledge while maintaining and protecting one's distinctiveness, also play an important role in helping the Annecy festival and market to maintain and reinforce its position. The current director of CITIA is a well-known former animation producer who is recognised as an expert at the interface between art and business. He and other members of the Annecy management regularly participate in panels and expert meetings on cultural policy and frequently act on the selection committees and juries of other animation events. According to the managing director of the event, Annecy does not face direct competition in the animation field today. It is clearly positioned as the leading event in terms of reputation, attractiveness, organisation and quality (including technical aspects like the quality of film projections). In this position, the Annecy management readily shares its expertise and knowledge and participates in other events, but it systematically refuses any kind of endorsement, labelling or co-inscription of films with other animation events in order to maintain its image of uniqueness.

Conclusion

This paper has presented an analysis of the Annecy International Animated Film Festival and International Animated Film Market, a major event in the global animation industry, from the vantage point of field-configuring events. It has identified three phases in the development of the event. Each phase is characterised by a particular constellation of industry environment, event characteristics and organisation and the particular contribution to field-configuration during this phase. The Annecy festival has moved from a community focus to a showcase event and from there to an industry event in which the festival organisation itself seeks to proceed as an industry actor. Development and brokerage of network ties and knowledge play an increasingly important role as the animation industry faces rapid aesthetic, technological and economic change and attracts large numbers of new actors. The multiplicity of artists, technical and aesthetic forms and organisations participating in the global animation industry creates an environment in which the market-making role of film festivals becomes particularly salient (Caves 2000). A key challenge for the festival organisers in this situation is to ensure that the event remains on the field participants 'event agenda'. This requires at the same time very close contacts to important field participants and deliberate positioning of the festival and market in relation to other events.

Acknowledgements

I would like to thank CITIA and the entire Annecy Festival and market staff, especially Dominique Puthod, Patrick Eveno and Tiziana Loschi for their availability, openness and support. I would also like to thank Vincent Mangematin, Amélie Boutinot, Carmelo Mazza and Jesper Strandgaard Pedersen who have provided valuable comments to earlier versions of this text.

Notes

[1]   Earlier versions of this paper have been presented at the 2nd annual conference on 'Cultural Production in a Global Context: The Worldwide Film Industries', Copenhagen, 29-31 May 2008, and at the 24th EGOS colloquium, Amsterdam, 10-12 July 2008.

[2]   'Plan Image': A strategic plan devised by the French Ministry of Culture (after a 1983 national summit of the animation industry and public administration) to revitalise and to develop the French animation industry.

Works Cited

Anand, Narasimhan and Mary R. Watson (2004) 'Tournament Rituals in the Evolution of Fields: The Case of the Grammy Awards', *Academy of Management Journal*, 47, 1, 59-80.

Benghozi, Pierre-Jean and Claire Nénert (1995) 'Création de Valeur Artistique ou Économique: du Festival International du Film de Cannes au Marché du Film', *Recherche et Applications en Marketing*, 10, 4, 65-76.

Caves, Richard E. (2000) *Creative Industries: Contracts between Art and Commerce*. Cambridge, MA: Harvard University Press.

Ciment, Gilles (1999) 'Le Festival International du Film d'Animation d'Annecy 1999', *Positif*, 465.
On-line. Available
http://gciment.free.fr/cafestivalsannecy99.htm
(9 May 2008).

____ (2001) 'Le Festival de Film d'Animation d'Annecy 2000', *Positif*, 480.
On-line. Available
HTTP: http://gciment.free.fr/cafestivalsannecy2000.htm
(12 May 2008).

Clarke, James (2004) *Animated Films*. London: Virgin Books.

Delacour, Hélène and Bernard Leca (2007) 'Le Processus de Désinstitutionalisation d'un Événement: Le Cas du Salon de Paris', in Anne-Laure Saives & Robert H. Desmarteau (eds), *Actes de la XVIème Conférence de l'AIMS*. Montréal: UQAM.

DiMaggio, Paul J. and Walter W. Powell (1983) 'The Ironic Age Revisited: Institutional Isomorphism and Collective Rationality in Organizational Fields', *American Sociological Review*, 48, 147-60.

Evans, Owen (2007) 'Border Exchanges: The Role of the European Film Festival', *Journal of Contemporary European Studies*, 15, 1, 23-33.

Gamson, Joshua (1996) 'The Organizational Shaping of Collective Identities: The Case of Lesbian and Gay Film Festivals in New York', *Sociological Forum*, 11, 2, 231-61.

Journées Internationales du Cinéma d'Animation (1985) *Festival d'Annecy 1960-1985*. Annecy.

Lampel, Joseph, Alan D. Meyer and Marc Ventresca (2005) 'Special Issue Call for Papers: Field-configuring Events as Structuring Mechanisms: How Conferences, Ceremonies and Trade Shows Constitute New Technologies, Industries, and Markets', *Journal of Management Studies*, 42, 5, 1099–100.

Langley, Ann (1999) 'Strategies for Theorizing from Process Data', *The Academy of Management Review*, 24, 4, 691-710.

Teninge, Annick (1997) 'Rendezvous in Annecy: An Interview with Jean-Luc Xiberras', *Animation World Magazine*, 1, 10, 16-19.

___ (2000). 'The Annecy Story: 40 years of Celebrating the Art of Animation', *Animation World Magazine*, 5, 4, 74-79.

Chapter Five

From Urban Bohemia to Euro Glamour: The Establishment and Early Years of The New York Film Festival[1]

Rahul Hamid

The founding of The New York Film Festival (NYFF) in 1963 marked a turning point in the cultural life of cinema in the United States, when serious art film escaped ghettoisation in college campuses and urban beatnik enclaves. The movies were ready to take their place on stage with ballet, opera and symphonic music. In New York City, cinema would very literally join them at the newly founded Lincoln Center for the Performing Arts.

The New York Film Festival premiered only one year after the now-famous 'Lincoln Center complex opened to the public. It was founded with a democratic impulse in keeping with the spirit of Lincoln Center to bring the best of World Cinema to audiences in New York. However; along with this sentiment and the wider audience to whom it catered came a necessity to conform to the taste of the city's bourgeoisie, both aesthetically and politically. The conflicts, issues and compromises that characterised the first years of the NYFF foreshadow the curatorial challenges still faced by the festival today and can offer insight into the epicurean world of contemporary film festival culture.

As film scholar Thomas Elsaesser describes, an international culture of cinephilia developed first through the network of A-list festivals in Venice, Cannes and Berlin and later through an expanding group of newer festivals in places like Karlovy Vary and Locarno. This alternative network of film distribution created new markets for art film in Europe and abroad by giving visibility and fame to *auteurs* like Luis Buñuel, Federico Fellini and Satyajit Ray, as well as to entire national film movements, such as New German Cinema and the French New Wave (Elsaesser 2005: 89-90).

Elsaesser describes the post-war film festival circuit as a direct response to the growing power and hegemony of Hollywood and the US film industry. This antagonistic relationship to Hollywood coloured much of the international discourse around festivals, situating festivals and the European art cinema they programmed as anti-commercial 'high art' and American cinema and theatrical distribution as the province of the masses and lowbrow commercialism (though famously, Jean-Luc Godard and François

Truffaut challenged this distinction). It was precisely this stereotype that the founders of the New York Film Festival sought to contradict.

In her study of post-war film festivals, Marijke de Valck also targets this simplistic notion as a starting point for a more nuanced understanding from the European perspective, revealing the European festival circuit to be as much about the economy of film distribution as it is about the development of cinema as an art (de Valck 2007: 14-15). Younger American critics who were attending the big European festivals somewhat naively idealised the film culture on the Continent and wanted to promote the new cinema coming out of these festivals. European art cinema had until then only appeared in the US in small venues, primarily in urban centres and university towns. The desire to give festival cinema a prominent place in American cultural life stemmed from both a romanticised perception of the seriousness and glamour of the European cinema scene and a resistance to the characterisation of American film culture as being synonymous with the crass commercialism of Hollywood.

Since the end of World War II, the distribution of new modernist cinema had been growing in the United States. In 1963 New York, serious films like these were primarily being shown at the Museum of Modern Art (MoMA) and at various small art-house cinemas, mostly in the downtown bohemian neighbourhood of Greenwich Village. By September of that year, just a few days before the inaugural New York Film Festival celebrated its opening night, these little theatres were showing everything from François Truffaut's *Jules et Jim* (France, 1962) to Mario Monicelli's *I Soliti ignoti* (*Big Deal on Madonna Street*, Italy, 1958), Sergei Eisenstein's *Ivan Groznyy I* (*Ivan the Terrible, Part I*, Soviet Union, 1944), Jean Renoir's *La Régle du Jeu* (*Rules of the Game*, France, 1939), Jonas Mekas's *Guns of the Trees* (USA, 1963) and an Ingmar Bergman retrospective (Film Listings 1963: 9). At these venues and at MoMA film was treated as an art worthy of study and deep appreciation. The New York Film Festival sought to tap into this downtown cinephile culture and move its growing art-house audience uptown into the cultural establishment. It was founded to give the largest city in the US a major international film event on par with its European counterparts in Berlin, Cannes and Venice. The establishment of Lincoln Center in 1962 as the hub of the performing arts in New York was an ideal moment at which to raise the issue of film as a serious art form and to institutionalise it as such.

Lincoln Center and the Founding of The New York Film Festival

Lincoln Center, which operates on a combination of public funding, private donations and ticket sales, is a complex of theatres on Manhattan's Upper West Side. Since its inception it has been at the heart of New York's high culture scene, housing the New York Ballet, the Metropolitan Opera, the

The New York Film Festival

New York Philharmonic, and the Juilliard School of Music. Lincoln Center owes its creation to two municipal needs. First, the city had already been 30 years into the search for a permanent home for the Metropolitan Opera after plans for a new house were derailed with the stock market crash in 1929. Second, Manhattan's West Side, where the proposed project would be housed, had begun to deteriorate into a slum and New York's infamous Park's commissioner, Robert Moses, wanted to clean up the area (Rich 1984: 13). But as Robert Caro argues in his biography of the commissioner, Moses' brand of 'cleaning' was deeply related to controlling where ethnic minorities and the poor were allowed to live in the city (Caro 1975). So, as the city fathers were promising a new venue for the arts open to all the people, they were concurrently gentrifying the West Side, preparing to raze housing for the poor and working class to create a community and centre aimed at the *haute bourgeoisie*.

In 1962, the second string film critic for *The New York Times*, Eugene Archer, interviewed the president of the newly built Lincoln Center and renowned American composer, Dr William Schuman. Archer asked Schuman about plans for including film at Lincoln Center. When Schuman responded affirmatively, Archer wrote to Richard Roud, then director of The London Film Festival, urging him to approach Schuman about starting a festival in New York similar to the one in London. After confirming that Roud was an American – an important consideration at Lincoln Center – Schuman agreed over the phone to sponsor a single festival. The first film festival was funded through the New Projects Underwriting Fund, a US$10 million Lincoln Center budget line set aside for the development of projects like the NYFF (Vogel 1989). Indeed, the NYFF benefited a great deal from being a part of New York's cultural establishment and many of the barriers that less well-connected curators might have had to face were eliminated.

When Roud met with Schuman and the executive director of programmes, Richard Leach, he asked them to hire a New York-based person to help coordinate the NYFF and suggested Amos Vogel (Corliss 1987: 38).[2] But while both Roud and Vogel were established figures in the art film world and certified cinephiles, their later curatorial conflicts over NYFF's direction encapsulate the conflict that this essay aims to highlight – that is, the desire to integrate film into the arts establishment of the United States versus a commitment to a politically engaged cinephilia.

Roud, born in Boston in 1929 into a 'family of film buffs', (Goldman 1988: 29) went to France as a Fulbright scholar. He lingered in Europe, shuttling between France and England, teaching English on Army bases, and eventually doing graduate work at the University of Manchester. During the 1950s, he became the London correspondent for the groundbreaking French film journal, *Cahiers du Cinéma*. He also worked as the film critic for the *Manchester Guardian* and held many other writing jobs in England. While working with the British Film Institute, he was made programme director of the London Film Festival, sponsored by the BFI (Anon. 1989: B18).

Chapter Five

Vogel also had an extensive film background. Born in Vienna in 1921, his involvement with film began when he was given a magic lantern as a boy. Later, he received a hand-cranked movie projector and began to put on shows of the 9.5 mm films of Charlie Chaplin and Mickey Mouse. As a young man before the war, Vogel belonged to a film society in Austria where he was able to see a wide variety of films from around the world. But in 1938, he was forced to flee Europe for the United States to escape the Nazis and spent the next 10 years in New York doing odd jobs. While in New York, he renewed his passion for cinema amidst a burgeoning film culture in the city and became familiar with the circulation of 16 mm films (Macdonald 1997: 49-83).

In 1947, Vogel and his wife Marcia began their film club, Cinema 16, as an outlet to exhibit American avant-garde films and documentaries, particularly the work of John Grierson and Alberto Cavalcanti. Maya Deren, her husband Alexander Hammid, Stan Brakhage, Kenneth Anger, Bruce Conner and Ed Emshwiller all debuted in New York through Cinema 16. The eclecticism that characterised his programming style will be familiar to those who have read his 1975 book *Film as a Subversive Art*. Part manifesto, part celebration, and part detailed cinematic catalogue, there is no better introduction to Vogel's curatorial philosophy, which prioritised the examination of form over content, allowing industrial film, experimental work and *auteur* cinema to be appreciated on an equal plane.

In addition to his interest in the avant garde, Vogel was proud of Cinema 16's role as the first New York venue for many feature films. The films of Robert Bresson, François Truffaut, Michelangelo Antonioni, John Cassavetes, Nagisa Oshima, Roman Polanski, Yasujiro Ozu, Alexander Kluge, Agnes Varda, Brian De Palma, Richard Lester, Tony Richardson, Jacques Rivette, Lindsay Anderson and Karol Reisz were all shown at Cinema 16. Vogel also showed industrial and training films, anything that held some spark of interest for him. While running the film club, he also became a distributor and began to learn how to cope with censors. As the reputation of Cinema 16 grew, people began to phone Vogel asking for prints of the films he was known for showing. He began to distribute films to other film clubs, repertory houses and film classes. Cinema 16 sponsored trips to MoMA and the George Eastman House in Rochester for special screenings of films from these archives that could not be seen elsewhere. Cinema 16 also promoted a film programme for children. 'At its height, Cinema 16 boasted seven thousand members who filled a sixteen-hundred-seat auditorium at the High School of Fashion Industries [in Manhattan's garment district] twice a night...' (Vogel quoted in MacDonald 1997: 3-48).

Unfortunately, around 1962, the costs for running Cinema 16 increased to the point that Vogel was forced to close it (Vogel 1989). Nevertheless, Vogel became known in New York as a booster of cinema as art and of the American avant garde in particular. After Cinema 16 ended, Vogel wrote to William Schuman about including film at Lincoln Center. His letter would be answered a year later. After Roud's recommendation, Vogel was the second person to whom Schuman spoke.

The selection of Roud and Vogel, each with a distinguished track record and many connections to the film world, was part of Lincoln Center's effort to give the festival an impeccable pedigree. Roud was named as 'programme director' and credited with the film selection, while Vogel was the 'festival coordinator' (Archer 1963, 'Major Fete': 18). It seems clear that Schuman wanted the collaboration of other established film entities. The festival was a co-presentation of MoMA, the British Film Institute through Roud, and the Lincoln Center arts organisation itself. As an example of the tenor of the times, in an interview given in 1993 Vogel recalls that when the idea of film's inclusion at Lincoln Center was first introduced, one of the board members supposedly said, 'Film at Lincoln Center? We might as well have baseball!' (Vogel 1989). Schuman cautiously agreed to start with one festival and if that was a success, it would be renewed and become a yearly event. Both Vogel and Roud agreed that by the time the first festival began in September, it was clear that Lincoln Center was pleased with the result and that the NYFF would continue.

Selection for the First Festival – Censorship and Content

Roud and Vogel were given great latitude to programme films for the festival. *The New York Times* describes the festival as including the best films 'presented at other festivals' (Archer 1963, 'Major Fete':18). The only criterion was quality. From the beginning, the festival had been intended to be non-competitive; it was simply an exhibition of cinematic art. This made the NYFF more attractive to the directors and served to reinforce the serious tone of the festival. The films were expected to cover 'the broadest possible range of experimental works by new directors to major achievements by established filmmakers' (ibid.).

Roud remembers that the only limitation was that Schuman wanted to be warned if a movie had strong sexual content since, '[i]n those days sex was a big problem' (Corliss 1987: 38). Still, there was no intention of preventing any film's inclusion. Vogel says that Schuman simply said he wanted to hear a justification for a questionable film so he could defend it when asked. Apparently, the issue only came up once during Vogel's time at the festival from 1963-69. Vogel and Roud felt the need to warn Lincoln Center about James Broughton's short, *The Bed* (1966), shown in the 1968 festival. The film contained a lot of nudity, but the audience responded well and the festival managed to avoid any significant controversy (Vogel 1989).

The festival did not have many problems with the censors because the films for NYFF were only in the country temporarily and would be shown in a non-profit venue; only films scheduled for commercial distribution could be legally blocked. *The New York Times* quotes Schuman as saying that the waivers from the censors 'mark[ed] a milestone in the recognition of film as an art form. Americans, like their counterparts abroad, will now be able to experience works of the cinematic art as their creators intended' (Archer 1963, 'Skirt Censors': 15). The waiver was obtained through August Heckscher, the White House Consultant on the Arts and chairman of the festival's sponsoring committee. Other notable members of the sponsoring committee included big Hollywood players such as John Ford, Samuel Goldwyn, Elia Kazan, Edward R. Murrow, Otto Preminger, Robert Rossen, David O. Selznick, Jack L. Warner, Billy Wilder, William Wyler, Darryl F. Zanuck and Fred Zinneman, as well as many well-to-do New Yorkers (Film Society 1976). The artistic freedom of the festival was ensured in large part through its connections with the wealthy and powerful in Hollywood, Washington and New York.

Roud and Vogel had to gain approval from Leach and Schuman for any funds spent, but while their expenditures were closely scrutinised, they were not denied anything significant. The other sponsors of the festival, whose advertisements appeared in the festival's programme, include *The New York Times*, Smith Barney and Company, Steinway and Sons, Baldwin Pianos and the Hamilton Watch Company (ibid.). Roud and Vogel spared no expense in setting up a huge screen and sophisticated sound system in Philharmonic Hall (now called Avery Fisher Hall). This process was lengthy and costly, since all the labour at the Lincoln Center was unionised. It took until four in the morning on the day of the festival's opening on 10 September to perfect the screening facilities. For the first few years, the New Projects Fund covered the entire cost of the NYFF. Although it enjoyed between 90 and 100 per cent attendance from the beginning, the festival was meant to be non-commercial. Vogel says that he would never have agreed to work for the festival if it had been any other way. Cinema 16 was a non-profit organisation dedicated to the exhibition of film as an art, not as a commodity. As Vogel puts it, 'box office and art do not mix' (Vogel 1989). He saw the programming of the NYFF as a continuation of his work at Cinema 16. In his book on Cinema 16, film scholar Scott MacDonald characterises Vogel's curatorial philosophy as being motivated much more out of a desire to educate, rather than to entertain (Macdonald 2002: 8).

The First New York Film Festival

The first festival featured 21 films selected by Roud and Vogel from festivals around the world. 'Nine distinguished films of the recent past never before shown theatrically in the United States' (Anon. 1963 'Museum Picks': 3) were chosen by Richard Griffith, curator of film at MoMA, for screening at the museum in conjunction with the festival. The main selections and the MoMA films were challenging and diverse. Although there are many from Western Europe, particularly France, there were a significant number of films from

Eastern Europe and a few from Asia and Latin America. While most of them had been shown at other film festivals, few had US distribution. The great film movements that had been mushrooming since the end of World War II – Italian Neo-Realism, the French New Wave and Brazilian Cinema Novo – were represented in the selections.

In addition, the inclusion of Emile De Antonio's *Point of Order* (USA, 1964) on the Army-McCarthy hearings and the screening of the blacklisted American expatriate Joseph Losey's *The Servant* (UK, 1963) revealed an unspoken leftist-progressive bent in the programming. In general, Roud and Vogel chose a wide selection of films: there were documentaries such as Chris Marker's *Le Joli Mai* (France, 1963) and Takis Mouzenidis's *Ilektra* (*Elektra at Epidaurus*, Greece/USA, 1962); films by established masters like Ozu, Buñuel, and Bresson and works completely new to the US, such as Roman Polanski's *Nóz w Wodzie* (*Knife in the Water*, Poland 1962). As one might expect, the films in the line-up heavily favoured European art cinema in fictional feature mode. New American Cinema and avant-garde films, suited to Vogel's more catholic and radical tastes, would have to wait until later years. Even then they would not take a place of primary importance.

Still with a nod to the subversive, Roud and Vogel selected Buñuel's black comedy, *El Ángel Exterminador* (*The Exterminating Angel*, Mexico, 1962) for opening night. The film is about a dinner party from which the wealthy guests cannot leave. As the situation continues for days and the guests are deprived of food, water and toilet facilities, they begin to devolve into savage beasts. The film was a fitting introduction to the festival, a challenging foreign film by a great director. It was also an inside joke between Vogel and Roud. The opening night audience would be of the same wealthy, bejewelled class represented in the film. Vogel remembers laughing with Roud as they watched the logjam of perturbed guests at the doors of Philharmonic Hall when the film ended (Vogel 1989). Their joke perfectly encapsulates the collision of cultures that the New York Film Festival represented. The values of New York high society, upon whose financial support Lincoln Center and the festival relied, stood in stark contrast to Roud and Vogel's Europhilic, left-leaning sensibilities.

Reception of the First Festival

Despite this cultural disjunction, the audience reception of the first film festival was exceedingly positive. Archer covered the festival in a series of articles, describing the overflowing crowds who were challenged by and sometimes critical of a variety of films. While Joseph Losey's *The Servant* (UK, 1963) was popular, Alain Resnais' *Muriel* (France/Italy, 1963) and Leopoldo Torre Nilsson's *La Terraza* (*The Terrace*, Argentina, 1963) gave the audience particular trouble. His concluding article states that the festival was a 'rousing success,' selling 50,000 tickets (Archer 1963: 47, 12, 31, 23, 26). Brendan Gill at the *New Yorker* wrote, 'There's no harm in my whispering that, at the halfway mark, the festival is proving a terrific success' (Gill 1963, 'Current Cinema': 113). A week later Gill wrote that the festival had three or four great films and three or four really boring films, but that:

> The chief discovery made at the festival was ... that a large and enthusiastic audience exists ... for the so-called art film. The discovery may cause Lincoln Center to embrace movies in a rather less gingerly fashion than heretofore. (Gill 1963, 'Current Cinema': 108)

Variety gave full-page coverage to the festival, commenting on 'Beatniks at Lincoln Center'. The writer noted that the audience was extremely knowledgeable and vocal about its likes and dislikes. There were boos and applause for certain films and filmmakers (Anon. 1963, from three Variety articles: 7). A younger educated audience was interested in the film festival and had invaded a bastion of high culture. The success was surprising because the films did not receive much individual coverage. They were advertised as part of the film festival, so it was difficult to ascertain whether it was the films or the idea of an international festival of new cinema in contrast to Hollywood that made the NYFF so successful. Another marker of the festival's success and the mainstream acceptance of a new conception of cinema was the front-page article by Brad Darrach in *Time* Magazine on the 'Cinema as an International Art'. The cover featured a still from Polanski's *Knife in the Water*, which premiered at the NYFF. The article passionately proclaims a universe of new films by directors from all over the world that were challenging and far more interesting than Hollywood product. Darrach triumphantly concluded that, 'The world is on its way to a great cinema culture' (Darrach 1963: 78).

The most noticeable aspect of the publicity, press coverage and programming of the NYFF was that it self-consciously pronounced film as art, separate from Hollywood and commerce. The original advertisement for the festival that appeared in *The New York Times* and *Village Voice* announced that:

> Most of these films must go back after one performance in the United States. Great films from all over the world are now being shown at the New York Film Festival. None of these films have ever been seen before in the United States. Each film will be shown once in Lincoln Center, in its original form. Then it must be returned. It may be the only opportunity you will ever have to see some of these great films. (Anon. 1963: *Times*, 10; *Voice*, 17)

The advertisement emphasised the international nature of the new cinema, that it was subject to censorship, and that it was 'great'. It appeared throughout the run of the festival, indicating that a substantial amount of money was spent on advertising. In addition to print announcements, a 16-

74

The New York Film Festival

by-10-foot canvas was installed on 65th Street and Broadway for a painting to proclaim the NYFF. Larry Rivers, described in *The New York Times* as 'one of the nation's leading artists' (Canaday 1963, 'Rivers': 38), was given the commission. John Canaday, an art reporter, wrote that the painting demonstrated a mixture of high and low culture. An original painting advertising the festival was mixed in on Broadway among billboards for *Palisades Park* and the *Petty Girl* (a pin-up girl created by illustrator George Petty for a variety of advertisements). Canaday noted that the design of the painting, which played with the forms of stencilled letters and an image of Jane Russell among other elements, exhibited a 'deftness and sportiveness [that] should delight the kind of person who is a potential customer for a film festival' (Canaday 1963, 'Art': 21). Furthermore he noted that in this age of Pop Art, where the images from advertising and popular culture were entering art studios, it seemed fitting that a studio painting should be out on the street. The theme of art and the definitions of high and low were never far from the NYFF, even in the advertising.

Taste and the idea of film as art was a polemical issue at this time and the programming of the NYFF was a major battleground in this war. Many of the younger critics actively advocated for the NYFF, heralding it as a banner for a sea change in American film culture. Andrew Sarris, the critic for the *Village Voice*, wrote in his column a month before the festival about the liberalising, positive effect of the Montreal Film Festival. He noted at the end of the column: 'It would be a shame if the New York Film Festival were to be buried by our old guard critics before it had a chance to exercise a similar liberalizing influence' (Sarris 1963a : 9). Archer, *The New York Times'* critic who proposed the festival to Schuman, had been a collaborator of Sarris' and, along with Roud and Vogel, did not see film as subordinate to the theatre or literature or any of the more established art forms. They were in conflict with the older critics, who they felt thought of film as a lesser form (Sarris 1999). The films that were included in the NYFF were the kinds of films that the new breed of critics championed. In a column two weeks later, Sarris wrote that Max Ophüls' *Lola Montès* (*The Fall of Lola Montes*, France/West Germany, 1955), being shown in the MoMA selection at the festival, 'is the greatest film of all time' (Sarris 1963, 'Film': 9). Years later, Sarris continued to stand by what he wrote, but he acknowledged that this proclamation was a thrust at the establishment. John Simon, film critic at the *New Leader*, in contrast, called the film a 'monstrosity' (Simon 1967: 86). A bone of contention in addition to these aesthetic differences between the festival and the old guard critics was the restriction on the writing of reviews of festival films in the commercial press while the festival was in progress. This constraint was imposed so that a negative review could not hurt a film's chances for distribution. It is unclear whether this was the choice of Roud and Vogel or a compromise made with the organisation of film distributors (Landry 1963: 7). *Variety*, the show business trade paper read by distributors, could and did include reviews.

Indeed, the first-string critic at *The New York Times*, Bosley Crowther, who was singled out by both Sarris and Vogel as one of the most recalcitrant members of the old guard, was positive about the NYFF. But he was also quick to point out that New York was the most important city in the country in terms of foreign film distribution and that a negative reception at the festival could kill a film's chances for US distribution (Crowther 1963: 1). On the second day of the festival in 1963, *Variety* expanded upon this rift between art and business considerations. They quoted people involved in distribution as resenting that the festival was too 'artsy-craftsy', organised by film buffs and not business people. *Variety* pointed out that quirky films and tastes had gone on to become popular and that the distributors should stay with the times, although they acknowledged that the NYFF organisers avoided talking about 'trade angles'. The article concluded that if the festival were to continue, the business people and the arts people will have to come together. Next to this article was an article with the headline, 'NY Fest Pre-Sells 30,000 Tickets', as though to prove the point that art has a business aspect as well (Anon. 1963: 3, 26). The more conservative and business-oriented critics noted the financial repercussions for the idea of film as art and took a rather cautious, negative view of any festival that did not consider the financial aspects of film. This was a far cry from the effusive aesthetic advocacy of critics such as Darrach, Sarris and Archer.

In the festivals of 1964 and 1965, Roud and Vogel, bolstered by the success of the first festival, ignored the criticisms and continued to programme according to their personal proclivities and interests. They included many of the same filmmakers that had been represented in the first festival and presented much new, interesting work. In the programmes written for these festivals, Roud and Vogel stressed the importance of exhibiting challenging cinema. Roud compared Godard with Samuel Beckett and Bernardo Bertolucci with William Faulkner. Vogel wrote about the need for cinema education in hopes that Lincoln Center and the festival could begin to fill this need. They were full of enthusiasm for the films and the cinema's relationship to other serious art movements, such as modernism in literature and the Theater of the Absurd. Both saw the filmmaking of the 1960s as finally catching up with the other arts. The Festival's programme noted, 'film is abandoning traditional narrative like the novel, in the same way that painting moved away from realism' (Film Society 1976).

Curatorial Controversy and the need for a Selection Committee

Along with the main slate of films shown in Philharmonic Hall, Vogel, mirroring his earlier commitment to the avant-garde at Cinema 16, added a programme called Special Events. These sidebars to the festival were presented at a 200-seat theatre around the corner from the festival on Amsterdam Avenue and 65th Street, where Vogel was able to show avant-garde films and other more specialised film. In the first years, Special Events were presented free of charge. According to Vogel, Roud had little interest in the special events and let Vogel have most of the responsibility for them. Roud's interest in limiting the festival exclusively to feature films and a few narrative shorts may have had much to with the increasing hostility that he, Vogel, faced. Roud's approach to programming was decidedly more pragmatic than Vogel's idealistic perspective.

The criticisms that were brought up by the business establishment and the older critics continued during 1964 and 1965. According to Sarris, the rule that films could not be reviewed during the festival (because this was too far in advance of their theatrical releases and therefore not useful for film promotion) grew to become a major cause of anger among critics, who were not primarily interested in the films' profitability. In addition, Roud was somewhat abrasive; he was unapologetic about his taste and took credit for selecting the films for the festival without the input of anyone else (Sarris 1999). While Sarris remembers Roud's passion for film and the writings of Bazin fondly, other critics found his monopoly to be insulting and began to attack Roud's and, to a lesser extent, Vogel's selections. Simon and Stanley Kauffman even went so far as to call for their resignations and to call Godard, a festival favourite, a 'fake' (Vogel 1989). Even in his reviews of the first festival, Simon attacked Roud's writing in the programme and his advocacy for the festival films. He called the festival 'meager and generally tiresome' (Simon 1967: 87). His vitriol continued as the years went by; he attacked Godard and most of the films in the first two years of the festival, writing that the selections disprove the idea that film is a 'fertile, vital art' (Simon 1967: 188).

In 1965, Kauffman viciously attacked the festival, homophobically complaining that Roud's descriptions of the films were written with a 'limp mind and wrist'. He called Special Events a 'circus sideshow', maintaining that festivals were for selling films and not for the display of art. Good films will be released, so ran his logic, and the rest were not worthy of the exalted status given to them by the festival in the first place. Kauffman argues that the festival films should be shown in small venues year-round like Vogel's Cinema 16 (Kauffman 1965, 30-32). It is true that many of the same directors, including Godard, were selected repeatedly, but the fury of these attacks attest to the painful changes occurring in film culture at this time.

The offensive against Roud and Vogel and their choices could not go unanswered and finally it was decided that a selection committee would be formed to pick the films. Both Vogel and Roud recall that this change was made as a direct result of the criticism that they were receiving. The first selection committee in 1966 consisted of Roud, Vogel, Arthur Knight, and Sarris. The next year, Susan Sontag joined them (Schickel 1987: 44).

The selection process began with Roud, Vogel and the other committee members attending various at the major festivals in Europe (Cannes, Locarno, Venice, and Berlin primarily) during the year before the festival in New York, which occurred in October. They would identify films that they wanted the committee to consider. When possible, the films would be re-

Chapter Five

screened for the selection committee in New York, during marathon sessions of watching and debating. Vogel recollects that Roud was very resistant to the idea of a selection committee at first, but in time he grew to enjoy it. Roud was very good at arguing passionately for the films he favoured and adept at convincing the committee that his opinions were correct (Vogel 1989). Sarris remembers that the discussions were extremely heated, but he never felt coerced into making any choices. Each member's vote received equal weight. They just fought it out and each member was allowed to pick one film that was immune from the vetoes of other members (Sarris 1999).

In the programme for the 1966 festival, Roud mentioned the criticism of Godard by an unnamed critic for the *New Republic* (whom anyone remotely familiar with film criticism would have recognised as Kauffman), publicly acknowledging the attacks on the festival and bemoaning the state of film in the United States. He regretted having to defend Godard against unsympathetic critics. He wrote that 'plot and motivation', the standbys of critics like this, were not the main concerns of new cinema and he hoped that one day these critics would catch up. Vogel mentioned the new selection committee members and advocated again for film education, which he hoped would take place in the newly built 1,000-seat Alice Tully Hall. The films selected in 1966 were not radically different from the selections of the prior three years (Film Society 1976). There was a new Bresson, a Bertolucci, a Buñuel, two Godards, two Pasolinis and a Torre Nilsson. There were some revivals such as De Mille's *The Cheat* (USA, 1915), Clarence Brown's *A Woman of Affairs* (USA, 1929) and Renoir's *La Chienne* (*The Bitch*, France, 1931). In addition, the festival included many films from Eastern Europe, particularly Czechoslovakia, and Sergei Paradjanov's unforgettable *Tini Zabutykh Predkiv* (*Shadows of Forgotten Ancestors*, Soviet Union, 1964) from the USSR. Roud continued to write his exuberant blurbs for the films in the programme. The special events were dedicated to the American avant-garde, Vogel's first love. The NYFF did not completely change in response to the established critics but rather gave them a few more targets at which to aim by spreading the selection duties among a committee.

As the years have passed, a cloud of confusion as to the respective roles played by Vogel and Roud has descended upon the history of the festival. In later interviews and writings, Roud took all the credit for the programming of the films, insinuating that Vogel was more involved with the logistics. In contrast, Vogel claimed that the two were on an equal footing and shared all the responsibilities around organising the NYFF. Vogel was made a temporary employee of Lincoln Center but with no benefits. Roud was not a Lincoln Center employee; he was paid a fee and given travel expenses, since he spent at least half of the year in Europe. Due to his fear of flying, he traversed the Atlantic by liner. Vogel explains that he and Roud each had an official title, festival director and programme director respectively, but that these were simply bureaucratic designations. The two had very little time, much less than a year, to organise the first festival, so it would seem likely that they must have done the bulk of the work together in a hurry and with few formal distinctions between them. Vogel recalls that the cost overrun for completing the remaining buildings of Lincoln Center in 1968 was US$30 million. As a result, the New Projects fund dried up and the continuation of the festival was imperilled. Eventually, the decision was made that the festival would continue but at a smaller venue with raised ticket prices for the main films and an imposition of a charge for the sidebar. Vogel did not want to charge for the special events and due to this and other changes, including a personal falling out with Roud, Vogel left after the 1968 festival.

Conclusion

The NYFF began as a well-funded, well-run festival with the backing of the business and cultural establishment. Roud and Vogel believed in promoting film as art and both had extensive knowledge of the cinema in all its forms. It does not appear that there was much conflict between them about what kinds of films should be included in the festival once it became clear that they would have to focus on feature length films. Vogel had initially wanted to include avant-garde and short films along with narrative feature length films. Their programming and publicity were single-minded in advancing the idea of a new artistic cinema unfettered by censors, old forms, and the demands of the marketplace. They saw the festival and festival culture as a bully pulpit for proclaiming this new cinema, and once the audiences responded favourably, they continued similar programming and advocacy. Roud and Vogel were aware of their own subjectivity and included it in the programmes and film notes, which made no attempt to be measured or objective; they were written by two people bowled over by the possibilities of cinema and by the films that they had selected. Their cinephilia is an unquestioned given. Ironically, the success of their collaboration may have tempered the innovation of their programming decisions, as they fell into familiar patterns and created a canon of directors whose films appeared again and again. Roud, for one, was very much affected by the *Cahiers du Cinéma* critics and the *auteur* theory – an allegiance quite evident in his selections for the festival.

The NYFF also pushed the culture of film festivals one step further by being, in a sense, a festival of festival movies. The films selected were for the most part self-consciously artistic, created for an educated international audience. On the other hand, the NYFF was non-competitive and stayed away from the hyperbolic atmosphere that surrounds festivals like Cannes and Venice. It was created as a haven for art appreciation. A staid and reverent atmosphere remains at the festival even today, as it approaches its fiftieth year. Further insulated from a promotion-crazed commercial atmosphere by the proliferation of festivals on this continent (Toronto in particular), the NYFF seldom hosts any North American premieres any more. Contemporary critics might also view the event as elitist and think of the festival as a completely bourgeois and irrelevant institution, but ironically that was part of the original point of the festival – to give film a place in the cultural establishment of the city.

Notes

[1]   I would like to thank The Film Society of Lincoln Center for providing access to their archive and to Andrew Sarris, for being a great teacher and for being so generous with his time.

[2]   This information comes from an interview of Richard Roud conducted to mark the 25th anniversary of the film festival. It is worth remembering that *Film Comment* is the official journal of the Film Society of Lincoln Center, the sponsors of the festival.

Works Cited

Anon. (1963) 'Advertisement for New York Film Festival', *Village Voice*, 12 September, 17; *New York Times*, 8 September, II, 10.

Anon. (1963) 'Film Front and Lincoln Center', *Variety*, 18 September, 7.

Anon. (1963) 'Film Listings and Advertisements', *Village Voice*, 5 September.

Anon. (1963) 'Lincoln Center Fest Dedicated to Art, for Public, Not Trade', *Variety*, 11 September, 3, 26.

Anon. (1963) 'Museum Picks Pix for NY Festival', *Variety*, 24 September, 3.

Anon. (1963) 'New York Film Trade Somewhat Miffed as Public Flocks to See One-time Screenings at Festival', *Variety*, 18 September, 7.

Anon. (1963) 'NY Fest Pre-sells 30,000 Tickets', *Variety*, 11 September, 3.

Anon. (1963) 'Vincent Canby', *Variety*, 18 September, 7.

Anon. (1989) 'Richard Roud, 59, First Director of New York Film Festival, Dies', *New York Times*, 16 February, B18.

Archer, Eugene (1963) 'Capacity Crowds Attend Film Fete', *New York Times*, 11 September, 47.

___ (1963) 'Film Series Here to Skirt Censors', *New York Times*, 28 May.

___ (1963) 'Major Film Fete Planned for City', *New York Times*, 1 May.

___ (1963) 'Moviegoers Laud British *Servant*', *New York Times*, 17 September, 31.

___ (1963) 'New French Film Baffles Festival', *New York Times*, 19 September, 23.

___ (1963) 'Screen Festival Ends in Success', *New York Times*, 20 September, 26.

___ (1963) 'Young Argentines in *Terrace* Disturb Film Festival Audience', *New York Times*, 14 September, 12.

The New York Film Festival

Canaday, John (1963) 'Art: Larry Rivers Juxtaposing the High and Low', *New York Times*, 26 August, 21.

___ (1963) 'Rivers is Painting Canvas Outdoors', *New York Times*, 21 August, 38.

Caro, Robert (1975) *The Powerbroker: Robert Moses and the Fall of New York City*. New York: Vintage.

Corliss, Richard (1987) '70-millimeter Nerves', *Film Comment*, 23, 5, September-October, 38.

Crowther, Bosley (1963) 'We Have a Festival', *New York Times*, 8 September, II, 1.

Darrach, Brad (1963) 'A Religion of Film', *Time*, 20 September, 78.

de Valck, Marijke (2007) *Film Festivals: From European Geopolitics to Global Cinephilia*. Amsterdam: University of Amsterdam Press.

Elsaesser, Thomas (2005) *European Cinema: Face to Face with Hollywood*. Amsterdam: Amsterdam University Press.

Gill, Brendan (1963) 'The Current Cinema', *The New Yorker*, 21 September, 113.

___ 'The Current Cinema', *The New Yorker*, 28 September, 108.

Goldman, Debra (1988) 'The Coup that Shook the New York Film Festival: Rough Cut', *Village Voice*, 27 September, 29.

Kauffman, Stanley (1965) 'Are We Doomed to Festivals?', *The New Republic*, 2 October, 30-32.

Landry, Robert J. (1963) 'New York Gets Festival Fever', *Variety*, 18 September, 7.

MacDonald, Scott (1997) 'An Interview with Amos Vogel', *Wide Angle*, 19, 1, 49-83.

___ (1997) 'Cinema 16: Documents Toward a History of the Film Society', *Wide Angle*, 19, 1, 3-48.

___ (2002) *Cinema 16: Documents Towards a History of the Film Society*. Philadelphia: Temple University Press.

Rich, Alan (1984) *The Lincoln Center Story*. New York: American Heritage Publishing.

Sarris, Andrew (1963a) 'Film', *Village Voice*, 15 August, 9.

___ (1963b) 'Films', *Village Voice*, 5 September, 9.

___ (1999) Personal communication, 23 December.

Simon, John (1967) *Private Screenings*. New York: MacMillan.

The Film Society of Lincoln Center (1976) *New York Film Festival: Programs 1963-1975*. New York: Arno Press.

Vogel, Amos. (unknown year) *Oral History with Amos Vogel conducted by Sharon Zane* in the Lincoln Center Archive.

Chapter Six

Toronto Women & Film International 1973

Kay Armatage[1]

The original aim for this article was much more ambitious than the discrete object indicated by its title. I had originally intended to produce documentation of women's film festivals across the decades and from a range of geographical sites and concentrate on their contribution to knowledge production of women's cinema. For the first time in my life, I found myself consumed with empirical desire; I craved hard data. To develop this research territory, I was counting on the admirably obsessive character of Debra Zimmerman, Executive Director of Women Make Movies, the oldest continuing distributor of women's films and, as such, the leader of the one organisation that has participated consistently in women's film festivals around the globe over the last thirty years.

I wasn't wrong to count on this. When I emailed Zimmerman to ask if she had a collection of women's film festival catalogues and told her what I was hoping to study, her response was ecstatic. She replied that she had boxes of catalogues that she had been saving for someone to make use of and offered the WMM boardroom as a research location. Yet when I said I was booking flights to New York to begin the research, she advised me to wait until she found the boxes.

A few weeks later, she sent me a devastating message. The women's film festival catalogues had been lost. Whether through water damage or repeated office moves as the organisation grew, they just could not be found.

This substantial loss, I believe, has profound effects for scholarship, for it is unlikely that there is another accumulation of this kind in the world. This loss is devastating not only for me but for the future scholars of women's film festivals who will seek precise documentation, mission statements, graphic images, original sources for films, mappings of popular texts, indications of institutional affiliations and networks, material evidence, and the films themselves.[2] In other words, with the disappearance of the WMM collection of women's film festival catalogues, also effectively lost, in hard copy at least, is the history of women's film festivals.

This is a serious point. Although this article is not about archives or librarianship, as this is not my field, I want to insist on the importance for history of what has been considered ephemera, of local events, fleeting encounters. If we don't retrieve what we can of this history now, in a few years that recent past will be even more lost to us than the silent era, a period in which we now pursue spectral traces of women cultural producers like ghosts in the machine.

In this piece, my aim is to contribute to the history of women's institutional and industrial production in cinema by considering some aspects of the Toronto Women & Film Festival (1973). I will argue that such single-issue (feminist) events have significant import for film and feminist film history as well as wider economic, national, federal, transnational and local ramifications.

Film History and Women's Films Festivals

The distressing evacuation of historical artefacts through the loss of the Women Make Movies collection of catalogues could be seen, paradoxically, as an inadvertent adjunct of the 'historical turn' in film studies, which massively shifted scholarly attention to the early decades of modernity. In the last decades, the women film pioneers' project has been substantially effective in its efforts to retrieve the history of women's participation in silent era cinema, and yet the lost objects of the 1970s feminist era are many. As Melinda Barlow writes, 'the legacies of ... [1970s film and] video and feminism are literally at peril ... It is obviously imperative that we prevent such losses by archiving key documents and artefacts and writing the histories that still remain unwritten' (Barlow 2003: 4). The potential losses from the 1970s and beyond include not only the film and video productions themselves but also the events that brought many of the films to the public: women's film festivals.

This results from multiple exigencies, including an underdeveloped sense of the historical significance of such ephemeral events coupled with the real-world economics of document storage, the social agendas of women's film festivals, the constraints of the media marketplace, and the scholarly agendas of film studies, which have begun to turn only recently to ancillary institutions such as film festivals. Let's take these in turn.

With a few exceptions, women's film festivals have usually existed on intermittent or volunteer labour, government grants and community centre venues and without permanent institutional homes. Like Toronto Women & Film 1973, often they have been one-off events. Thus they have come and gone, with their erstwhile founders caching old catalogues in their basements (if they had basements) or not at all.[3] The loss of the WMM collection dramatically underlines this lack. Ragan Rhyne also saw a similar trend in the gay and lesbian festivals of the 70s and 80s, 'which of course changed as the years progressed. But it had a profound influence on the kinds of materials I was able to access and I think [it] speaks to larger important points about the way that new social movements have been organized through these kinds of institutions' (Rhyne 2007).

The social agendas of women's film festivals are intertwined with the boundaries of interest from the media marketplace. In contradistinction to mainstream festivals, where industry sales and press coverage are the measures of international standing, women's film festivals have tended to operate within a feminist protocol and thus their programming directives are distinctive. One could chart specific genres that appear at women's film festivals – e.g. generational chronicles, tributes to women artists, critiques of the beauty and femininity imperative (often by young women filmmakers), films about labour exploitation, domestic violence, women's civil rights, and so on.[4] Many of the locally made films exhibited in women's film festivals are short video documentaries and therefore ignored by the world of international film circulation. With the exception of Women Make Movies (New York), which services North American organisations and institutions that consume non-commercial, educational media in their programmes, relatively few distributors either attend women's film festivals or buy the sorts of films they exhibit.

Furthermore, little scholarly research has attended to women's film festivals, although there have been two recent forays into this long-forgotten territory. In her article on the New York Women's Video Festival 1972-80, Melinda Barlow writes that research in this ephemeral territory 'means examining an absence, an occurrence neither physically present nor open to bodily experience' (Barlow 2003: 8). Barlow's article perforce relies on an ethnographical methodology: personal interviews with the original organisers and participants, and recollected descriptions of the undocumented viewing environments and the exhibited works, for many of them have either disappeared or disintegrated. She concludes: 'Researching this history is both challenging and invigorating. It involves finding and interviewing living artists, examining their personal archives, imaginatively restoring tapes that no longer play by following their trails of documentation, and, perhaps most importantly, remembering that history is always a romance, and that the search for lost objects is driven by desire' (Barlow 2003: 28).

Archival Absences

As Barlow suggests, a significant problem for research on women's film festivals is the lack of archives and documentation. Even given the existence of archives of specialist interests, as attested to by Ann Cvetkovich's work on lesbian archives, ephemera, affect and *Watermelon Woman*, the film object she examines, the frustrations can be enormous (Cvetkovich 2002: 107-47). Underlining the current paucity of documentation that Barlow notes, Patricia White therefore imagines an 'archive for the future' as including 'the concrete, material practices and spaces of 1970s "cinefeminism", the women's films and festivals, as well as the publications and distribution and activist organizations that sprang up not only in Great Britain and the United States but also in Australia, Canada, France, Germany, Mexico, and elsewhere' (White 2006: 146).

There are at least two significant exceptions to the archival absence of the present. One is the Créteil Festival International de Films de Femmes. Founded in 1978 with the first festival in 1979, Créteil (like Cannes, known by its location) has benefited from its institutionalisation in the cultural centres established by French Cultural Minister Andre Malraux and the emphasis on women developed by Health Minister Simone Weill in the 1970s. The festival was founded in Sceaux, a suburb in the south-west of Paris, but in 1984 it moved to larger accommodations in the Maison des Arts et Culture in the south-easterly suburb of Créteil, which has been its permanent home ever since. In these new digs, the festival is afforded offices for a full-time staff of seven as well as storage space for the archives. Their catalogue collection from 30 years of the Créteil festivals is missing only documentation of the first two years, and their videotape collection of interviews with filmmakers is impressive. Although the Créteil Women's Film Festival has begun to save catalogues from other women's film festivals, their holdings date back only a few years and many of the catalogues in their collection are from relatively new festivals (from Germany, India, Israel, Palestine, Seoul and Turkey in their first five or so years).

The other women's film festival that has archival holdings is the Seoul International Women's Film Festival, entering its eleventh year in 2009 and offering (selected) on-line archives in English from its first year (http://www.wffis.or.kr; 9 October 2008). Other women's film festivals have websites that include documentation from previous years, but websites are perhaps even more ephemeral than stashes of catalogues in basements, for they tend to disappear with each annual upload. Past logos (always semiotically telling) and graphic designs, previous mission statements, film selections, managing personnel and programmers, criteria for submission, funders, venues and so on vanish into cyber-space.

History and Memory

In the absence of the WMM archive, I had to abandon the project of compiling hard data on women's film festivals and knowledge production of women's cinema, at least for now. Instead, I will attend to a history of one of the first women's film festivals, the Women and Film International Festival, Toronto 1973.[5] Full disclosure: I am listed among the organising committee credits, as I co-wrote two of the catalogue essays and co-edited the programme book. Although many scholars have pointed out the problematical and permeable relations between memoir and history, that's nevertheless just what I will attempt to negotiate here.[6]

Chapter Six

But first a conjunctural summary quoted at length from Melinda Barlow's overview of feminist art activism in the U.S.:

> By 1972, feminism had trickled into the mainstream and was gathering force in conferences, caucuses, collectives, alternative spaces, protests and publications of all kinds ... One year after Judy Chicago and Miriam Schapiro founded the Feminist Art Program at the California Institute of the Arts, 1972 was the year Chicago, Schapiro, and twenty-one of their students created a collaborative art environment ... and called it *Womanhouse*. Other important collective endeavours appeared the same year: following the model of the Women's Interart Centre in New York (1970), galleries featuring women's work were founded in New York (A.I.R.) and Los Angeles (Womanspace); women picketed the Corcoran Gallery in Washington, DC, for excluding women artists from its 1971 biennial and also organized the first conference on Women in the Visual Arts at the Corcoran School of Art; the College Art Association established the Women's Caucus for Art; Women Make Movies was founded in New York to teach film production to neighbourhood women; and *Feminist Art Journal, Ms. magazine*, and *Women and Film* published their first issues. (Barlow 2003: 10-11)

In other parts of the world besides the USA, similar historic art events were occurring. In Great Britain, the Edinburgh International Film Festival mounted a special Women's Film Event (1972). Parallel with the founding of New Day Films and the Women's Film Coop in the USA, Women In Media and the Women's Film Project were established as similar distribution cooperatives in the UK. In Canada, multi-media artist/filmmaker Joyce Wieland explored women's 'home totems' using traditional crafts (quilting, embroidery) as the principal artistic media in her monumental exhibition, *True Patriot Love/Véritable Amour Patriotique*, the first major exhibition by a woman artist in the National Gallery of Canada (1971); A Space, an avant-garde video and performance gallery, was co-founded by Marien Lewis in Toronto; and Lisa Steele made her first ground-breaking videotape, *Birthday Suit – with scars and defects* (1972). Like other film journals located elsewhere, *Take One Magazine* published a special issue on women's cinema (Armatage and Platt 1972).

On the heels of that special journal issue, which I co-edited, I inserted myself into the small group of enterprising young women who had been inspired by the New York event to mount a similar festival.[7] This small network, with its political, social and media nodes and vectors, is worth unpacking and especially worth situating in the socio-economic and cultural conjuncture, notably baby-boomer economics, federalism and feminism.

With Pierre Eliot Trudeau's election as Prime Minister of Canada in 1968, something of an Obama-like surge occurred among young Canadians, many of whom had flocked to Ottawa to work on Trudeau's campaign, and whose hopes for change were indeed soon supported by liberal policies that faced up to the economic and social tensions of the era. By 1972, there was a significant demographic of university-educated twenty-somethings who were not quite yet recognised as baby-boomers, but who were largely out of work. In their support, the Local Initiatives Program (LIP) was established by the federal government in 1971 as 'a creative solution' to 'the massive unemployment' afflicting the country and specifically targeted to supporting cultural activity. In 1973 in Toronto alone, LIP handed out $800,000 to 27 organisations, including Toronto Women & Film, who received just over $25,000 to defray administration and salary costs (Fraser 1973).[8]

Another significant vector was the North American women's movement. Contrary to the monolithic views of feminism purveyed by the popular press of the time, feminism was a complex and contradictory movement, including Women's Liberationists, Radical Feminists (American-style consciousness-raising), Revolutionary Marxist Group Maoism, old-girl NOW (National Organization for Women, with Betty Friedan as its first President), and other splinter and service groups. The Trudeau government had responded to professional activist women's demands for a Royal Commission on the Status of Women (1970) and as a result, as in France, feminism was then in its eminence as a governmentally sanctioned movement in Canada. Capitalising on the opportunity, one of the first funding proposals for Women & Film began with a quote from the Royal Commission: 'The future of our country will be determined substantially by the directions we Canadians choose to take now. If women are to be able to make use of their full capabilities, help is needed for the whole society. Even so, women themselves must work for change' (Women & Film document). The renewal of Canadian nationalism was aligned in these documents with feminism.

Feminism and Federalism I

Spurred by these social, cultural, political and economic incentives, Toronto International Women and Film was financed through federal, provincial and municipal grants dedicated to job-creation for baby-boomers and the instauration of cultural industries in Canada. With LIP in for $25,251 to cover salaries, funding rolled in from the Ontario Arts Council ($5,750), the Province of Ontario Ministry of Community and Social Services, Youth & Recreation Branch ($7,500), and Toronto City Council ($750). In retrospect, it is clear that, as with other 'alternative' festivals founded in the 1970s, as Ragan Rhyne points out, 'cultural production and the circulation of images are central to the legal and institutional practices of governance and liberation' (Rhyne 2007: 7). We were blithely and unwittingly celebrating governmentality (Foucault's term).

Yet for some of the Toronto Women & Film organisers, Canadian media and politics were what they had been brought up on. Publicity surrounding the event often centred on the media genealogies of the organisers, especially Jill Frayne, whose parents June Callwood and Trent Frayne were respected Canadian journalists; Penny Berton, whose father Pierre Berton was famous as a radio personality and popular writer of Canadian histories; Suzanne DePoe, whose father Norman DePoe was a high-profile news correspondent for CBC-TV and a pioneering figure in Canadian television front-line journalism, and Deanne Taylor, who had been a child star in the formative days of the CBC and had recently returned from film school in England.[9] Although a minority on the staff, their participation sparked several gossipy media exchanges. The national newspaper, *The Globe and Mail*, found the celebrity-fodder newsworthy enough that it ran a series of letters to the editor. These two snide rallies from Paul M. Dickie of London, ON, a riposte from Norman DePoe, who offered to meet Dickie on the sidewalk, and a factoid from Marni Jackson, writing for Women & Film (Fraser 1973, Dickie 1973; DePoe 1973, Jackson 1973). As usual, although the organisers bridled at being identified as 'daughters of', the publicity didn't hurt.

The group also included Marien Lewis (video artist and co-founder of A-Space, an artist-run-centre specialising in performance and video art), Lisa Steele (a pioneering video artist), university friends, and others who, like myself, had just come forward upon hearing of the project. Nine women worked for six months in a dank rented basement office crammed with desks and phones. On two of the desks there were new model rented IBM Selectrics ($15 each per month); the bookkeeper had a rented adding machine; and on a third desk was an old clunker of a typewriter. This technological hierarchisation within the working group caused such dissention that, at a reunion 35 years later, one of the staff said she could still recall coveting the red Selectric and trying to insinuate herself into its possession.[10]

Around the corner in the large A-Space gallery, the staff met weekly with a 'festival committee' that included women filmmakers, video artists, writers and interested feminists. After a few meetings (with attendance up to 40), some political cleavages became apparent. There were arguments that only collective decisions should hold sway, that only 'feminist' films (positive women's content) should be included in the selection, and that no men should be allowed to attend. This was the early 1970s after all, when the North American theoretical apparatus cleaved to the white liberal feminist agenda: positive role models, consciousness-raising, sexism and gender inequities. In Canada, the National Film Board's Studio D – the women's studio – was in its lobbying stage. Spurred by the recommendations of the Royal Commission on the Status of Women (1970), Studio D was launched in 1974 on a directive of films 'by, for and about women', hinging on the mode of realist documentation of women's struggles for liberation. Many women's film festivals steer by this mandate still, especially in Southern and Eastern countries where women's equality is considerably more in jeopardy than in the West.

Feminist Scholarship, Feminist Programming

The political agendas of various feminist groups stimulated many different cultural modes, but the USA, especially in the feminist movement, dominated certainly cultural currency in Canada then, as now. A few years after the Toronto Festival, Julia LeSage outlined the generic elements of feminist documentary, citing as significant the presentation of 'a picture of the ordinary details of women's lives' and extending this generalisation with the observation that 'feminist filmmaking has often led to entirely new demands in the areas of health care, welfare, poverty programs, work, and law (especially rape)' (Lesage 1978: 507-23).[11] Lesage also noted the strategy and processes of consciousness-raising, and of collective work in particular, as providing the 'deep structure' of feminist documentary. This rubric was, for all intents and purposes, what was defined as feminist film production, in North America at least. The 'thrill of negativity' in the avant-garde ushered in by Laura Mulvey's now-canonical article was still in the future, although not so distant.

In this climate, representational politics were hotly contested. I was a fan of Stephanie Rothman's *The Student Nurses* (USA, 1970) and *The Velvet Vampire* (USA, 1971) but had to argue long and hard to get Rothman's newest, *Terminal Island* (USA, 1973) (an early foray into masculinity set in a men's prison) programmed amongst the uplifting feminist and avant-garde films. After much debate, we made the decision to concentrate on production by women directors, despite their 'women's content' or lack of it (Shirley Clarke's oeuvre and Stephanie Rothman's latest as cases in point). We sought out women's filmic production on many subjects and in diverse cinematic modes, and in the end, notwithstanding the collective meetings, the paid staff and volunteer programmers made the decisions.[12]

Unlike the New York Women's Film Festival, the Toronto mandate included a retrospective of work by women filmmakers over the history of cinema. This was a significant undertaking. At the time, there was a dearth of published history regarding women's participation in film production. The only source the researchers and programmers had to go on was Anthony Slide's *Early Women Directors* and a woefully incomplete filmography of 150 women filmmakers (Henshaw 1972). As B. Ruby Rich writes: 'Back then, organizing a women's film festival was first and foremost a research project ... [C]abals of programmers were ... literally rescuing films from a life on the shelf: they were dusting off the cans to show women's work for the first time in months, years, decades, *ever'* (Rich 1998: 29; italics in original). Toronto Women & Film had a stellar researcher who found hundreds of women filmmakers and tracked down prints of films long considered lost. Anne Mackenzie, whose research apparatus was the telephone, unearthed good prints of *Back to God's Country* (Nell Shipman, USA, 1919), *Working Girls* (Dorothy Arzner, USA, 1930), which Arzner said was her favourite although never commercially distributed, and, from a private collector, *Das Blaue Licht* (*The Blue Light*, Leni Riefenstahl, Germany, 1921).

8-17 June 1973

Coming after the Women's Cinema event at Edinburgh (1972) and the New York Women's Video Festival (June 1972), Toronto International Women & Film (June 1973) was the largest women's film festival thus far: 10 days, noon to midnight. As a result of advance pieces on national radio, gossipy notices in the press, and the ubiquitous posters (10,000 printed in three colours) and programme books (25,000 printed on newsprint so they could be free – available later for $0.50), it was a well-publicised affair. Perhaps even more significantly for its local prominence and press attention, it was held in the newest and largest cultural edifice in Toronto, the St. Lawrence Centre, which was usually home to the ballet and the opera. For Women & Film, its lobbies were fitted out with monitors for the video programme, notice boards for announcements of feminist services and personal messages, an exhibition of women's photographs, and an organic food concession. The whole affair was redolent with the 1970s *zeitgeist*: collective administration by grant-savvy women and avant-garde artists, parties every night, free admission and free full-time daycare run by men. The accessibility of the festival, as a result of free admission and onsite day-care, set Toronto apart from the New York event, which had been criticised for its hefty ticket price and lack of daycare (Edwards et al. 1973: 14).

Many guests were invited: one early list included Simone de Beauvoir, Marguerite Duras, Ruth Gordon, Ida Lupino and Vera Chytilova – with the proviso that 'in the case of those who could be expected to afford it, [they have been asked] to consider paying their own way' (Taylor, Berton, Jackson, undated newsletter, 1973). In fact, although few paid their own way, there were many guests, including Freude Bartlett, Joyce Chopra, Shirley and Wendy Clarke, Martha Coolidge, Mireille Dansereau, Alanis Obomsawin, Stephanie Rothman, Amalie Rothschild, Sylvia Spring, Viva Superstar and Agnes Varda. Many participated in discussions and workshops.[13]

The opening night selection in Toronto began with *What I Want* (Sharon Hennessey, USA) (8 minutes), *Orange* (Karen Johnston, USA) (6 minutes), *How the Hell Are You* (Veronica Soul, Canada) (20 minutes) and *Bridal Shower* (Sandy Wilson, Canada, 1972) (20 minutes), all leading to the feature gala presentation of *La Vie Revée* (*Dream Life*, Mireille Dansereau, Canada, 1972). I include these details here precisely because such records aren't widely available and because these titles denote an era-specific aesthetic and politics. The Canadian shorts leading to a Canadian feature promoted national identity, while the infusion of U.S. shorts enabled a transnational connection and display of diversity of filmmaking modes. *What I Want* was a long slow zoom from a close-up to a wide shot that eventually revealed a woman reading from a floor-length scroll. *Orange* was an erotic montage of close-ups in the style of Ansel Adams' peppers but in colour. *How the Hell Are You* is one of the great animations of the period, and *The Bridal Shower* is a faux documentary, acerbically humorous in its castigation of contemporary marriage rituals. One report is worth quoting for its summary of the successes of the event:

> These four well-selected teasers prepared the audience for a festival in which they would be constantly amazed, delighted and occasionally overwhelmed by the diversity, the skill, the cleverness and depth, originality and capabilities of women's work in the world of film. The intention of the festival was to create an awareness of what women could do, and what they have done, in film. Right from the beginning it became apparent they would succeed ... The week became a celebration ... I'd love to go on and on about each film, each showing, the shorts, the documentaries, the audience reactions, discussions, panels, and interviews, but since the films alone numbered 200 selections from the 450 considered, the writing would be endless. (Edwards et al. 1974: 17)

Nationalism and Regionalism

In addition to the 10-day event in Toronto, Women & Film sent three teams carrying films out to 18 cities across Canada. The tour was a significant organisational undertaking. First, in addition to the 10-day Toronto event, it necessitated raising funding support for a total budget of more than $125,000 in 1973 dollars, equivalent to over $500,000 in 2007 dollars (the latest figures I could get). Originally planned as a nine-week tour with nine features and 30 shorts going to each city consecutively, the tour had to be rethought in order not to tie up prints for such a long period. Instead, teams went out on three circuits, East, West and Quebec, with different films and paraphernalia. The Toronto coordinators, who then carried the 16 mm prints and other exhibition materials to the regions of Canada from Labrador to the North West Territories, handled exhibition, shipping, advertising and travel costs as well as the logistics of the tour.

Local committees worked in all cities, organising the volunteers, workshops and daycare, booking venues and curating exhibitions by local artists. The report from Edmonton is typical:

> 'A couple of women ...organized the video-tape display ... Two local film makers ... worked on ... liaison with Toronto. Several women ... collected, arranged and hung the local submissions of art and photography. Various women's groups set up information tables outside the theatre ... A local bookstore sold feminist paperbacks of current interest' (Edwards et al., 1974: 14).

After the tour, which followed the Toronto festival in the summer of 1973, the local coordinators came to Toronto in October for an evaluation and future planning conference. Although the event had been ambitious in scope already, the plans didn't end there. The institutional vision included a continuing national organisation, a newsletter/magazine, a distribution circuit for regular circulating packages of films by women, an access catalogue listing all available films by women with sources and continuing events over the next few years.[14] Not all of it came about, but Women & Film obtained further funding for events and conferences in 1974 and 1975.

Most reports from the tour cities were pretty positive. The Edmonton and Halifax summaries are typical in reporting outcomes such as women who had felt isolated in their artistic activities coming together, instructional workshops mounted for women on video and film equipment, the beginnings of a Women's Photo Co-op, lobbying for a women's centre, and other continuing projects. The imbrications of women's cinema with feminist politics seemed diverse and specifically local and yet consistent across a national geography. As Julian Stringer remarks of the contemporary film festival network, the events are conceptually similar and yet culturally specific (Stringer 2001: 129).

Federalism and Feminism II

In terms of local, regional and national Canadian politics, however, ripples on the surface leaked indications of the tidal whirlpool lurking beneath. A multi-authored article in *Cinema Canada*, Canada's first film journal, surveyed the event. Here is a ripple example, from the Vancouver report: 'We had some problems in regionalism vs. nationalism – hard not to have a say in the selection of films and scheduling. We want to do our own, yet are tied to [Toronto] purse strings – as selection and quantity would have been different had it all been under our control' (Edwards et al. 1974: 14). Another from Whitehorse, Yukon, illustrates geographical disconnects in terms of geo-thermal dynamics: 'The lack of participation by [Women's Groups] was due to the timing of the festival; by mid-May all organizations in the north have recessed until mid-September, in order to enjoy to the fullest the short summer, and no one is willing to re-organize for any specific project such as the Festival' (Edwards et al. 1974: 17).

The more formidable national and regional crosscurrents are signalled first by an absence, the lack of a report from a Quebec location in the festival wrap-up in the national film journal (Edwards et al. 1974: 14-?). Another flag is raised by a quickly glossed-over topic for potential discussion at the evaluation conference later that year: 'What did you think of the way in which liaison between you and Toronto proceeded? Is the "remote control" method of organizing an event of this kind satisfactory?' (document).

It was at the level of feminism and federalism that the greatest rifts occurred. A stunning 11-page document entitled 'Report on Montreal Festival Organization: in reply to a brief submitted Sept./73 by Montreal coordinators Lise Daoust, Helene Girard, Lisa Labreque' reveals the forms and sources of the schisms in great detail, as the Toronto organisers respond to the Montreal report point by point and add some of their own. In the first paragraphs of the text the Toronto organisers express chagrin that they had overlooked 'the unique political atmosphere in Quebec ... [which] should have been given special consideration when the budget was drawn up' (document). In the budget, 18 tour cities were allocated one to three-day events, depending on the size of the city. But as the events approached and communications between centres accumulated, it had become apparent that 'each city had its own specific needs' (document). The Montreal organisers seemed to think that their festival, in a larger city than Toronto with a more developed film industry at the time, should have been at least equivalent to Toronto's. As the initiators, fund-raisers and principal organisers in this document, the Toronto committee treads this territory on tiptoe.

But the rhetorical tone of the Toronto response hardens quickly, as the organisers compare the Quebec position to the responses of other cities, for whom enthusiasm for the women's event appears to outweigh local or regional grievances: 'For the Montreal women, however, it was a case of trying to get as big a piece of the pie as they could: strictly a business arrangement. They wanted Montreal's festival to be unique and had little interest in the national aspect of the event. The political importance to them of having a festival that not only rivalled those in other cities (Toronto included) but also differed from them as much as possible took precedence over their personal sympathies with the women's movement in Canada' (Report).

Setting aside feminism, youthful bravado and Toronto media-centrist arrogance as political explanations just for a moment, it is important to remember some historical ironies that subtended these feminist and federalist vicissitudes. The 1968 election of Trudeau government, which had initiated the grant structures that were funding Women & Film, had coincided with the founding of the Parti Québecois. That advocated political, economic and social independence for the province of Québec, and in 1973 the Québec separatist movement remained very strong. Another historical irony is that the Royal Commission on the Status of Women, whose recommendations had installed feminism as a federal undertaking, had been tabled in the House of Commons in December 1970, less than two months after the October Crisis during which terrorist activities in Québec had prompted Prime Minister Trudeau to invoke the War Measures Act and the deployment of the army in the province. Hundreds of suspected Front Liberation du Québec members and sympathisers were arrested without warrants, and in the years following, support for independence increased.

To counter the federalist failure to establish equality between English and French within the operations of government, Trudeau had made the language issue one of his first priorities. He established the Official Languages Act in 1969, one of whose most significant briefs was to designate Canada as an officially bilingual nation. Somewhat surprisingly, Women & Film paid little heed to this policy, acceding to its claims by translating 'women and film' as 'la femme et le film' only on the cover page of the catalogue; perhaps the policy was not being as strictly enforced in 1973 as it was later. Nevertheless, it was a minimalist capitulation, to say the least. Neither, by the way, is 'Toronto' designated on the cover page, suggesting a universal purview from an unidentified global site. The charges of Toronto media centrism and financial control rankle the regions to this day, to the crippling of the federal government.

The Toronto committee admitted, 'We realized too late our mistake in not designing a completely bilingual poster' (Report: 3). Moreover, there was no provision in the budget for translation (a line item that would be required for a national project nowadays). The Toronto group made an effort to translate the programme notes into French for the Quebec cities on the tour, but apparently the translation was neither accurate nor timely – 'a rush job' (Report: 4). When the Montreal committee received the translated notes, 'they hit the roof' (Report: 4) but by this time it was too late and the translated notes were never printed. From the large issues of translation and the allocation of federal funding to nit-picking quarrels over $100 petty cash and a $40 beer permit, the stress-points outlined in the Toronto response seem endless.

In addition, there were divergences in forms of feminism that drove another wedge into the federally troubled project. The festival poster, catalogue cover and postcards that were designed and approved by the central committee indicate the Toronto feminist formation graphically. The Women & Film logo was a graphic of a woman hoisting a huge film reel, suggesting Atlas carrying the world on his shoulders. Like Atlas, she is naked and voluptuous in contour, but unlike the iconic depictions of Atlas, who seems to struggle under the burden of the world, the woman wears a wide smile, big hair and 1970s-style-graphic tripping toes. The illustration offered a celebratory (and liberal) substitute for the more radical fists-in-the-air feminist logos of the era. Some postcards bore the official logo, while others offered an alternative that featured paper doll-type clothing for the naked figure. Tinged just a bit with a hippie-ish playfulness, these publicity materials spoke from a non-militant, unthreatening, and definitely femme feminism.

The Montreal committee, on the other hand, was divided internally. The Toronto document does not characterise the factions politically in terms of feminism, but it seems possible to read them that way. One faction, whom the Toronto document described as having a vision for the festival as 'a glamorous, prestigious event for the film elite of the city', might be read as aligned with the politically conservative feminism that sought change through legislation, job progress through the ranks to positions of power, and the professionalisation of women's lives. Another group, according to the Toronto document, wanted 'a more grass roots happening', perhaps indicating similarities either with more left-wing strategies or with the American-style consciousness-raising of Radical Feminism. The first 'finally resigned in protest over Toronto's "unprofessional approach'" (Report: 3), but ultimately neither of the Montreal groups got along with Toronto.

In the end, feminism and federalism was an uneasy coupling, at least for the Women & Film project. Even though the Quebec women agreed to remain within the proposed national organisation, they made it clear that 'this would be mainly a business arrangement for economic reasons' – i.e. for access to federal funding for their own projects. Ironically, as the decades progressed and Canada elected conservative governments, it became increasingly clear that there would be very little federal cultural funding for the rest of the country if Quebec were not demanding 'their piece of the pie'.

In the ensuing efforts to galvanise a national organisation, the centre vs. regions problems became increasingly exacerbated. The 1974 follow-up conference, for which the Toronto organisers garnered more government funding, became a pitched battle between centre and regions. The Toronto committee came to see itself as the embattled federalists harangued for resources by local and regional claims. Eventually the committee concluded that a national organisation with a centralised structure feeding local committees was not workable: 'Any future "national organization" that develops from here on in will be a network of autonomous committees each managing their own project and budgets' (Post-Tour Conference document).

The Women & Film national organisation folded its tents in 1975. While the demise of Women & Film 1973 may be specific to the uneasy and everlastingly fraught federalism of Canada, its passing is also symptomatic of a particular moment in the history of film festivals. Many of the ad hoc and grass roots events of the 1970s died and were replaced in the 1980s by more institutionalised and more professionalised non-profit organisations established as networks or international circuits (de Valck 2007: 19). There are now two women's films festivals of size and stature in Canada, St. John's (Newfoundland), a five-day annual event <womensfilmfestival.com> and Herland (Calgary, Alberta), a seven-day event and one of the largest film festivals in the western region <herlandfestival.com>. Both were founded in 1989, around the time of establishment of many women's film festivals now thriving on a transnational scale.

Notes

1   I want to thank Joceline Andersen, M.A. student in the Cinema Studies Institute, University of Toronto, for her invaluable research assistance.

2   In a graduate course on women's film festivals, I gave a 'lost films' assignment. One of the students, Joceline Andersen, researched films whose sources were listed in the Toronto Women & Film catalogue as 'filmmaker's print'. Many of the films, as we can predict, have been lost. Anne Wheeler, well-known Canadian filmmaker, responded to

Andersen's query that she had thrown the only print of her first film off a bridge. Other filmmakers' prints have not suffered such violent ends, but simply disintegrated under beds.

3   It is only because one of the organisers, Penny Berton, was taught by her historian father and archivist mother to value documents that we have the present materials relating to Toronto Women & Film 1973.

4   One of my formative memories of such films is *Amor, Mujeres y Flores* (*Love, Women & Flowers*, Marta Rodríguez & Jorge Silva, 1988) which instructed me never to buy carnations again. Fortunately the film is in distribution with Women Make Movies.

5   Following the Edinburgh Women's Film Event (1972), a sidebar of the Edinburgh International Film Festival, and the New York Women's Film and Video Festival (1972).

6   See, for just a few examples, Stewart 1993, Gilmore 2001, Hastie 2007.

7   Sylvia Spring, who had directed the first feature-length film by a Canadian woman, suggested the event, but the organisation fell to her followers.

8   Equivalent to approximately $3.25 million and $102,000 respectively.

9   Star of Maggie Muggins 1956-59, an iconic and much-loved children's adventure show that ran in print, on radio and then TV from 1947 to 1962.

10 On 5 December 2008, many of the Toronto staff gathered, bringing photos, super-8 films reels, and any other materials they could retrieve. Present: Kay Armatage, Penny Berton, Suzanne DePoe, Jill Frayne, Marni Jackson, Marien Lewis, Anne Mackenzie, Deanne Taylor, Lydia Wazana. Much of the anecdotal material of this paper was gathered on that evening.

11 Many of the feminist documentaries that Lesage attends to as central to the genre – *Growing Up Female* (Julia Reichert and Jim Klein, USA, 1971), *The Woman's Film* (Judy Smith, Louise Alaimo and Ellen Sorin, USA, 1971), *I Am Somebody* (Madeline Anderson, USA, 1970) – were exhibited in Toronto Women & Film, 1973.

12 Hot Gossip from 1973: In a workshop on directing, Stephanie Rothman (in pastel sweater set and pearls) and Shirley Clarke (wearing black skinny pants and turtle-neck) traded tips: Clarke emphasised the importance of good solid shoes, and Rothman demonstrated a yoga posture to take the strain off the back over long hours of standing. In the workshop, they got along well, but later Clarke, who had never heard of Rothman, was horrified to discover the kinds of films Rothman directed: American International flicks. After Clarke saw *Terminal Island* on the first weekend of the festival, she didn't speak to Rothman again. This was, in spades, the standoff of avant-garde vs. B-movie, New York vs. L.A., groovy vs. square, not to mention class privilege (the opposite of what their chosen vestimentary codes might suggest: Rothman's was a masquerade). Yet there was no discussion of feminist content, which Rothman's early films would have won hands-down. While her films

conformed to the Roger Corman model of sex or violence every seven minutes, they presented commanding women characters and dealt with women's issues (e.g., the abortion scene in *The Student Nurses*, in which the inadvertently pregnant character hallucinates the evacuation of commodity consumption – boxes of laundry detergent, fridges).

[13] Freude Bartlett and Viva Superstar, with Deanne Taylor and Marien Lewis, participated memorably in a live commentary during a midnight screening of *Near the Big Chakra* (Anne Severson, USA, 1971) (40 minutes), usually screened silent. The notoriety of the screening in Toronto is in no small measure due to their participation, compared with the boredom (or was it the hour?) indicated by the report from Regina: 'Comic relief was needed and wasn't forthcoming. At 2 o'clock in the morning *Near the Big Chakra* was shown – what was left of the audience got up one by one and left' (Bergles et al. 1974: 15).

[14] Relevant documents have been collected and are housed in the University of Toronto Media Archives, but they are not catalogued or numbered yet.

Works Cited

Anon. (Undated) 'Report on Montreal Festival Organization', 11.

Armatage, Kay and Phyllis Platt (eds) (1972) 'Women in Film Special Issue: Take One', 3, 2.

Barlow, Melinda (2003) 'Feminism 101: The New York Women's Video Festival, 1972–1980', *Camera Obscura*, 54, 18, 3, 2-38.

Cvetkovich, Ann (2002) 'In the Archives of Lesbian Feeling: Documentary and Popular Culture', *Camera Obscura*, 49, 17, 1, 107-47.

de Valck, Marijke (2007) *Film Festivals: From European Geopolitics to Global Cinephilia.* Amsterdam: Amsterdam University Press.

DePoe, Norman (1973) 'LIP Grants', *Toronto Globe & Mail*, 17 March, n.p.

Dickie, Paul M. (1973) 'LIP Grants', *Toronto Globe & Mail*, 12 March, n.p.

___ (1973) 'LIP Grants', *Toronto Globe & Mail*, 21 March, n. p.

Edwards, Nathalie, Frances Bergles, Jan Cornflower, Joyce Hayden, Janet Hone, Nora Hutchinson, Jay Maclean, and Andrea Rogers (1973) 'Women & Film Festival', *Cinema Canada*, 9, 14-18.

Fraser, John (1973) 'Are Those LIP Grants Really Helping the Arts?', *Toronto Globe & Mail*, 3 March, n.p.

Gilmore, Leigh (2001) *The Limits of Autobiography: Trauma and Testimony.* New York: Cornell University Press.

Hastie, Amelie (2007) *Cupboards of Curiosity: Women, Recollection and Film History.* Durham: Duke University Press.

Henshaw, Richard (1972) 'Women Directors: 150 Filmographies', *Film Comment*, 8, 4, 33-45.

Chapter Six

Jackson, Marni (1973) 'LIP Grants', *Toronto Globe & Mail*, 17 March, n.p.

Lesage, Julia (1990 [1978]) 'The Political Aesthetics of the Feminist Documentary Film', in Patricia Erens (ed.) *Issues in Feminist Film Criticism*. Bloomington: Indiana University Press, 222-23.

Rhyne, Ragan (2007) 'Pink dollars: Gay and Lesbian Film Festivals and the Economy of Visibility', unpublished PhD dissertation, New York University.

Rich, B. Ruby (1998) *Chick Flicks*. Durham: Duke University Press.

Slide, Anthony (1984 [1972]) *Early Women Directors*. New York: Da Capo Press.

Stewart, Susan (1993) *On Longing: Narratives of the Miniature, the Gigantic, the Souvenir, the Collection*. Durham: Duke University Press.

Stringer, Julian (2001) 'Global Cities and International Film Festival Economy', in Mark Shiel and Tony Fitzmaurice (eds) *Cinema and the City: Film and Urban Societies in a Global Context*. Oxford: Blackwell, 134-44.

White, Patricia (2006) 'The Last Days of Women's Cinema', *Camera Obscura*, 63, 21, 3, 145-51.

Chapter Seven

Corporatising a Film Festival: Hong Kong

Ruby Cheung

Introduction

While scholars such as Thomas Elsaesser (2005: 88), Julian Stringer (2006: 202) and Kenneth Turan (2002: 8) have proposed that the film festival circuit offers an alternative distribution network for cinema, it is the local and institutional politics of operating a festival that particularly interests me. In this essay, I will examine the evolution of one such institution, the Hong Kong International Film Festival (HKIFF), as it underwent a process of corporatisation after 27 years of governmental operation. This corporatisation, I will argue, has had significant implications for the ways that we might understand the function of the film festival as an alternative distribution network, a government policy vehicle, and a cinematic art event for local audiences.

The corporatisation of the HKIFF has had a significant effect on the festival's two primary stakeholders: the film industry and the local government. The influx of commercial sponsorships that were introduced to replace public funding challenged the high-art aspirations of the festival, turning it into a more populist, film industry-driven, market-oriented event. But while the additional funding from the commercial sector that has come with corporatisation has helped to boost the festival's international profile, it has not necessarily facilitated its role as a node in any kind of alternative film distribution network. Moreover, while the corporatisation of the festival from a government-owned-and-administered event to one heavily supported by private sponsorships has fulfilled the goals of the local government to 'streamline' its bureaucracy, it has also brought into relief the politics of programming, as the festival's audience might have changed along with its administrative structure.

I will first take a look at the brief history of the HKIFF leading up to the time when the government decided to corporatise it. I will then turn to discussing the possible rationale of the corporatisation. Exploration of the effects of such an initiative on the film industry and local government will come next via comparing the contents of three publicly available annual reports of the corporatised festival. Finally, I will scrutinise the programming strategy of the HKIFF before and after the corporatisation and address the issues of a possible change in the audience profile by comparing the programme catalogues in the HKIFF's pre- and post-corporatisation years. Due to the scarcity of scholarly work on the HKIFF, most of my investigation is based on the festival publications, promotional materials and loose-leaf pamphlets that I have collected during the years (from the early 1990s to early 2000s) when I was a regular festival-goer in Hong Kong.

Film Festival Corporatisation

Since its inception in 1977, the HKIFF has operated as a non-competitive event, focusing primarily on screening non-mainstream overseas films to its local audience. According to one of the founders of the HKIFF, Chan Pak-sung (Hong Kong Film Critics Association 2003: 4; my romanisation of his name and paraphrasing of this Chinese-language interview), the idea of hosting a film festival in Hong Kong was first initiated by the then programme manager of City Hall (a local high-art cultural venue run by the government), Yeung Yu-ping, whose office was responsible for all cultural programmes hosted by the Urban Council in Hong Kong. Chan recalls that Yeung, being a film buff, was inspired by those most successful film festivals in the West to organise such an event in Hong Kong. The festival did not have a clear direction back then and the three coordinators who were involved in the festival organisation worked voluntarily without getting paid. However, as most of the 46 films presented were screened without being subtitled, the festival was not readily accessible to a mass audience. In addition, the film industry workers were not interested in attending these screenings, according to Chan, as they were either not willing to exchange with the overseas film productions or they did not see many films beyond their work remit. Hence, whereas the first season of the HKIFF can be regarded as being run in a loosely centralised model of cultural and funding management (Colbert 2000: 54) for the benefits of the general public, such an initiative was criticised by public opinions as catering to a small group of film buffs (Hong Kong Film Critics Association 2003: 4). According to an official record published in 2003, the first season of the HKIFF in 1977 screened only 37 films (instead of 46 titles as what Chan recalls) to an audience of 16,000 (Chen 2003: 3).

Moreover, the HKIFF has not given out awards that are guarantees of commercial success for films on the festival circuit. The individual tastes of festival curators almost exclusively determined the selection of films. Throughout the entire 27 years of operation under the aegis of the local government from 1977 to 2004, the HKIFF has gradually developed into one of the most famous, well-established film festivals and the oldest of its kind in East Asia. Yet due to the absence of long-term cultural policy on the part of the government, several government departments have taken turns to organise the HKIFF. Initiated by Yeung under the Urban Council of the Hong Kong colonial government, the HKIFF was later organised by the Provisional Urban Council from 1997-98. Further changes took place in 1999-2000, when the HKIFF came under the administration of the Leisure and Cultural Services Department. In 2001-04, the Hong Kong Arts Development Council took the reins to manage the HKIFF.

In the twenty-first century, corporatisation became a buzzword in the HKIFF's publications, officials' speeches, press releases and so on. The word 'corporatisation' refers to '[t]he act of reorganizing the structure of government owned entity into a legal entity with the corporate structure found in publicly trade companies' (*Investopedia*). That is to say, the corporatised units do not belong to the government structure any more. Instead, they have their own corporate practices modelled on that of profit-making commercial enterprises. As they are not publicly traded, many of them may still be under strong influence from governments.

Certainly, there are a lot of reasons why governments corporatise their former units: there may be strategic reasons to grow the corporatised units separately, financial reasons to reduce the costs of running these units by allowing them to take care of their own income and expenditure, or administrative reasons to streamline bureaucracy. In Hong Kong, no full clarification was given as to why the local government decided to corporatise the once government-owned-and-administered, already well-established festival. The only reasons that have been given as rationale for this government initiative were (a) to have the event managed more flexibly, and (b) to attract more commercial sponsorships to the event.

In many Western countries, corporatisation has existed since the 1980s in public service sectors such as water management and national railway systems. For example, in Canada most of these corporatised units, called crown corporations or state-owned enterprises, are clustered in various public services and strategic fields like oil and gas provision, land transportation and aviation, where the ultimate goal of maximising the general public interest is often upheld (Bozec and Breton 2003). The corporatised entities are thus essentially different from privately owned enterprises, which usually have their first and foremost objectives of maximising their private profits and/or minimising their operating costs. As such, corporatisation allows the public goods and service providers to maintain their production standard (if not excellence) while shedding unnecessary bureaucracy and complicated administrative procedures.

Identifying corporatisation as the main mechanism used for the reform of state-owned enterprises (or SOEs) in 1990s China, Donald Clarke (2003: 27), a professor at the University of Washington School of Law, highlights three key trends:

- The raising of equity for SOEs following conversion to the corporate form;

- The expansion of state control in some sectors through leverage; and
- The improvement of the management of state assets through the implementation of a new organisational form

As Hong Kong is still operating in a market economy mode under the 'one country, two systems' framework after the 1997 sovereignty handover, the rationale of corporatising HKIFF is likely to be more in line with what has happened in the public sector in the Western countries rather than with the three trends Clarke identifies.

As far as commercial sponsorship is concerned, arts management scholar François Colbert, in writing about the corporate contributions and sponsorships for cultural institutions, argues that:

> A contribution is normally a philanthropic act, whereas sponsorship is a promotional initiative in exchange for publicity or advertising. Sponsorships are undertaken according to promotional benefits calculated in advance. The corporate sponsor then judges the performance of the investment in terms of visibility, top-of-the-mind awareness, and the vehicle's reach – that is, the number of consumers receiving the message ... Today, companies such as the Toronto Film Festival, the Chicago Symphony Orchestra, and the Salzburg Festival are so successful that major private-sector corporations do not hesitate to associate themselves with these events, which not only reach a large number of spectators, but also enjoy tremendous public approval and appeal. (2000: 56)

The cases mentioned here thus show us the positive aspects of commercial sponsorships which are closely linked to arts bodies' corporatisation. Known for the absence of a clearly defined, long-term cultural policy and for regularly failing to support sizable cultural projects, Hong Kong government's decision of corporatising the HKIFF and separating it from government structures prompted suspicion about the government's real motives behind the corporatisation initiative. For instance, those who are familiar with the contestable cultural development in Hong Kong would immediately think of the controversial project of developing the West Kowloon Cultural District by the Hong Kong government since the late 1990s. The project was first proposed in 1998 by the then Chief Executive (the government head of the Hong Kong Special Administrative Region after the 1997 Handover), Tung Chee-hwa, to turn the West Kowloon area of Hong Kong into a cultural district in the hope of establishing Hong Kong's image as the culture and art centre of Asia. Public consultation was conducted on this extravagant project, which has since generated a huge amount of debate, yet no solid conclusion has been reached a decade later (Information Note 2004; Hong Kong Government Press Release 2008).

Corporatising a Film Festival: Hong Kong

The corporatisation of the HKIFF began in 2002 and was completed in 2005 – before the government laid out the coporatisation plan for the HKIFF, three other arts bodies (the Hong Kong Chinese Orchestra, the Hong Kong Dance Company, and the Hong Kong Repertory Theatre) had left the government structure and become corporatised. Since 2005, the HKIFF has been independently managed by a non-profit, non-governmental corporation called The Hong Kong International Film Festival Society Limited. Today, the organisation receives about 30 per cent of its operating budget from a government statutory body, the Hong Kong Arts Development Council. Another government department, the Leisure and Cultural Services Department, assists this 32-year-old festival indirectly by renting out venues at a reduced rental rate for festival screenings during the March-April festival season. The new company managing the corporatised HKIFF continues to employ important members of the previous staff of the festival to carry out such work as programming and art direction.

Most scholarly studies of the impacts of corporatisation generate positive evidence to support governments' strategies of corporatising parts of their former units of public goods and service provision. They focus on the organisational level (Laux and Molot 1988; Gordon 1981), and on the efficiency and financial performance of the corporatised units as measured by the criteria of privately-owned enterprises (Bozec and Breton 2003). Similar methodologies may be applicable to evaluate the performance of the corporatised arts service providers, though there would be some adjustments in practice because of the specifics of arts institutions. There are certainly a lot of advantages of bringing market approaches to an arts scene originally sponsored by public money. By abiding to the basic market economy rules of supply and demand, the arts events are expected to prosper while allowing stakeholders to engage into mutually beneficial exchanges and forge constructive collaborations. However; there are also complications that arise during the process of arts and cultural corporatisations, mostly because the multiple stakeholders are bringing along competing agendas.

It is in this regard that the HKIFF offers an interesting case study for the topic of corporatisation. It is an event of a triple nature: (a) a site for film business, (b) a public policy initiative, and (c) a cinematic art event known as an 'audience festival' (*Screen International* 2008: 20).

Firstly, according to this tripartite function, the corporatised HKIFF has become a site where art-house and mainstream filmmakers display their latest productions and find potential producers and buyers for their new projects. This function was particularly evident when the HKIFF began the corporate transition in 2002. In April of that year, the festival took place concurrently with the Hong Kong-Asia Film Financing Forum (HAF). The Hong Kong Film Awards, the local equivalent to the Oscar Awards, started in 1982 as an independent event and were later rescheduled to take place during the same month as the HKIFF. Filmmakers, film producers, distributors and potential buyers thus came to see the HKIFF as a kind of trade show where they could find opportunities for film promotion. It is, however, worth noting that the three main film-related events under the banner of Entertainment Expo Hong Kong – the HKIFF, the HAF, and Hong Kong International Film & TV Market (Hong Kong Filmart) – finally synchronised after years of discrepancy in timing and kicked off on the same day on 20 March 2007 to capitalise fully on the promotion and distribution opportunities that these events help facilitate (*Screen International* 2007: 13). This strategy allowed Hong Kong to compete with the Pusan International Film Festival's (PIFF) up-and-coming Asian Film Market, which was inaugurated in 2006 (Shackleton 2007: 17).

Secondly, upon the full corportisation of the HKIFF, the Hong Kong government is still maintaining its remote control over the operation of the HKIFF through partial funding, sponsorship of screening venues, and secondment of government personnel to some of the administrative positions of the corporatised HKIFF. It is thus arguable that the government viewed corporatising HKIFF as a strategic move to ensure that quality cultural activities are brought to the general audience at reduced government expenditure and via the introduction of significant amount of commercial sponsorships to cover the necessary costs of running the festival. This governmental goal makes the HKIFF different from its successful Western counterparts, such as Venice, Cannes, and Berlin, which started in politicised contexts (Elsaesser 2005: 89). For politicisation was probably one of the last items on the HKIFF's priority list when it was first established by the Hong Kong colonial government, which had a policy of censoring films conveying explicit political messages (Lo 1999, Sek 1988, Teo 1988).

Thirdly, the HKIFF is an important occasion offering the general public an opportunity to appreciate films from different parts of the world. The event has been an alternative to the local mainstream cinema houses, where screenings are primarily limited to Hollywood blockbusters and popular films made in Hong Kong and neighbouring territories. It is almost an act of pilgrimage when audiences, film buffs and tourists alike attend the festival annually to enjoy their favourite films. The opportunity of seeing different films is undeniably very important to these festival-goers. In the coming sections, I shall look into each one of these aspects and discuss the effect of corporatisation.

Stakeholders in Festival Corporatisation: The Film Industry and the Government

In 'Film Festival Networks: The New Topographies of Cinema in Europe' (2005), Elsaesser argues that the festival circuit is post-national, transcending national borders while maintaining certain elements for understanding European cinema. For Elsaesser, the concept of film festivals brings along other concerns, such as the author and national cinema in the field of film studies. Probing whether the film festival circuit can emulate the Hollywood model with its own film business platform that involves production, distribution and exhibition while also maintaining 'European' traits, the author believes that the answers can be both yes and no. His 'yes' considerations acknowledge that both systems do have a lot in common; the film festival circuit displays some of the qualities necessary to become an alternative distribution network to Hollywood, and the commissioning of films for festivals is analogous to the control that commercial distributors exert over Hollywood production. On the other hand, Elsaesser's 'no' argument refers mainly to the discrepancy in the sheer size and media visibility between Hollywood and film festivals (Elsaesser 2005: 93).

Writing about the ways in which mainstream blockbusters exploit major film festivals to advance their international promotions, Stringer remarks that there is indeed 'a sense of unease among all concerned' (Stringer 2006: 204), for these festival-participating blockbusters are too glamorous to go with the flow, yet they are not highbrow enough to be on a par with international art cinema. Not only does their presence at film festivals become an embarrassment, it also elicits the issue of unequal power relations among different filmmaking territories (ibid.: 204-5).

The premise of these arguments is that there are at least two distinct, if not mutually exclusive, global circulation routes for cinema. One is the mainstream (Hollywood) network and the other the film festival circuit. Indeed, this distinction is quite useful if we consider those biggest and most prominent international film festivals such as Cannes, Venice and Berlin. The situation, however, becomes different when it comes to film festivals that have strong regional focus. A clear-cut distinction between mainstream film circulation and the festival circuit would be too simplistic to show the actual, complex circumstances. Here, both the mainstream film distribution network and the festival circuit become branches of a larger distribution network. These branches of different natures help each other to reach mutually beneficial goals. Blockbusters are welcome to share the spotlight with highly-praised art-house films in film festivals. This larger network thus grants additional exhibition opportunities to the mega-budget mainstream films to reach not only mass audiences but also art-house audiences who may despise the lower cultural value of mainstream films. On the other side, festival films can utilise mainstream theatrical channels to draw audiences to which they normally cannot reach out. Instead of being antithesis, the mainstream film network is working hand in hand with the festivals to reach out to a much wider audience. The catalytic effect of the HKIFF corporatisation in blurring the distinction between the mainstream and festival circuit helps illustrate this point.

Let me go back a little in time to look at the original high-art aspirations of the Hong Kong colonial government in establishing the HKIFF in 1977. They have been mentioned in two messages since the plan of corporatising the HKIFF has come to light. The first message was given in 2003 by Darwin Chen, the Chairman of the Hong Kong Arts Development Council, in one of the most important publications of the 27th HKIFF – *Hong Kong Panorama*. In the very first paragraph of his English-Chinese bilingual message, Chen said:

> Hong Kong's cultural and arts events began to flourish in the 1970's, with the establishment of professional troupes and arts groups. This was also the period during which the Hong Kong International Film Festival was first launched – in 1977. Despite its small scale and with only 37 films being screened at the City Hall Theatre, the public response was overwhelming. Tickets sold out in four days to highly appreciative audiences totalling over 16,000. As the government official responsible for cultural services at the time, I dedicated myself to the challenging task of organising the Festival, working closely with the Urban Council to launch the Film Festival. That was an experience I will never forget. (Chen 2003: 3)

Besides giving the facts that 'only 37 films' were screened in the first year of the HKIFF and that the only screen was the City Hall Theatre, Chen does not hide his pride as speaking from a government official's position. In this statement he also indirectly gives the HKIFF the same privileged standing as high-art groups, like the Hong Kong Ballet and the Hong Kong Philharmonic Orchestra that flourished in the 1970s under the support of the local government. In referring to the burgeoning arts scene of 1970s Hong Kong, however, Chen, fails to acknowledge vernacular local cultural activities, like the long-established Cantonese opera performances, which were mostly organised by local troupes without financial or administrative support from the government.

The second utterance of similar nature appeared in the Chairman's Statement in the 2005-06 annual report of the Hong Kong International Film Festival Society after the HKIFF was completely corporatised. It was again emphasised at the front part (second paragraph) of this English-Chinese bilingual message:

> The Film Festival was first initiated to bring Hong Kong audiences closer to the international film scene and to present artistic films which would otherwise not be shown in commercial cinemas. (*Hong Kong International Film Festival Society Annual Report* 2005-06: 1)

The privileged origin of the HKIFF is deliberately distinguished from the 'commercial cinemas' by the chairman of the mother company of the HKIFF, Wilfred Wong, who is a high-profile official figure from Hong Kong's colonial era. Wong is currently the Executive Vice Chairman & C.E.O. of Mission Hills Group, a company focusing on golf and diversified leisure industry investments.

These two messages from the authorities indicate quite clearly that the HKIFF was originally separated from the general theatrical exhibition. What was happening to the film industry and how film professionals were to be assisted in distributing, producing and acquiring films were not part of the concerns of the HKIFF's organisers. Li Cheuk-to (Hong Kong Film Critics Association 2003: 3), the long-term HKIFF programmer and current artistic director of the event, and a reputable local film critic, confirms this objective of the pre-corporatised HKIFF. He emphasises that box office takings were not the dominant criteria of choosing a film for the festival during the period it was run by the government. He would be more concerned about how diversified the films were.

Yet the HKIFF corporatisation blurs the boundary between art and commerce, crystallising and accelerating the commodification process of the cinematic event. This is similar to Janet Harbord's commentary on Berlinale's specifics as a result of the 'strategic development of the film festival as a global city, the economic significance of which is masked by the emphasis on cultural exchange' (Harbord 2002: 66). The case of corporatising the HKIFF renders an example that branches off from Harbord's argument in that Hong Kong does not rely on the HKIFF to become a global city. Rather, it is more appropriate to say that it is Hong Kong's established status as a global city that enhances the glamour of the newly corporatised HKIFF.

With corporatisation, there were some abrupt changes in the timing of the HKIFF and other film-related events. The first annual report of the Hong Kong International Film Festival Society (2004-05) shows that the Asian Independent Films Screenings at the Hong Kong Filmart were re-scheduled from late June 2004 to late April 2005, whereas the HKIFF in 2005 was held between 22 March and 6 April. The lack of synchronisation between the HKIFF and Hong Kong Filmart was effectively toned down, though the latter is still unlike other film markets that run in conjunction with film festivals in terms of temporal and geographical immediacy. The actual 426 screenings of 298 films from 47 countries were held in the government-owned cultural venues such as Hong Kong Cultural Centre Grand Theatre, Hong Kong City Hall, and Hong Kong Science Museum Lecture Hall *alongside* mainstream cinema houses, for instance, UA Cityplaza, UA Langham Place, UA Pacific Place, and Grand Ocean Theatre. This was a true breakthrough from the past, when screenings of films had been confined to government-run cultural venues and art-house cinemas.

Moreover, instead of highlighting the diversified viewing experience that the HKIFF could bring to its attendees, this annual report on the 2004-05 season of the HKIFF covers widely the festival's public relations and promotional efforts over a span of eight pages, with only a single page left for the listing of programmes and screenings. The report cover reveals a high-angled photo featuring a red-carpeted, outdoor platform where megastars like Jackie Chan and senior government officials greet event participants under a confetti shower. The whole report is suffused with photos of local stars and actors/actresses attending promotional events. Looking at the Income and Expenditure Account at the back of this report, one cannot help thinking that such emphasis on promotion is closely connected with the significant amount of commercial sponsorships and donations (22 per cent of the total income) which the festival attracted in that year. Ticket proceeds in 2005 amounted to 22.7 per cent of the overall income.

Public relations and promotional campaigns continue to be the main thrusts in the next two annual reports. It is shown in the report of 2005-06 that the number of films that year went down by 33 titles to 265 (with 437 screenings). No information is available regarding the number of countries where these films were from. Programme highlights take up only one page again in this second report, with wider and more detailed coverage of promotional activities such as press conferences, gala dinners and red carpet events, spanning across 13 full pages (including one page of event photos) out of a total of 33 pages in the report. Commercial sponsorship and donations in that year increased to 24 per cent of the total income, while ticket proceeds stayed at roughly the same level of 22 per cent.

The effects of corporatisation were even more evident in the HKIFF 2006-07 season, allowing more films to be shown (379 films with 25 world and international premières from a total of 52 countries) against a backup of more forceful marketing efforts. In that year's annual report, there is more information on programme highlights and awards (two pages out of a total of 42 pages). Coverage on promotional activities, however, decreases to 10 pages, three pages fewer than the previous year's coverage. There is coverage on the newly established Asian Film Awards (three pages) and highlights of the HAF (nine pages), whose organisation has just been taken over by the Hong Kong International Film Festival Society (Shackleton 2007a: 18).

The table below presents the income and expenditure from the first three years of HKIFF's corporatisation. This financial chart with the oldest financial data aligning right is a combination of the financial spreadsheets found at the back of the annual reports. It is presented in a format normally adopted by the financial annual reports of publicly traded companies. The top part of the chart shows a rather stable cash grant given by the government to this annual event. Ticket proceeds have also increased gradually over these three years. However, particularly striking in this table are substantial increases in income in 2007 from 'Commercial and Individual Sponsorships and Donations' (up 61.8 per cent from 2005 and 33.7 per cent from 2006 respectively) as well as 'Other Public Section Subvention' (fifteen times that of 2005 and more than five times that of 2006). No breakdown of such public subvention is given. The bottom half of this table shows the main expenses of running such a festival in Hong Kong. While payroll expenses remain relatively stable throughout these three years, the production cost and marketing expenses increase considerably. Production costs in 2007 increase by 178 per cent in comparison with 2005 and 98 per cent in comparison with 2006. The increase in marketing expenses (for public

Corporatising a Film Festival: Hong Kong

relations functions, red carpet events and so on) stands at 66.4 per cent compared with 2005 and 37.2 per cent compared with 2006.

No such information was publicly available before the corporatisation took place:

Income	2007 HK$	2006 HK$	2005 HK$
Grants from Hong Kong Arts Development Council	7,164,000	7,164,000	7,489,850
Ticket Proceeds	5,762,674	4,341,973	4,030,174
Commercial and Individual Sponsorships and Donations	6,464,354	4,833,529	3,995,155
Other Public Sector Subvention	8,013,806	1,500,000	530,000
Service Fees from Public Sector	1,001,200	980,000	1,300,000
Other Revenue	597,843	826,577	398,730
Total Income	**29,003,877**	**19,646,079**	**17,743,909**
Expenditure			
Production Expenses	19,558,514	9,888,141	7,027,419
Payroll and Related Expenses	5,380,548	5,072,681	5,103,484
Marketing Expenses	2,111,125	1,741,384	1,268,903
Other Operating Expenses	1,754,394	1,658,372	1,472,108
Total Expenditure	**28,804,581**	**18,360,578**	**14,871,914**
Surplus	**199,296**	**1,285,501**	**2,871,995**

Source: Hong Kong International Film Festival Society Annual Reports 2004-05, 2005-06, 2006-07

These comparisons suggest that within the three years following the corporatisation, the HKIFF tremendously increased its public profile. From previously emphasising diversified film choices for festival-goers to becoming a show of celebrities' and actors' glamour, the corporatised HKIFF gives the impression of changing from a high-art event to a populist occasion led primarily by the local filmmaking industry and the appeal of individual stars in all sorts of promotional events. Commercial sponsorships and marketing expenses also reveal the corporatised HKIFF's increasing dependency on the commercial sector.

On the other hand, although the government remains the largest sponsor of the event with a contribution amounting to 52.5 per cent of HKIFF's total income in 2005, 49 per cent in 2006, and 55.8 per cent in 2007, it has successfully passed about half of its financial burden over to the Hong Kong International Film Festival Society. As far as administrative tasks are concerned, operating and payroll expenses remain relatively stable. This indicates that the festival has not increased the number of staff members. Major positions, such as executive director, artistic director and curatorial roles, were kept by the same individuals (who were once parts of the civil servant structure) after corporatisation was completed. There is no information in any of the three annual reports as to how surplus funds were used.

Hence, within a relatively short period of time, the corporatisation of the HKIFF multiplied the capacity of the film festival to promote a select group of films to potential producers, buyers, distributors, exhibitors and journalists. In this regard, the corporatised HKIFF has become another commodity alongside the films it shows, offering not just film distribution channels but also the advertising spaces for its commercial sponsors and donors (Colbert 2000: 54-7). At the same time, just when the corporatised HKIFF started to rent theatres from a mainstream theatrical chain, its distinction from the mainstream film distribution was effectively blurred. Contrarily, by letting out specific theatres to do festival screenings, mainstream exhibitors and their working partners in distribution may have found a way to associate mainstream blockbusters with the art-house film circle and negotiate their cultural status without causing too much unease. Seen in this light, corporatisation appears to create win-win situations both for the government (reducing its financial and administrative burden) and for the film industry (distributors mobilising the well-established system to circulate world premières of both non-mainstream films and blockbusters, and forging new collaborations with potential filmmakers and producers alike). In this seemingly victorious formula, however, the predilection of the target audiences is often difficult to estimate. Ticket proceeds shown in the HKIFF's annual reports suggest that the size of the audience remains relatively stable over this three years' period. They do not show, for instance, the demographic profile of audiences nor their likes and dislikes. I shall turn next to see what the corporatisation of the HKIFF would possibly mean to festival-goers.

Festival Programming: Number of Films vs. Freedom of Choice

Corporatisation has certainly helped to strengthen the HKIFF financially. The festival previously operated on a tight budget, something typical for Hong Kong, where cultural activities have never been on the top of government's agenda. However, with the example of London Film Festival re-creating in its audience the exclusive and privileged pleasures of watching classical Hollywood movies, Stringer reminds us that a major function of film festivals is to generate the 'aura of exclusivity' for festival-goers (Stringer 2006: 209; Stringer 2003). Such a viewing experience may not be easily quantified by the sheer number of films shown during the festival period. The relatively unrestrained freedom of choosing different types of films in festivals also gratifies the festival-goers.

In the case of the corporatised HKIFF, such complete freedom of choice on the part of the attendees might be curbed at the outset when the curators start to plan the programmes, given both direct and indirect influences from the commercial sponsors. Hence, even if the additional sum of private sponsorships can help to bring more titles to the festival, the increase in the number of films shown does not necessarily give the festival-goers more freedom to choose their favourites. My research on the festival programmes before and after the HKIFF corporatisation clearly reveals that the premières of mainstream blockbusters have gradually pushed art-house films aside and become the festival's main features. One might argue that attending the festival is no longer an experience that is distinct from attending mainstream theatrical screenings.

The festival's programming strategies in the pre- and post-corporatisation period of the HKIFF are worth considering. In 2002, when the news of the imminent corporatisation was announced, the HKIFF was still solely run by the Hong Kong Arts Development Council. The season of that year opened with Tom Tykwer's *Heaven* (Germany/USA, 2002) and Fruit Chan's *Heung Gong Yau Gok Hor Lei Wood* (*Hollywood Hong Kong*, Hong Kong, 2001), and closed with Tsai Ming-liang's *Ni Na Bian Ji Dian* (*What Time Is It There?*, Taiwan/France, 2001). These highlights were all regarded as art-house films. Gala presentations included Iwai Shunji's *Riri Shushu No Subete* (*All about Lily Chou-Chou*, Japan, 2001), Ray Lawrence's *Lantana* (Australia, 2001) and so on. The 'Global Vision' section showed films from as far afield as Tunisia, Morocco, Kirghizstan, Iran and Albania, all of which might not have been shown in Hong Kong had it not been for the festival. The films listed attest to Li's statement in the interview granted to *Film Critics Quarterly* (Hong Kong Film Critics Association 2003: 3) that diversification was once the main concern of the festival programming. By extension, the diversification of films in the pre-corporatised HKIFF gave rise to the 'aura of exclusivity' that attracted festival-goers to attend the festival.

In 2007, two years after the initial corporatisation, the HKIFF kept its Asian focus unchanged. Contrary to its practice of opening the festival with art-house films in the pre-corporatisation years, the HKIFF this year opened with two box-office surefire hits that featured top Asian stars: Yau Nai-hoi's *Gun Chung* (*Eye in the Sky*, Hong Kong, 2007) and Pak Chan-wook's *Saibogujiman Kwenchana* (*I am a Cyborg but That's OK*, South Korea, 2006). The usual closing film section was replaced by the Hong Kong Film Awards (Shackleton 2007: 19), a ceremony which focused on the glitz and glamour of local stars. 'Gala Presentations' became a showcase for European and US premières, including Joachim Lafosse's *Nue Propriété* (*Private Property*, Belgium/France, 2006), Andrea Arnold's *Red Road* (UK, 2006), and Marc Foster's *Stranger than Fiction* (USA, 2006). There were films from small nations such as Bosnia, Herzegovina, Chad and Egypt, but the festival in that year showed a strong tendency for geographical clustering, like 'Nordic Lights', 'Lost in Place: Petro Costa', 'Chinese Renaissance', 'Young Romanian Cinema', perhaps at the expense of some other, even smaller national cinemas. With the curatorial personnel remaining unchanged after the corporatisation and the choice of art-house Western titles still being upheld, the regional bias and clustering of Western titles, and the incorporation of East Asian blockbusters in the HKIFF (which has previously avoided featuring any such films) suggest subtly that corporatisation has facilitated, if not causing it directly, a lessened 'aura of exclusivity' that festival-goers and cinephiles once enjoyed. In turn, such a change in the festival's programming strategy has likely drawn a different group of local audience, whose profile and predilection are different from that of the festival-goers in the pre-corporatisation period.

Certainly, we can see here quite clearly that commercial money helps to enhance the viewing experience by increasing the number of film titles, allowing the event to hire high-end mainstream theatre halls for screenings, and conducting majestic air-screen outdoor screenings at the Tamar site in Admiralty, Hong Kong. However, it does not necessarily enhance the complete freedom of film choice for the audiences or, therefore, the 'aura of exclusivity' unique to festival-going.

Gains and Losses of Festival Corporatisation

Corporatisation has effectively enabled the HKIFF to achieve what it could not do previously. The first thing is the extensive media coverage it now benefits from with its multiplied marketing budget. All three annual reports stress the increasing number of press representatives and journalists who were present in Hong Kong to cover the event – a likely source of satisfaction for the board of directors and the commercial sponsors whose commitment is vindicated by unprecedented media exposure. Moreover, the co-operation among the government, commercial sector and film industry conveys the optimistic message to project investors and filmmaking professionals that Hong Kong cinema is still vibrant and promising.

Certainly, the corporatisation of the HKIFF has made the event more prominent. There are, however, still a lot of uncertainties that film distributors and promoters need to take into account in opting for this circulation route. One such consideration is that corporatisation may not guarantee film distributors more alternative choices in circuiting their films via the HKIFF. There are several reasons for this: firstly, the blurred boundary between the mainstream network and festival circuit in Hong Kong may actually worsen the festival's role as an alternative to the mainstream film distribution network. Secondly, there are still no world-recognised awards like Palme d'Or, the Golden Lion or the Golden Bear in place to give the HKIFF a supreme status as an alternative choice to its mainstream counterparts. Thirdly, there is no guarantee of quality films to be made, and subsequently circulated, with the funding that film projects can attract in the Hong Kong Filmart.

As for the local government, the case is simpler due to the very nature of corporatisation – to decentralise its administrative control and cut down its financial responsibilities in offering a quality film festival to its citizens. By setting up an independent company to look after this annual event, the government has stepped down from its prominent role of festival organiser to become a mere supporter through giving subsidies and renting low-cost screening venues to the festival.

From the festival-goers' point of view, the corporatised HKIFF may not necessarily further improve their chances to see films from every possible corner of the world. Indeed, audiences may in effect move down from the top of the festival's stakeholder list to be replaced by film industry practitioners and commercial sponsors. This shift of power from a government to a commercial enterprise has inevitably forced the high-art aims of the film festival to spiral downwards while its commercialism and stronger links with the mainstream film distribution network have grown up. The consequence could be a counterbalance of the corporatised HKIFF's attempt to build a profile more in line with those most esteemed film festivals, which have their explicit and primary goals of catering for art-house and *auteur* cinemas.

Works Cited

Bozec, Richard and Gaétan Breton (2003) 'The Impact of the Corporatization Process on the Financial Performance of Canadian State-owned Enterprises', *The International Journal of Public Sector Management*, 16, 1, 27-47.

Chen, Darwin (2003) 'Message' by the Chairman of the Hong Kong Arts Development Council, *Hong Kong Panorama 2002-2003*. Hong Kong: Hong Kong Arts Development Council, 3.

Clarke, Donald (2003) 'Corporatisation, not Privatisation', *China Economic Quarterly*, 7, 3, 27-30.

Colbert, François, with Jacques Nantel, Suzanne Bilodeau and J. Dennis Rich (2000) *Marketing Culture and the Arts*, foreword by William D. Poole, second edition. Montreal: Presses HEG.

Elsaesser, Thomas (2005 [2005]) 'Film Festival Networks: the New Topographics of Cinema in Europe', in *European Cinema: Face to Face with Hollywood*. Amsterdam: Amsterdam University Press, 82-107.

'Entertainment Expo Hong Kong Special' (2007) *Screen International*, 16 March, 13-19.

'Entertainment Expo Hong Kong' (2008) *Screen International*, 7 March, 15-23.

Gordon, Marsha (1981) *Government in Business*. Montréal: C.D. Howe Institute.

Harbord, Janet (2002) *Film Cultures*. London: Sage.

'HKADC Decides to Corporatise Film Festival' (2002) The International Federation of Arts Councils and Culture Agencies – National Arts Agency News (posted 13 September). On-line. Available HTTP:http://www.ifacca.org/national_agency_news/2002/09/13/hkadc-decides-to-corporatise-film-festival/ (15 January 2009).

'HKIFF to Form New Company' (2002), Press Release 20 September by Hong Kong Arts Development Council. On-line. Available HTTP: http://www.hkadc.org.hk/en/infocentre/press/press_20020920 (15 January 2009).

'Hong Kong Entertainment Expo 2006: Pull-out Special' (2006) *Screen International*, 10 March 2006.

Hong Kong Film Critics Association (2003) 'An interview with Chan Pak-sung', *Film Critics Quarterly* (in Chinese), 20, April. Hong Kong: Hong Kong Film Critics Association, 4.

____ (2003) 'An interview with Li Cheuk-to', *Film Critics Quarterly* (in Chinese), 20, April. Hong Kong: Hong Kong Film Critics Association, 3.

Hong Kong Government Press Release, 'LCQ2: The Work of West Kowloon Cultural District Authority', posted 19 November 2008. On-line. Available HTTP:http://www.info.gov.hk/gia/general/200811/19/P200811190183.htm (3 March 2009).

Hong Kong International Film Festival Society Annual Report (2004-05) Hong Kong: The Hong Kong International Film Festival Society Limited.

Hong Kong International Film Festival Society Annual Report (2005-06) Hong Kong: The Hong Kong International Film Festival Society Limited.

Hong Kong International Film Festival Society Annual Report (2006-07) Hong Kong: The Hong Kong International Film Festival Society Limited.

'Information Note: Financial Study on the West Kowloon Cultural District' (completed 15 December 2004). Hong Kong: Hong Kong Legislative Council, 2004. On-line. Available HTTP:http://www.legco.gov.hk/yr04-05/english/sec/library/0405in11e.pdf (3 March 2009).

Corporatising a Film Festival: Hong Kong

Investopedia: A Forbes Digital Company (Financial Dictionary). Definition of 'Corporatisation'. On-line. Available HTTP:http://www.investopedia.com/terms/c/coporatization.asp   (24 February 2009).

Laux, Jeanne Kirk and Maureen Appel Molot (1988) *State Capitalism: Public Enterprise in Canada*. Ithaca, NY: Cornell University.

Lo, Yu-lai (1999) 'Some Notes about Film Censorship in Hong Kong', *The 21st Hong Kong International Film Festival*. Hong Kong: Urban Council, 60-3.

Sek, Kei (1988) 'The Social Psychology of Hongkong Cinema', *Changes in Hongkong Society through Cinema*, The 10th Hong Kong International Film Festival. Hong Kong: Urban Council, 15-20.

Shackleton, Liz (2007) 'HK Market Stakes Global Claim', *Screen International*, 16 March, 17.

___ (2007a) 'Matchmakers', *Screen International*, 16 March, 18.

Stringer, Julian (2001) 'Global Cities and the International Film Festival Economy', in Mark Shiel and Tony Fitzmaurice (eds) *Cinema and the City: Film and Urban Societies in a Gobal Context*. Oxford: Blackwell, 134-44.

___ (2003) 'Raiding the Archive: Film Festivals and the Revival of Classic Hollywood', in Paul Grainge (ed.) *Memory and Popular Film*. Manchester and New York: Manchester University Press, 81-96.

___ (2006) 'Neither One Thing nor the Other: Blockbusters at Film Festivals', in Julian Stringer (ed.) *Movie Blockbusters*. New York: Routledge, 202-13.

Teo, Stephen (1988) 'Politics and Social Issues in Hongkong Cinema', *Changes in Hongkong Society through Cinema*, The 10th Hong Kong International Film Festival. Hong Kong: Urban Council, 38-41.

Turan, Kenneth (2002) *Sundance to Saravejo: Film Festivals and the World They Made*. Berkeley: University of California Press.

Chapter Eight

Rethinking Festival Film:
Urban Generation Chinese Cinema on
the Film Festival Circuit

Ma Ran

Introduction

Following in the footsteps of their Fifth Generation predecessors, The independent Chinese filmmakers of the Post-Tian'anmen era won worldwide acclaim through the international film festival circuit in the early 1990s. The new generation's enfant terrible, the Urban Generation,[1] were mostly known for their low-budget, urban-themed, realistic underground works, at least until their legitimisation in 2004. Most of the award-winning indie works that came out of the Urban Generation directors have been cynically tagged 'festival film' because they are neither officially visible within China nor viable beyond the festival circuit.

Some scholars attribute this success overseas to misinterpretation by 'Western critics of the cultural and political meanings of these films' (Dai, quoted in Chen & Xiao 2006: 147). In this essay, however, I will rethink the concept of the 'festival film' as a critical device in order to map out the global trajectory and politics of Urban Generation Chinese films.[2] While it is true that most independent Chinese film is destined for distribution overseas, to accuse them of 'selling out' – either ideologically or aesthetically – in order to win a global audience is to ignore the changing topography and dynamics of the contemporary international film festival system itself.

Therefore, in the first part of this essay, I shall deploy Thomas Elsaesser and Marijke de Valck's arguments about the international film festival network in order to outline what I understand as a reconfigured global visual industry. Orchestrated discourses permeate the festival as an ongoing event. Nevertheless, the ideological and cultural mechanisms embedded in the valorisation of films and the politics of programming as an integral component of festival discourse need to be highlighted in any analysis of the contemporary festival circuit, which pertains particularly to the circulation of contemporary Chinese film through it.

In the second section, I will examine the global/domestic circulation of Urban Generation films and its various components through the film festival network. Then Zhang Yingjin's formulation of post-socialist filmmaking will help to illustrate the dynamics between *politics, marginality, capital, art* and the *market*, offering a Bourdieuian perspective through which to observe Chinese independent filmmaking without effacing the critique of filmmakers' autonomy (2007). In focus here will be a discussion of the nexus between *politics* and *marginality*; troubles with censors have often been translated by the Urban Generation into what we might understand as 'critical capital' (Czach 2004: 82).

The third section of this essay will foreground festival film as a unique mode of filmmaking, understanding it as a response to the growth of a global niche market and a practice closely related to image-branding among festivals themselves. That is to say, the festival circuit has functioned as the crucial link enabling Chinese independent films to enter into the global visual production/consumption chain; but in order to understand this process, stereotyped visions of 'festival film' need to be revised, or even debunked entirely.

Film Festivals in Perspective

In the early 1980s, Hollywood mobilised to 'strike back' and recapture an audience that had been profoundly transformed by the presence of multimedia. Since then, the festival circuit has also undergone considerable metamorphosis. As Marijke de Valck describes, over the two decades that followed, a 'global proliferation of film festivals' created 'a worldwide alternative film circuit in which a few festivals became the major marketplace and media events' (2005: 101). Festivals thus became intricately 'embedded within the global system of the film festival circuit' and strategically dependent on each other (de Valck 2007: 68-9). In a similar vein, Thomas Elsaesser argues that 'the international film festival must be seen as a network (with nodes, flows and exchanges)' and with 'a capillary action and osmosis between the various layers' (2005: 84-7).

As these scholars describe, the international film festival system has not only played a crucial role in rejuvenating European and other regional and national film traditions but also in counterbalancing the juggernaut of Hollywood. Wu Chia-chi emphasises that European film festivals once 'worked closely with European new waves and Third World films', both of which 'consciously entrenched themselves in ideological and formal otherness to classic Hollywood narratives' (2004: 17). One case in point for such Third-World film culture discovered on the festival circuit is the New Iranian Cinema, which culminated with art-house *auteur* Abbas Kiarostami's Golden Palm at the Cannes Film Festival in 1997. Ten years later, Cannes has redefined the 'trend' by celebrating Romanian film *4 luni, 3 săptămâni şi 2 zile* (*4 Months, 3 Weeks and 2 Days*, 2007). The International Film Festival

Rotterdam (IFFR), for example, has nurtured independent filmmaking in southeastern Asia for over a decade and even expected the burst of Malaysian New Wave in recent years.

As well as dominating film festival programmes, extremely hierarchical structures are replicated in the pecking order of the film festivals themselves (Czach 2004). However, it may also be that their status is determined by their history, prestige and potential for discovering brilliant films and outstanding new talent. FIAPF (*Fedération International des Associations de Producteurs de Films* or *International Federation of Film Producers Associations*), a Paris-based international organisation that supervises and accredits international film festivals, used to classify film festivals into a strict hierarchy, though today the A-list festivals are neutrally designated as *Competitive Feature Film Festivals.*[3] Nevertheless, it is argued even in Europe that the model of the Cannes Film Festival seems too totalising in Elsaesser's conceptualisation of the 'festival network'.

The existence of associations such as the *European Coordination of Film Festivals Network* (ECFF), which 'protects and promotes the interests of 250 of the smaller regional festivals across the continent', must be noted if characteristics of European film festivals are to be adequately differentiated and understood (Owen 2007: 2). As de Valck observes, despite the fact that the festival network functions as an exclusive zone outside of which films are not considered commercially viable, festivals 'produce their own material' and are in the 'business of cultural prestige'. Films may travel after their premieres at major festivals to smaller, regional events, or after being discovered at specialised festivals (like IFFR), they might 'move on to prestigious competition programs of the A festivals'. This cultural idiosyncrasy could even be translated into economic value 'through competition programs and awards' (de Valck 2007: 106).

While film festival programming, selection and competition criteria embrace the idea of polycentric or alternative aesthetics (Shohat & Stam 2002: 37), the valorisation of film at Euro-American film festivals is infused with value judgments saturated with a yearning for progress, democracy, justice and human rights, though the criteria themselves are often revised or upgraded with the prevalent *leitmotif* of multiculturalism and political-correctness. Selection or exclusion decisions with regard to festival programming and film awards are never purely aesthetic or artistic but often complicated by contesting ideologies, value systems and other sociopolitical issues. For instance, the Golden Bear film of the 58th edition Berlinale (February 2008) was Brazilian entry *Tropa de Elite* (*Elite Squad*, José Padilha, 2007). This film aroused outrage among critics because of its problematic pro-fascist politics,[4] though it was positively received in Brazil. With the global proliferation of film festivals, the hegemonic taste and gaze are being profoundly re-territorialised. However, an analysis of the discourse of film festivals and their politics can push our understanding of 'festival film' somewhat further, as we understand how the aesthetics and politics of festival film generate new layers of meaning through circulation within the festival network.

Urban Generation Chinese Cinema on the Festival Circuit

US film critic Jonathan Rosenbaum once remarked that the industry term 'festival film' originally referred to 'a film destined to be seen by professionals, specialists, or cultists but not by the general public because some of these professionals decide it won't or can't be sufficiently profitable to warrant distribution' (Rosenbaum 2002: 161). Under the planned economy scheme,[5] however, Fifth Generation Chinese films were widely circulated and distributed domestically. Nevertheless, Rosenbaum's generalisation on festival film's exclusion of a general audience reads somewhat true with regard to the Urban Generation during its underground stage. While the disengagement of Chinese underground films with the domestic market and audience renders its marginality an invalid political stance, the critical acclaim that Chinese indie film received at major film festivals has been identified more as an endorsement of its ideologically challenging orientation.

Questions of whether underground filmmakers 'have surrendered themselves to Western cultural hegemony' or 'their films smack of self-Orientalism' have been keenly debated (Chen & Xiao 2006: 149). It is true that global conceptions and receptions of Chinese art cinema have been significantly changed with the emergence of the Urban Generation; nevertheless, the 'truths' of China and of independent filmmaking itself have been turned into consumable ingredients fuelling its global circulation. Therefore an in-depth examination of Chinese underground cinema and its circulation within the festival network can help to clarify the socio-political dynamics of post-socialist filmmaking and of the festival film itself.[6] In this essay, I will examine the components of the festival network: individual film festivals, funding schemes and film funds, the film market; cultural organisations (governmental ones and NGOs); production, distribution and exhibition entities, underground (illegal) distribution mechanisms and cinephile clubs, among others.

Since its inception in China, independent filmmaking has been notoriously 'underground', though filmmakers were reluctant to admit their shadowy status at home.[7] This underground period nominally ended in 2004, when previously blacklisted filmmakers such as Jia Zhangke and Wang Xiaoshuai were finally given authorisation by the state to produce films. Shot with equipment borrowed from TV stations or film studios (digital equipment was not introduced until late 1990s), most of the early independent films were made on a shoestring budget in a hit-and-run guerilla manner (though it was also possible to purchase the production quota from the state studios). Being 'underground' did not necessarily mean the state was blind to the activities of these filmmakers, but that the production of their films had been evasively regulated and addressed by official channels. Thus, these films were not given legitimacy through the media until the popularisation of Internet and the emergence of pirated visual products.

During the underground stage, few indie *auteurs* had the opportunity to screen their films at theatres.[8] Previews of underground titles had been highly exclusive events in which only certain circles of film professionals, including filmmakers, festival programmers, intellectuals and cinephiles were invited to participate. However, with the appearance of bootlegged independent films – particularly award-winning ones – the circulation of Chinese indie films expanded considerably. The internet has not only facilitated the dissemination of independent films (most of the time illegally); it has also created a virtual public sphere where knowledge about Chinese underground and banned films are exchanged and accumulated.

As Guangzhou-based art curator Ou Ning commented, 'pirated VCDs and DVDs also played a significant role in establishing the independent film culture in the mid-1990s ... because now what kinds of films are circulated is not determined by centralized policy, but instead by market forces in the pirated VCD/DVD market' (Cheung 2007). Cafes, bars, or other itinerant venues – usually an extension of culturally liberal colleges and universities, artist communities and the peripheral areas – became exhibition/screening venues, where serious cinephile groups organised screenings and relevant activities, though in recent years some once influential film clubs were disbanded and venues were gradually commercialised' (Nakajima 2006: 184-6). Fortunately, domestic film festivals encouraging independent filmmaking have emerged in their place.[9] Various kinds of independent or documentary film forums or conferences are regularly organised in Beijing, Shanghai and other culturally vibrant cities.

Individual film festivals constitute a vital part of the global circulation of Urban Generation Cinema. I shall not go into detail in talking about the 'Big Three' – Cannes, Berlin and Venice; my focus instead will be on several other specialised Euro-American film festivals, funds or institutions. Nantes Film Festival Three Continents, for example, has been a major showcase venue since 1980 for the national cinemas of Asia, Africa and Latin America. The influential International Film Festival Rotterdam (IFFR), which celebrated its 38th edition in January 2009, is itself quite an open and adventurous film festival famous for its uncompromising, rebellious and experimental vision in global visual industry. IFFR has for quite a long time kept an eye on promoting independent films from developing countries and remains a staunch advocate for Chinese independent films in particular.

Art-house directors like Zhang Ming, He Jianjun, Zhang Yuan and Lou Ye have had their projects funded by IFFR's renowned *Hubert Bals Fund* (HBF, since 1988), which has fuelled Asian independent filmmaking not only in China but also in other Southeast Asian countries, including the Philippines, Indonesia and Malaysia. Some of those HBF-funded Chinese films later on walked away with Tiger Awards.[10] Furthermore, *The*

International Forum of New Cinema or *Forum* of the Berlin International Film Festival, which aims for 'everything new and unconventional',[11] functions in a similar way by encouraging and funding young filmmakers' projects. Vancouver International Film Festival (VIFF) has been another significant venue for showcasing Chinese independent films on a global level for the last two decades. Other international film festivals in Toronto (Canada), Locarno (Switzerland), San Sebastian (Spain) and New York (Tribeca Film Festival) have long kept an eye on mainland Chinese indie films. The list is even longer if we consider documentary film festivals.

In addition to the HBF of IFFR and its film market CineMart (since 1984)[12], the French film funding mechanism Fonds Sud also serves as a vital link in bolstering Urban Generation film talents.[13] Pusan International Film Festival's (PIFF) Pusan Promotion Plan (PPP, since 1998), is another weighty funding scheme which has been successful in luring young Chinese directors. The Asia Film Financing Forum (HAF), initiated by Hong Kong International Film Festival, is a film project market that aspires to bring together 'Asia's top filmmaking talents to meet with the world's premier film financiers, producers, bankers, distributors, buyers and funding bodies' (Anon. 2008). PIFF launched a similar film market, the Asia Cinema Fund (ACF) in 2007. While one may argue that Pusan's ACF emulates and competes with the HAF with an view to enhancing the individual 'festival's brand image' (Elsaesser 2005: 88), we should also realise that such a competition works in order to interrelate and integrate within a regional and global festival network, despite the subtle differentiation of the scale or scheme concept.[14]

It might not be surprising to see that these financing schemes are not to any extent contending with each other for attracting talents and premieres. For instance, HBF would love to see film projects funded by them also seek grants from and be programmed by other major film festivals.[15] This recalls Elsaesser's supposition that the international film festival must be seen as a network with nodes, flows and exchanges (2005: 84). When it comes to film distribution, Amsterdam/Hong Kong-based company Fortissimo Film Sales,[16] which boasts a passion for films, professional instinct and 'excellent relationships with key distributors, film festivals and international and local journalists',[17] has indeed identified and nurtured several new directors of the Urban Generation. Fortissimo still bases its selection of potential films at high-profile international film festivals, and it works closely with the film markets at Berlin, Cannes, Venice, Rotterdam and Hong Kong's FILMART. Also keen on producing and distributing Urban Generation films[18] is Hong Kong/mainland-based Huayi Xinmeiti (Asian Union New Media Group). In addition, Hong Kong-based Yingyi Yule (Focus Film), founded by Asian megastar Andy Lau in 2002, has launched a HD project Yazhou Xinxingdao (FOCUS First Cut) targeting 'new and upcoming directors from across China, Hong Kong, Malaysia, Singapore and Taiwan' (Anon. 2005).[19]

Big 'Ban' Theory

Zhang Yingjin has formulated a diagram that demonstrates the political economics of post-socialism in the age of World Trade Organisation (WTO). In figure 1, four players, *art* ('characterised by imagination and generated by creativity'), *capital* ('characterised by money and motivated by the market'), *politics* ('characterised by power and sustained by censorship') and *marginality* ('characterised by 'truth' and inspired by dissent')[20] have been interwoven into the post-socialist filmmaking scene with *market* as the magnetic centre of all four parties (2007: 73). Although this diagram recalls Pierre Bourdieu's sociological analysis about the field of cultural production, the four players roughly correspond to various positions that the actors should take into consideration when entangled within complicated power play.

Particularly, Zhang Yingjin posits, 'the nexus of *politics* and *marginality* is the only site where dissent and resistance are possible', but 'as a result of the prohibition by politics and dismissal by art, the impact of marginality and its pictures of reality have been largely felt overseas at international film festivals' (2007: 72). The PRC's censorship organ basically consists of two committees affiliated to the Film Bureau of The State Administration of Radio, Film and Television (SARFT)[21]. Since the 1990s, film regulations have been under constant review spurred by the intensification of Opening-up, especially after China's entry into the WTO in 2002.[22] In the first place, the constringent and sometimes unpredictable film policies were ignorant of and even reluctant to react to the socio-political vacuum generated during re-territorialisation, where alternative filmmaking is both a cultural and economic phenomena.

At the operational level, which has inherited a bureaucratic inertia, the censorship committee's decision-making on film bans lacks transparency, and complicates intervention at different levels of local bureaucratic bodies.[23] Also, regulations concerning so-called 'content-correctness' (or, more accurately, ideological-correctness) are too generally written and cannot help to clarify reasons why a certain film does not get a permit despite official prescriptions; explanations often must be sought out elsewhere. Any decision to ban a certain film, then, is interpreted as a subjective and capricious vengeance targeted at the cinematic outlaws, though these speculations may also turn out false. The already tense relationship between filmmakers and censors was compromised even further when, at a later stage, they didn't bother the Film Bureau to get the official permission when their films were invited to film festivals overseas. Instead, they would smuggle their film copies out of the country in the hope of garnering further distribution and funding opportunities, a practice which remains quite common even in the post-underground stage. During this period, most of the young generation's works were banned within China despite their mobility and visibility on the circuit. According to film scholar Zhang Xianmin's research on banned indie films made between 1992 and 2002, there are around forty titles such films.[24] Ironically, this list features a high proportion of winners at major international film festivals.

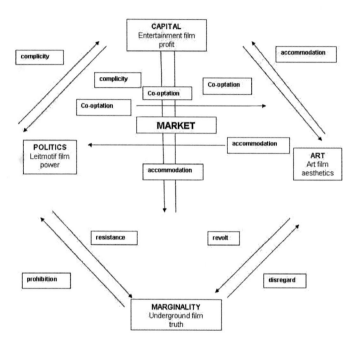

Figure 1: A representation of co-optation and complicity in the new millennium. See Zhang Yingjin (2007).

Cloaked within the ambiguously defined category of 'art cinema', most of the first or second feature films by Chinese indie helmers are not only appreciated because of their Cinéma Vérité outlook and the spiritual core reverberating the dazzlingly changing reality of China, but also because of another layer of 'reality' about their filmmaking. They are shooting independent films in a socialist regime, a gesture which is in itself an outrageous challenge to the state authority, even though the filmmakers themselves seldom harbour any specific political agenda when launching these projects. As admitted by Ou Ning, 'the changing Chinese society in the PRC is already a provocative subject for local independent filmmakers. Just shooting people's lives on the streets is already provocative enough to make a good documentary' (Cheung 2007). Ou's perception might sound an exaggeration; nevertheless it demonstrates the reasons why, beyond obvious economic considerations, independent filmmakers would favour realist aesthetics in portraying a changing China. As Zhang Yingjin points out, 'Independent filmmakers turned their financial disadvantages into ideological advantages and negotiated their ways through the cracks and fissures opened up by their market economy' (2007: 54).

Underground filmmaking or film culture in mainland China since 1989 is often regarded by some Western mainstream critics and scholars as a Chinese version of the Soviet 'dissident culture', and the frictions between filmmakers and the authorities are seen as an illustration of an anti-'violet prison' allegory (Pickowicz 1995 and 2006). Intriguingly, this very indirect ideological play between Western intellectuals, who tend to situate China within a lingering Cold-War landscape and Chinese censors annoyed by the transgression of indie filmmakers, has actually facilitated the circulation of Chinese independent films at international film festivals and via pirated VCDs and DVDs. It might not be too far-fetched to conclude that state-party censorship has in fact worked to promote the global circulation of films labelled 'Chinese underground' or 'Chinese indie'.

Towards the Post-underground Period

The post-underground period, as it were, figuratively started in 2004 with the state's legitimisation of Jia Zhangke and Wang Xiaoshuai's filmmaking and a further revision of film regulations.[25] That year also witnessed Jia and Wang's completion of their first 'overground' works, namely *Shijie* (*The World*, 2004) and *Qinghong* (*Shanghai Dreams*, 2004), which were nominated for 2004's Golden Lion and presented the Cannes Jury Prize, respectively. As the 'surprise film' for the 63rd Venice Film Festival, Jia Zhangke's second 'overground' work, *Sanxia Haoren* (*Still Life*, literally translated as *The Good Folks Of Sanxia*, 2006) sustained the surprise by grabbing the Golden Lion. In February 2007, Wang Quan'an's *Tuya de Hunshi* (*Tuya's Marriage*, 2006) was awarded a Golden Bear at the 57th

Berlinale, and at the 58th edition of Berlinale the Silver Bear for Best Script went to Wang Xiaoshuai's *Zuoyou* (*In Love We Trust,* 2007).

Endorsements from top film festivals suggest this might be the right time to talk about the 'coming of age' for the Urban Generation after its first ten years. This 'coming of age' is reminiscent of the fact that when the Fifth Generation filmmakers triumphed at major film festivals during the 1993-94 season, independent films by Zhang Yang, He Jianjun and Wang Xiaoshuai had just premiered at film festivals in Vancouver, Rotterdam, Locarno and San Sebastian. However, my argument is that Jia and Wang's recognition at Venice and Berlin, each with their state-sanctioned independent films, has further problematised rather than consolidated the 'overground' status of independent filmmaking. Undoubtedly, Jia's new legitimacy facilitated the fervent domestic media coverage, infusing his win at Venice with a nationalistic and patriotic tone.

In his article on *Still Life*, Shelly Kraicer observes, 'Chinese press reaction to the Venice win was predictable, universally lionizing Jia as the latest exponent of national pride and then deftly subsuming him into the pantheon of contemporary cultural heroes' (Kraicer 2008: para. 12). By contrast, the ambiguity and conservative attitude expressed in Western publicity towards *Still Life*'s golden prize was also instantly translated into an expression of surprise at its win.[26] *Variety*'s Derek Elley even commented, 'The surprise film at this year's Venice fest offered no surprises ... It will appeal to the most faithful of the director's camp-followers and no one else' (Elley 2006: para. 1). Responses from film critics like Derek Elley have mirrored the Western mainstream media's paradoxical reasoning and their suspicion regarding the 'coming of age' of the Urban Generation at major film festivals, which essentially supposes that legitimised Chinese independent films have, to certain degree, compromised their value as authentic cinematic representations of Chinese reality. However, the state-sanctioned-film-turned-festival-winner in the age of independent filmmaking has not only challenged the Western media's stereotyped knowledge of Chinese underground films as festival darlings but also characterised the dilemma the Urban Generation has had to deal with in their post-underground transition.

At the end of Jia Zhangke's *The World*, there is an intriguing dialogue between the female protagonist Tao and her boyfriend Taisheng:

Tao: '*Are we dead*'?
Taisheng: '*No, this is just the beginning*'.

Inspired by Jia Zhangke's optimism towards his post-underground career, I would rather consider the thaw a signal of the transitional period for the Urban Generation but not necessarily an end of underground film culture itself. Though the label of 'underground' has gradually lost its socio-political critical edge and the risky, anti-establishment connotation in an era of all sorts of 'coming-out', I suggest that the spiritual core of Chinese underground culture would be reincarnated among younger filmmakers in their independent works while the culture itself is also highly heterogeneous in having assimilated various or conflicting discourses and ideological undercurrents in the post-socialist era. Undoubtedly the infiltration of global/local capital has made this out-of-system filmmaking in mainland China an even more unexpectedly complicated phenomenon in the new millennium. Nevertheless, I see the collective legitimisation in the case of both Jia (Zhangke) and Wang (Xiaoshuai) as at least partially the result of the re-territorialisation of China's film industry as it moves to re-adjust itself to the remapped global film industry and world film culture.

More importantly, without the recognition the Urban Generation secured at the international level, mainly through festival exhibitions, their emergence from the underground in China would have been unimaginable. Their bravado of 'smuggling' their film copies abroad to screen their works at worldwide film festivals has helped nurture a niche market (most probably an already-existing art-house market for international indie films) and a global audience for Chinese independent films. When the State officially embraced 'Chinese indie film' by legitimising it, it was less of an ideological campaign characterised by sugar-coated co-optation; the changing socio-political dynamism with market as the driving force should not be underestimated. Excepting those spectacular Chinese costume epics by Zhang Yimou or Chen Kaige, the most globally visible Chinese films have been independently produced, art-house works.

Underground film (and filmmaking) has also initiated changes in post-socialist filmmaking. Today, the Chinese capital Beijing and its time-honoured Beijing Film Academy (BFA) indisputably continue to play a leading role in PRC's independent film scene in terms of professional networking, production, distribution or exhibition channels. Nevertheless, a new movement of grassroots DV (Digital Video) and amateur filmmaking has unsurprisingly triggered a decentralising flow by bringing new film talents centre stage. Most of these grassroots *auteurs* have not obtained any degree in relevant field and many are actually based in Chinese cities other than Beijing (Ying Liang is based on Zigong, Sichuan Province; Yang Heng is based on Jishou, Hunan province etc.).

Festival Film Reconsidered

In Bill Nichols' study, the international film festival circuit itself has become an integral part of the circulation and exchange of global image economy. Within the 'global overlay' of festival context prevails the 'dialectic of comprehension / miscomprehension, understanding / misunderstanding, recognition / misrecognition'. Nevertheless, more often 'it is this dialectic itself and specific aspects of the interdependent, [the] interpenetrating combination of localism and globalism that is misrecognised – particularly in those gestures that would lift veil of international circulation to rediscover local origins' (1994: 69). As asserted by Nichols, 'though made locally, film production is always a site at which the global penetrates the local, the traditional, the national'. Nevertheless, Nichols also points out: 'Local films need not, however, be made with an eye toward escape from this global net of capital, technology, and style' (1994: 77). The emergence of the genre of 'festival film' is thus closely related to the desire of local filmmakers to embrace the 'global net of capital, technology, and style'; however the cultural hierarchy and the politics of selection have been decisive for the less privileged side in formulating strategies to participate in the global image production and consumption.

Thomas Elsaesser argues that one strategy for the festivals to bolster their brand image is to offer 'competitive production funds' and 'development money' in order to attract and stimulate young talents to shoot 'interesting, innovative or otherwise noteworthy films' (2005: 88). Being a 'genuine phenomenon', 'festival film' also signifies films 'made to measure' and 'made to order' to such an extent that filmmakers could even 'internalize and target' a certain film festival or festival circuit schedule for their work. Elsaesser's reflection has indeed offered a different angle from which to approach the Urban Generation Cinema – festival film is a model that demonstrates how the Chinese indie could survive at the festival circuit. It should be noted, though, that the advantages of being a 'festival film' may also turn out to be limitations for artistic freedom, or the genre itself may lead to narrow interpretations. However, just as the Fifth Generation has been through two seemingly disparate development stages from maverick experimentation to the next stage of the Zhang Yimou Model, it is also significant to ask if the Urban Generation will evolve similarly from aesthetic experimentations to a mannerism – by mannerism I mean 'questions of convention, content, manner and style' (Overbey 1979: 20).

In his thought-provoking introduction to Italian Neo-realism, David Overbey agrees that Neorealism could be regarded only as 'one way of making films' and could become a mannerism detachable from the movement itself (1979: 24). In the same vein, whereas people tend to attach labels such as 'post-socialist realism', 'neo-Bazinian realism' or 'international style of aestheticized realism' (McGrath 2004: 103) to Jia Zhangke's oeuvre and other Urban Generation works, it is also tempting to consider the dominant realist aesthetics and stylisation as 'one way of making films'. To put it another way, when such formulas or patterns become exploitable, there are, at the same time, convenient manipulations of the salient aestheticism characterising the Urban Generation Cinema: in terms of cinematic chronotope (time-space), there have always been recurrent temporal-spatial preferences, such as 'hometown' imaginary vis-à-vis monstrous urbanisation; contrasting spatial configurations; 'real-time intervals between narrative actions' (McGrath 2004: 104).

When it comes to stylisation, favoured ingredients have been: documentary realism, camerawork pieced together by long-takes, sparse conversation and minimalist narrative, vernacular-speaking non-professional casts etc. Moreover, Urban Generation films are often reviewed within the reference framework of transnational art film tradition and of such maestros as Ozu, Mizoguchi and Hou Hsiao-hsien. Thematic concerns have obviously covered the anxiety, *ennui* and alienation found in the quotidian life of the urbanite; the marginal groups' previously unrepresented and bleak life; or the potentially controversial marginal lifestyle and youth subculture. However, the elusiveness, aloofness and ambiguity in most of the Urban Generation films invite multiple interpretations. Therefore, while it is not difficult to formulate the aesthetic and thematic characteristics of those films,[27] it seems rather challenging to cite certain films as they have deliberately fashioned in order to be noticed at the international festival circuit.

Despite the production mode, the aesthetic formulas and urban-themed narratives characterising the new generation's 'festival film' could be defined as imitable patterns and varieties of Urban Generation Cinema should be further differentiated. Such a realisation is based on understanding that the realities of post-socialist China are intricately multilayered; also, independent filmmaking is complicated both by the state's capricious regulating and the free flow of transnational capital. For instance, works by Zhang Yang, Shi Runjiu, Jin Shen and Zhang Yibai are more market-viable, with a very intense urban texture and commercial appeal. Zhang Yang (*Aiqing Malatang/Spicy Love Soup*, 1998; *Xizao/Shower*, 1999; *Zuotian/Quitting*, 2001) and Shi Runjiu (*Meili Xinshijie/Beautiful New World*, 1998; *Zoudaodi/All The Way*, 2001) are both active figures of New Mainstream Cinema (*Xin Zhuxuanlu Dianying*) and have been closely associated with *Imar Films* and its founder, American producer Peter Loehr (Chinese name: Luo Yi).[28] Together with filmmakers like Li Xin and Zhang Yibai, this branch of Urban Generation directors is more concerned with modern love and city lifestyles, appealing to both local and global audiences. Zhang Yang's urban films have also garnered film awards at international film festivals,[29] whereas his *Spicy Love Soup* (1998) ranked second in that year's domestic box office with a gross profit ten times its budget, losing only to the Hollywood blockbuster *Titanic* (James Cameron, USA, 1997).

Conclusion

Zhang Yingjin has pointed out that the observable changes of Urban Generation works could arguably be summarised as the 'inconsistency' of 'artistic style (from avant-garde to melodramatic)', 'ideological positions (from radical to conservative)', 'genre experiments (from comedy to crime thriller)', and 'thematic choices (from misplaced love to social criticism)' (2007: 74). Whereas Zhang has insightfully mapped out the vital role that the post-socialist 'market' in a WTO age is playing in initiating those aesthetics and production transformations, it should be noticed that some of those observable 'new' features have characterised certain indie works even at an early stage of Urban Generation filmmaking. Stimulated by the global capital flow as well as the international film festival network(ing), independent filmmaking in mainland China is flourishing and constantly emerging film talents are rewriting Zhang's generalisation with their works.[30] Therefore the transformations of Urban Generation are not to be simply understood as linear evolution but rather as much more diversified, negotiable movement characterised by its unique fluidity and openness. In other words, I would also see those changes or 'inconsistency' have, to a greater extent, reflected the polyvocal nature of postsocialist filmmaking. Shi Runjiu (backed up by Loehr and Imar Film) and Zhang Yibai showed acute market-consciousness even in the early stage of their filmmaking 'experimentation', when several of their Urban Generation peers were more avant-garde and artistically adventurous.

After his 2001 road movie *All the Way,* Shi Runjiu diverted to documentary filmmaking, seemingly having distanced himself from his time on the festival circuit as a once promising Urban Generation filmmaker. Meanwhile Zhang Yibai, who is more often identified as a very commercially-oriented, mainstream director, has paradoxically showed the ambition to establish himself as an *auteur* trying to transcend his previous melodramatic urban love formulas; his latest work *Mi'an (Lost, Indulgence,* 2008*)* boasts an enviable cast including Karen Mok, Eason Chan, Jiang Wenli and Eric Tsang and was described by *Variety*'s Ronnie Scheib as being '...more claustrophobic, arty and surreal than Zhang's previous efforts' (2008: para. 1). Talking about the Urban Generation 'in transition', a conclusion has yet to be drawn and the 'inconsistency' as perceived in their works needs to be further addressed: would the module of the 'four players' be adequate in dismantling *auteur's* subjectivity investment of individual film?

Put into transnational/transregional perspective, I argue that transformations in Urban Generation works are also closely related to those of international art film community/market (McGrath 2007: 106-7) and of Chinese society and urban space – the leading 'character' of most Urban Generation works. The mannerism of Urban Generation is thus symptomatic of the anxiety of coping with the power relation in the post-socialist market. Furthermore, the film festival network in a global age has understandably functioned to regenerate China's independent film scene: in attracting younger talents and showcasing their works, the film festival has provided a vital platform through which independent filmmakers could become more closely involved in the global image consumption economy. 'Festival film' of the Urban Generation is therefore one way for the young filmmakers to articulate their contradictory condition as a global-game player/actor.

Notes

[1] I shall use the term 'Urban Generation' rather than the 'Sixth Generation' or 'the Newborn Generation' etc. in this essay to talk about the continuing and prosperous independent filmmaking scene in mainland China, which could be said to date back to the early 1990s. I would mainly focus on feature films by the new generation's helmers, but it should be remembered that broadly speaking, the Urban Generation also included from an early stage such avant-garde documentary filmmakers as Wu Wenguang (*Liulang Beijing: Zuihou De* (*Bumming in Beijing – The Last Dreamers*, 1990), Du Haibin (*The Lu Yan Xian* (*Along the Railroad*, 2001); *San* [*Umbrella*, 2007]). In the later stages Wang Bing (*Tie Xi Qu* (*West of the Track*, 2003); *He Fengming: A Memoir of a Chinese Intellectual*, 2007) and Li Ying (*Yasukuni, 2007*) etc. were involved.

[2] In order to facilitate the discussion, the film festivals mentioned here are mostly European. However, in the later sections on festival network I mention film festivals in Asia.

[3] Those twelve 'competitive feature film festivals' are international film festivals at Berlin, Cannes, Shanghai, Moscow, Karlovy Vary, Locarno, Montreal, Venice, San Sebastian, Tokyo, Cairo and Mar del Plata. See FIAPF official webpage, http://www.fiapf.org/intfilmfestivals.asp.

[4] See the reviews of Berlin International Film Festival 2008 at *Variety.com*. On-line. Available HTTP: http://www.variety.com/blog/1390000339/post/480022048.html.

[5] Before PRC launched the Reform and opened up in the late 1970s, the socialist state was in full control of the economy, fixing prices and production. Every aspect of the film industry 'from the censorship of the individual films right through to the distribution, the sales, where the films are shown, when they're shown, how they're shown, how they're exported' was state-controlled and mandated. See Tony Rayns' interview with the online film magazine *Offscreen* reminiscing PRC's film history since 1978. On-line. Available HTTP: http://www.offscreen.com/biblio/phile/essays/tony_rayns/.

[6] As succinctly summarised by Zhang Yingjin (2007), post-socialism can be differentiated by (1) a label of historical periodisation; (2) a structure of feelings; (3) a set of aesthetic practices; (4) a regime of political economy. Presupposing socialism, this new framework illuminates Chinese culture in the 1980s, when it contained the vestiges of late imperial culture, the remnants of the modern or bourgeois culture of the republican era, the residue of traditional socialist culture, and elements of both modernism and postmodernism.

[7] In Paul G. Pickowicz's reflection on underground filmmaking in China, he poses such questions as 'what do we mean by "underground film" (dixia dianying) and "Is it a useful term?"' (2006: 2). He claims that in the case

of China, the exclusive use of the term 'independent' indicates independence from the Chinese state rather than independence from the sort of powerful private conglomerates – which is what defines the American independent filmmaking. Pickowicz extends his arguments by taking a close look at the early stage of Chinese filmmaking from the early twentieth century to 1937, when the filmmaking was 'almost totally controlled by the private sector' (2006: 3). In the decades following 1949, private filmmaking in China became impossible because of the 'exclusively state-controlled socialist film production' (2006: 3).

[8] There were exceptions, of course. Emerging filmmakers such as Hu Xueyang, Guan Hu, Lou Ye, Wang Rui, Jiang Ge and Lu Xuechang have jobs inside the state film industry. See Chen and Xiao (2006).

[9] For instance, first held in the early spring of 2003, the biannual Yunnan Multi Culture Visual Festival is a young and pre-eminent documentary film festival in China. Financed by cultural foundations, it has aimed to promote and showcase domestic documentary filmmaking. (http://www.yunfest.org); the DOChina in Beijing (*Zhongguo Jilupian Dianyingjie*) which has its fifth edition in September 2008; *Mecooon Film Festival* 2008 (*Micang Dianyingjie*) based in Shanghai; CNEX (*Chinese Next* or *Huaren Xinshidai*) in Taiwan, which could be visited at http://www.cnex.org.tw/about_us.php.

[10] *Youchai (Postman*, He Jianjun, 1995), *Er'zi* (*Sons*, Zhang Yuan, 1996), *Suzhou He* (*Suzhou River*, Lou Ye, 2000).

[11] See the official website of Berlin International Film Festival: http://www.berlinale.de/en/das_festival/sektionen_und_reihen/forum/Forum.html.

[12] See the official webpage of CineMart of IFFR: http://www.filmfestivalrotterdam.com/professionals/cinemine.aspx.

[13] *Fonds Sud* has been commissioned by the French Ministry of Cultural Affairs and the National de la Cinematographie (CNC) to promote the cultural diversity that is inherent in World Cinema, an initiative directly at odds with Hollywood's commercially-driven agenda to standardise global entertainment consumption patterns. It has, over the past 20 years, co-financed well over 300 thematically diverse and culturally rich films helmed by 260 directors from nearly 70 countries. See the official sites: http://www.diplomatie.gouv.fr/en/france-priorities_1/cinema_2/cinematographic-cooperation_9/production-support-funding_10/fonds-sud-cinema_11/index.html.

[14] In fact, HAF's international partners include CineMart and Hubert Bals Fund of Rotterdam International Film Festival, Italy's Rome International Film Festival and Pusan Film Festival's PPP. See the official website of HAF: http://www.hkfilmart.com/haf/review.htm.

[15] Personal interview at the 37th Rotterdam International Film Festival on January 2008.

[16] Noticeably, transnational entities such as Fortissimo, though originally Dutch, could hardly be differentiated as such. Having many branches in both Europe and Asia, Fortissimo is mainly based in Hong Kong and Amsterdam.

[17] See the introduction on the official website of Fortissimo: http://www.fortissimo.nl/companyprofile/.

[18] Works such as *Guizi Laile* (*Devils On The Door*, 1999) by Jiang Wen, *Yige Mosheng Nvren De Laixin* (*A Letter from an Unknown Woman,* 2004*)* by Xu Jinglei and *Li Chun (And the Spring Comes,* 2007*)* by Gu Changwei.

[19] See its official website: http://www.focusfilms.cc/aboutus.htm. Films included in FOCUS FINAL CUT are, *Fengkuang de Shitou/Crazy Stone* (China, 2006), *Duk Haan Yum Cha/I'll Call You*(Chi Chung Lam, Hong Kong, 2006), *Seelai Ng Yi Cho /My Mother is A Belly Dancer* (Kung-Lok Lee, Hong Kong, 2006), *Taiyangyu/Rain Dogs* (Yuhang Ho, Hong Kong/Malaysia, 2006) and *Love Story* (Kelvin Tong, Singapore, 2006).

[20] Italics by Zhang Yingjin.

[21] According to the updated *Regulations* that came into force in 2006, the two committees are the *Film Examination Commission* and the *Re-Examination Commission*. To obtain the government's permission to show their films in national cinema lines, a Chinese filmmaker must meet several requirements: they must purchase a quota number from a state-owned studio (though it is not necessary that the studio agrees to produce or finance the film. However, selling the quota number also enables the studio to make profit); they must submit both a plot synopsis (until late 2003, a full script was required, but new policies in force since early 2005 prefer the synopsis. In 2006, a new policy for censorship called 'archiving' was introduced, details to follow) and the completed film to government censors; they must not make the film public – including submitting it to international festivals – until the censors' approval is guaranteed. Filmmakers who fail on any of these counts can expect their film to be banned and themselves to be forbidden to make any more films in China until further notice.

[22] Following its 'Regulations on Film Examination' (*Dianying Shencha Guiding*, English provided by official website) in 1997, the *Regulation on Film Management* has become effective since 2002. In 2006 the State set out *The Regulations for Administration of the Records of Screenplay (Outline) and Films,* and the previous key regulations were nullified. See http://fec2.mofcom.gov.cn/aarticle/laws/200609/20060903168864.html.

[23] In September 2006, after the reconfiguration led by the SARFT, a new 37-member film censorship committee, which would, in a sense, have the final say on which films the 1.3 billion people in China could watch, was formed. Its members' professional backgrounds differ but are closely related to the state ideology establishment.

[24] See Zhang Xianmin's online article on contemporary Chinese banned films (in Chinese):
http://sh.netsh.com/bbs/2901/messages/10595.html.

[25] See sina.com.cn news (in Chinese), 'The Thaw Of The Sixth Generation' (Dianying Diliudai Jiedong) in 2004: http://news.sina.com.cn/c/2004-02-03/11432752760.shtml.

[26] See the festival report at *International Herald Tribune* on 9 September 2006:
http://www.iht.com/articles/2006/09/09/frontpage/web.0910film.php.

[27] Jenny Kwok Wah Lau has argued that three aspects of this new generation's films deserve attention: *no epic*; *stream of life* and *disengagement*; *free market* or *globalization* (Lau 2003: 17-9).

[28] See the report on *Imar Films* at the website of *Beijingscene* (*Xin Beijing*):
http://www.beijingscene.com/v06i004/feature/feature.html

[29] In 2001, Zhang Yang's *Zuotian (Yesterday,* 2001) won Netpac Award at Venice Film Festival; *Xizao (Shower,* 1999) won International Critics' Award (FIPRESCI) at Toronto International Film Festival; this film also garnered Golden Alexander at Thessaloniki Film Festival in 1999; Audience Award at Rotterdam International Film Festival (2000); Golden Space Needle Award at Seattle International Film Festival in 2000. *Xiangrikui (Sunflower,* 2005) won the Silver Seashell at San Sebastián International Film Festival in 2005. *Luoye Guigen (Going Home,* 2006) won Prize of the Ecumenical Jury at Berlin International Film Festival in 2007.

[30] Mostly they are reflected in the premiered films (including documentary films) at cutting-edge, independent-oriented film festivals in Pusan or Rotterdam. But they are also screened at alternative venues such as universities or cinephile clubs. The aforementioned non-governmental annual film forum in Beijing (BiFF, funded by *Li Xianting Film Fund*) and Nanjing-based China Independent Film Festival (CIFF, *Zhongguo Duliyingxiang Nianduzhan*) also constitutes the ideal platform for showcasing the latest new indie works.

Works Cited

Chen, Mo and Xiao Zhiwei (2006) 'Chinese Underground Films: Critical Views from China', in Paul G. Pickowicz and Yingjin Zhang (eds) *From Underground to Independent: Alternative Film Culture in Contemporary China.* Lanham: Rowman & Littlefield, 143-60.

Cheung, Esther M. K. (2007) 'Dialogues with Critics on Chinese Independent Cinemas', *Jump Cut: A Review of Contemporary Media*, 49, On-line. Available
HTTP: http://www.ejumpcut.org/currentissue/index.html#c (May 2007).

Czach, Liz (2004) 'Film Festivals, Programming, and the Building of a National Cinema', *the Moving Image*. 4, 1, 76-88.

de Valck, Marijke (2005) 'Drowning in Popcorn at the International Film Festival Rotterdam? The Festival as a Multiplex of Cinephilia', in Marijke de Valck and Malte Hagener (eds) *Cinephilia: Movies, Love and Memory*. Amsterdam: Amsterdam University Press, 97-110.

___ (2007) *Film Festivals: From European Geopolitics to Global Cinephilia*. Amsterdam: Amsterdam University Press.

Elley, Derek (2006). 'Still Life', *Variety*, 8 September. On-line. Available HTTP: http://www.variety.com/review/VE1117931509.html?categoryid=31&cs=1 (May 2007).

Elsaesser, Thomas (2005) 'Film Festival Networks: The New Topographies of Cinema In Europe', in *European Cinema: Face to Face with Hollywood*. Amsterdam: Amsterdam University Press, 82-107.

Evans, Owen (2007) 'Border Exchanges: The Role of the European Film Festival', *Journal of Contemporary European Studies*, April, 15, 1, 23-33.

Kraicer, Shelly (2008) 'Chinese Wasteland: Jiazhangke's *Still Life*', *Cinemascope*, 29. Online. Available HTTP: http://www.cinema-scope.com/cs29/feat_kraicer_still.html (March 2008).

Lau, Jenny Kwok Wah (2003) 'Globalization and Youthful Subculture: The Chinese Sixth Generation Films at the Dawn of the New Century', in Jenny Kwok Wah Lau (ed.) *Multiple Modernities: Cinemas and Popular Media in Transcultural East Asia*. Philadelphia: Temple University Press, 13-27.

Lu, Tonglin (2002) *Confronting Modernity in the Cinemas of Taiwan and Mainland China*. Cambridge, UK; New York: Cambridge University Press.

McGrath, Jason (2004) 'Culture and the Market in Contemporary China: Cinema, Literature, and Criticism of the 1990s', unpublished PhD thesis, University of Chicago. On-line. Available HTTP: http://pqdd.sinica.edu.tw/twdaoeng/servlet/advanced?query=313653 (June 2006).

___ (2007) 'The Independent Cinema of Jia Zhangke: From Postsocialist Realism to a Transnational Aesthetic', in Zhang Zhen (ed.) *The Urban Generation: Chinese Cinema and Society at the Turn of the Twenty-first Century*. Durham; London: Duke University Press, 81-114.

Nakajima, Seio (2006) 'Film Clubs in Beijing: The Cultural Consumption of Chinese Independent Films', in Paul G. Pickowicz and Yingjin Zhang (eds) *From Underground to Independent: Alternative Film Culture in Contemporary China*. Lanham: Rowman & Littlefield, 161-87.

Nichols, Bill (1994) 'Global Image Consumption in the Age of Late Capitalism', *East-West Film Journal*, 8, 1, 68-85.

Overbey, David (1979) 'Introduction', in David Overbey (ed.) *Springtime in Italy: A Reader on Neo-realism*. London: Talisman Books, 1-33.

Pickowicz, Paul G. (1995) 'Velvet Prison and the Political Economy of Chinese Filmmaking', in Deborah S. Davis, et al. (eds) *Urban Spaces in*

Contemporary China: The Potential for Autonomy and Community in Post-Mao China. Washington, D.C.: Woodrow Wilson Center Press; Cambridge: Cambridge University Press, 193-220.

___ (2006) 'Social and Political Dynamics of Underground Filmmaking in China', in Paul G. Pickowicz and Yingjin Zhang (eds) *From Underground to Independent: Alternative Film Culture in Contemporary China*. Lanham: Rowman & Littlefield, 1-22.

Rosenbaum, Jonathan (2002*) Movie Wars: How Hollywood and the Media Conspire to Limit What Films We Can See*. Chicago: A Cappella.

Scheib, Ronnie (2008) 'Lost, Indulgence', *Variety*, 15 May. On-line. Available HTTP: http://www.varietyasiaonline.com/content/view/6089/ (30 June 30 2008).

Shohat, Ella and Robert Stam (2002) 'Narrativizing Visual Culture: Towards a Polycentric Aesthetics', in Nicholas Mirzoeff (ed.) *The Visual Culture Reader*. London: Routledge, 37-59.

Wu, Chia-chi (2004) 'Chinese Language Cinemas in Transnational Flux', unpublished PhD thesis, University of Southern California. On-line. Available HTTP: http://pqdd.sinica.edu.tw/twdaoeng/servlet/advanced?query=3140 574 (March 2007).

Zhang, Yingjin (2002) 'Chinese Cinema and Transnational Cultural Politics: Reflections on Film Festivals, Film Productions, and Film Studies', *Journal of Modern Literature in Chinese*, 2, 1, July, 105-32 (Rpt. in Zhang (2002) *Screening China: Critical Interventions, Cinematic Reconfigurations, and the Transnational Imaginary in Contemporary Chinese Cinema*. Ann Arbor: Center for Chinese Studies, University of Michigan, 4-15).

___ (2007) 'Rebel without a Cause? China's New Urban Generation and Postsocialist Filmmaking', in Zhang Zhen (ed.) *The Urban Generation: Chinese Cinema and Society at the Turn of the Twenty-first Century*. Durham; London: Duke University Press, 49-80.

Chapter Nine

Film and/as Culture:
The Use of Cultural Discourses at
Two African Film Festivals[1]

J. David Slocum

The objective of this paper is to elucidate how culture operates as a defining idea at film festivals, particularly in the Global South. To do so, it will reference two African festivals, FESPACO and the Zanzibar International Film Festival (ZIFF), as touchstones to discuss three related concerns: (1) the status of film, a technological medium and social institution, as the primary basis for conceptualising events in which culture is explicitly invoked as an organisational rubric; (2) the roles assumed by festivals in determining and shaping given cultural formations or communities; and (3) the extension of concerns about culture to illuminate contemporary approaches to development and democracy at festivals and in their home regions.

Festivals of Ideas

To discuss culture, it is useful to tease out a distinction developed during international debates over cultural diversity from the early 2000s that addressed cinema directly. Culture can be approached in terms of expressive or artistic production, institutional structures that support this creativity, and external practices that enable their consumption. Yet as a 2004 UNESCO report put it, culture should be 'thought of more in terms of ... deeply internalised and identity-creating ways of thinking, feeling, perceiving, and being in the world' (Stenou 2004: 3). This far-reaching conception relates culture to political participation and public life as well as to individual engagement with worlds local and distant. These terms also push us to expand our conception of film from being a medium of artistry and expression to an integral part of individual identities and social lives.

That expanded idea of culture proves particularly relevant to film festivals in the Global South. Consider two African events: FESPACO in Burkina Faso and the Zanzibar International Film Festival in Tanzania.

Two African Film Festivals

The first, older, and arguably best-known African festival is FESPACO, Le Festival panafricain du cinéma et de la télévision de Ouagadougou. In 1969, a group of cineastes representing five West African countries, including director Ousmane Sembène, held a festival, the 'Semaine du Cinéma Africain,' to celebrate and publicly exhibit African film in the capital of what was then Upper Volta. A year later, a second festival was held under the same name with nearly double the number of films and countries represented. The third festival, held in 1972, was the first to use the name FESPACO and, with government aid, it nearly doubled again in size to include both non-Francophone African and European countries.[2] Festivals continued to take place and grow at irregular intervals throughout the 1970s, until a biannual format was adopted in 1979. The following decade saw more growth and the cultivation of the festival as Africa's premiere cinematic event with the increased support of President Thomas Sankara (who also changed the host country's name to Burkina Faso in 1984). By the 1990s, FESPACO was the continent's largest recurring cultural event, with over 5,000 official participants and an economic impact of over €100 million (Buch-Jepsen 2003).

As its name conveys, FESPACO was founded as a 'Pan-African' event. The social, political, and cultural ideas guiding the festival were thus complex and diffused. Typically understood to have emerged in the late nineteenth and early twentieth centuries, Pan-Africanism presumed, or acknowledged the importance of debate over, a loose unity of values and worldviews across the continent and diaspora that could empower social and political movement, resist exploitation, and embrace African heritage. During the post-war years of independence, several major postcolonial leaders updated Pan-Africanism: Kwame Nkrumah in Ghana, Julius Nyerere in Tanzania, and Ahmed Sékuo Touré in Guinea among them. Indigenous cultural production and public engagement with culture became important strategies for overcoming colonial legacies and celebrating African cultures.

From its beginnings in February 1969, FESPACO retained the purpose stipulated during the original Semaine du Cinéma Africain: 'to make people discover and to promote African film which for the most part was ignored. The purpose of this encounter was therefore to show that there exists an African cinema, which was made in Africa, by Africans, on African subjects' (qtd. in Diawara 1992: 129). In the preamble of FESPACO, the festival's objective was 'to facilitate the dissemination of African films so as to allow contacts and confrontations of ideas between the filmmakers. The aim was also to contribute to the development of cinema as a means of expression, education, and a means to raise consciousness' (Diawara 1992: 130).

The guiding viewpoint, Pan-Africanism, has not often been subject to direct scrutiny within the FESPACO programme. Instead, themes related to filmmaking and African social and cultural life and politics were assigned to the festivals starting in 1985, with colloquia and conferences added to engage them and other topics. The 1980s also saw other types of institutionalisation. A marketplace, Le Marché International du Cinéma et de la Télévision Africains (MICA), was established in 1983 and, six years later, the festival funded the construction of a film archive, La Cinémathèque Africaine de Ouagadougou. While hardly acting alone, Thomas Sankara was an especially significant contributor to these efforts. He believed in Pan-African self-determination (refusing any foreign aid to his country while president) and sought to further both the material facilitation of indigenous culture, including filmmaking, and the consciousness-raising of which cultural media were capable.

A second and more recently organised event, the Zanzibar International Film Festival (ZIFF), was established in 1998 as a site for celebrating the cosmopolitan culture of the Indian Ocean basin.[3] With the subtitle 'Films of the Dhow Countries', the inaugural event featured film screenings and other activities including 'Village Panoramas, Youth and Children's Events, Indian Panorama, Music, Drama, and an Intellectual Property Rights Workshop'. In the years since, 'Dhow culture', with Zanzibar as its crucible, has continued with varying emphasis to orient the event and its approaches to cinema and the public culture of the island and region.

'Dhow culture' has developed as a concept at ZIFF and its programming and against the historical backdrop of a much older Indian Ocean culture. By the end of the first festival in 1998, the jury produced a brief position paper for the festival and for evaluations to be made about films and other programming. With the seagoing dhow as emblem of the region's identity, the Jury Report read:

> The Dhow as the icon of the festival is the symbol of a long history of communication, migration and interaction which has produced a cosmopolitan culture as the manifestation of human experience and expression of the region. This we understand as 'Dhow Culture'. It is a culture owned by no one and by everyone. (ZIFF Jury Report 1998: 2)

Since that early formulation, successive festivals and conferences have explored facets of Dhow culture, history and experience, devoting special attention to hybrid cultural forms and practices. In 1999, the 'Festival Overview' cast the event as 'a remembrance and celebration of this rich legacy [of Indian Ocean interactions over the centuries] as it is expressed in the music, film, crafts, dance, video, photography, sculpture, painting and other art forms of people from the dhow region' (1999: 5). Yet how these diverse activities and productions together constitute a given culture has remained under-theorised. Scholarly workshops, as well, have examined Dhow culture through historical and other research into specific events and customs. It is film, though, that has enjoyed a pride of place among cultural forms at ZIFF since the organisation's founding.

The invocation of the Indian Ocean past at the founding of ZIFF occurred at a historical moment in the late 1990s influenced by particular conditions. In 1995, for the first time since independence, the country held multi-party elections that promised further liberalisation of the economy. Mainland Tanzania (Tanganyika) and Zanzibar had vexed relations in the years immediately following these elections. Among the disagreements was the matter of how to develop tourism in Zanzibar, where the development of new hotels both on the east coast of the larger island, Unguja, and in and around Stone Town aimed to support high-end Western tourism. One strategy sought to celebrate the islands' separate identity and culture and to showcase their historical linkages not only to the African mainland but to the Indian Ocean region as a whole. What for some was the apparent 'branding' of Zanzibar as an 'exotic' travel destination for European and U.S. tourists occurred at the same time that Unguja emerged as a distinctive heritage site that could benefit from 'cultural tourism'. ZIFF benefited from the widespread local development of Zanzibari tourism but has also been affected by the differing priorities brought to that process.

The respective founding moments of FESPACO and ZIFF yield two important insights. One is that festival organisers from these African events have sought to acknowledge affinities, if not build formal alliances, with counterparts elsewhere in the Global South. The founders of FESPACO aimed to promote cinemas that would offer alternative visions of African life and address vital issues of social justice around the world. Sankara would sharpen this effort during the 1980s, self-consciously supporting cinema as an expressive medium of the people after the example of Latin American political filmmakers (and leaders). Likewise, from the beginning, 'Dhow culture' was intended to embrace the longstanding integrity of experiences in the Indian Ocean world. Part of this manifested the political solidarity of the region in the face of the hegemony of Europe and the United States (and, earlier, the Soviet bloc). The finer point, though, is that these festivals approached culture in the broad terms of identity-creation. Sharing an understanding of how film and culture are linked therefore entails more than countering the predominance of neo-colonial economics or images. It fosters solidarity around the expanded idea of culture as a political project of recovering identity and heritage.

A related second point concerns the unstable relationship between the overarching cultural categories employed by organisers to distinguish their events and the cultural elements constituting them. Despite being an event celebrating Pan-African film, FESPACO has continued to rely on the national origin of films and participants (and support of many of their governments). This tension between the whole and the parts, between African culture and multiple national or sub-national cultures, has historically tied cultural claims to other social and historical concerns. The definition and emphasis of 'Dhow culture' has shifted since 1998, and its formulation in regard to Africa, Oman and the Middle East, and the Indian sub-continent remains unfixed. While taking pains to address this question, the first ZIFF Jury Report ultimately did not offer a compelling conclusion:

Each *cultural* arena consists of several distinct cultures ... We group them together and speak of culture in the singular. In this way, we can permit ourselves to speak of the Dhow Culture and to signify the numerous cultures of the Indian Ocean Basin. (ZIFF Jury Report 1998: 1)

As Andrew Apter shows in a trenchant analysis of FESTAC, a cultural festival held in Nigeria in 1977, supranational categories of culture are often constructed and staged according to very particular national or regional political and economic agendas (2005).

Art and Commerce

The lack of a film industry and infrastructure in many countries in Africa, and notably in Ouagadougou and Zanzibar, compounds the challenge of analysing festival engagement with politics and economics. Founded in the late 1960s heyday of Pan-African politics and Third Cinema filmmaking, FESPACO not only claims roots in an ideological project essential to postcolonial Africa but also at a moment when film held a privileged status in communicating indigenous social values to local and global audiences. Film also meant celluloid. As technologies have evolved, the festival has steadfastly remained loyal to the standards of traditional *auteur* filmmaking. In 1999, for example, young Nigerian videomakers disdainfully announced the festival offered them no meaningful reward for participating (Adewara 1999: 30). Serious discussions about the status of video and television productions had been ongoing since the 1980s but went so far, by 2003, as to generate a proposal that a separate festival be held in intervening years to feature a television screening programme and market (Barlet 2003). By 2007, some grassroots filmmakers alleged an economic bias by the festival against those who could access digital cameras but not afford filmstock.

Yet another layer of nostalgia operates in the aesthetics of films celebrated over the festival's four decades. In a review of the 1993 instalment, Manthia Diawara stressed the importance of celebratory renderings of the pre-colonial African past to the West African cinematic imagination highlighted at the event (1993: 22-5). Imagining village life, indigenous social and political mores, and oral traditions were crucial to reconstructing African histories and imagining pre-colonial life on-screen. Scholars like Frank Ukadike have observed that the generation of filmmakers who grew up with FESPACO and addressed the years of post-colonial independence and Pan-Africanism firsthand is passing. Younger film- (or video) makers differently focused on pre-European experience carry the potential for new visions that will increase the range of cinematic engagements with the past (Ukadike 1994).

The changing status of film exhibition in Ouagadougou parallels this generational change. By one account, West African film viewing is increasingly class-based: while the wealthy rarely venture into public spaces and prefer to watch satellite or DVD films on home plasma screens, the middle class attend the dwindling number of movie theatres, and the poor watch television or attend video clubs. In Burkina Faso, a passionate film-going country that boasted 3.5 million viewers in a country of 10 million as recently as 1995, theatre owners have increasingly been struggling. Declining attendance, often corrupt management, and aging theatres make it easier to sell spaces for conversion into supermarkets or offices than renovate. Recalling that the country is one of the world's poorest, the most impoverished citizens, who would still need CFA 125 to go to a video club, also cannot be counted on for regular attendance. The overall result is that the once robust Burkinabé audience has splintered and the image of consistent filmgoers in theatres is increasingly one of the past (Barlet 2007).

At ZIFF, the historical dearth of East African productions has meant that few local and particularly Zanzibar-produced films have been featured at the festival, conspicuously in the nightly public screenings intended for locals. The island's last three commercial cinemas closed over the first 10 years of ZIFF's existence, meaning that the festival's public screenings have become the main opportunity each year for Zanzibaris to watch films in large public groups and on a large screen. This situation contrasts the already well-entrenched tendency among viewers at other times to watch films on television and especially DVDs. Contemporary distribution networks, while varied, traffic almost exclusively in DVDs rather than films on celluloid and provide Nollywood, Hollywood, Bollywood, and Hong Kong productions for sale or rental for domestic viewing. Several videohalls in and around Stone Town offer another inexpensive small group viewing option; the cost of a theatre ticket was, before their closing, 6,000 Tz, while the cost of watching a DVD at a videohall is 50 Tz (Deckard 2006). Local and mainland television stations provide further non-theatrical opportunities for filmviewing.

Nostalgia for the past role of cinema in local social life also shapes contemporary perceptions of film. For some, an imagined cinematic cosmopolitanism links film in the early twenty-first century to pre- and early revolutionary days still fondly remembered by older locals and, as Jan-Georg Deutsch argues, even by some of those born after 1964 (2008). While few productions are overtly about that historical period (chiefly documentaries made mostly by non-East Africans), the *idea* of cinema as central to an earlier cosmopolitan moment has continuing relevance. That nostalgia for a time of social and political hope appears to remain a strong motivator for festival organisers. Despite being a relative newcomer among cultural events compared with FESPACO, both festivals share an important engagement with the imagined communities and markets of the 1950s and 1960s.

A second aspect of the relationship constructed at festivals involves the way cinema as cultural production and practice operates *within* or *as* the basis of a festival itself. Significant here is the lived experience of festivals that transcends the objects and artefacts they publicly exhibit (Harvey 2006:

1). Both FESPACO and ZIFF are themselves recurrent productions that operate as venues for showcasing cultural experience and (re-) constituting history. Organisers in Burkina Faso have had more than four decades to manage expectations of their event and relied on an idea, of Africa as unity, more longstanding and more familiar. Their counterparts in Zanzibar have more directly addressed and re-shaped their founding cultural idea, in part because of its lesser familiarity in the region and beyond.

Self-definition is not only important for marketing a specific festival brand to tourists or filmmakers and distributors. The emergence of a worldwide festival circuit since the late 1980s has foregrounded the question of how local or regional film cultures and burgeoning industries operate vis-à-vis an increasingly complicated global network of cultural events and markets. 'Inequality is...built into the very structure of the international film festival circuit', Julian Stringer writes. 'The astonishing growth of such events in the 1980s and beyond' suggests 'not so much a parliament of national film industries as a series of diverse, sometimes competing, sometimes cooperating, public spheres' (2001: 138). While this often translates into efforts to articulate cultural formations in various regional terms, the national designation of productions has persisted in the presentation and cataloguing of films. At the tenth ZIFF in 2007, a 'festival of festivals' programme went further in screening packages of films from festivals from Africa and elsewhere in the Global South (though originally advertised as part of the programme, FESPACO was not ultimately included).[4] Beyond enriching the overall slate of screenings and consolidating an institutional network, the basis for the selection of partners and the solidarities among the festivals and their respective missions remained unclear.

A potential basis for solidarity among the festivals is the inequality observed by Stringer. In marked contrast to Hollywood and European commercial films, productions from the Global South have been programmed as alternatives to the globalising tendencies wrought in the North. The analysis of films produced in the South thus often turns on questions of distinctive aesthetics and politics (e.g., diasporic, African, transnational) that can be defined in terms of hybridity or what Martin Roberts calls the 'affirmation of difference' (1999: 78). We might similarly ask how an annual or bi-annual event, itself a cultural production, can be approached as a site where common meanings and understandings are communicated and explored and also viewed as an alternative to the various and expanding array of distribution practices for commercial films in Africa.

The dual deliberative and economic character of culture re-emerges here. Shared ideas and creative practices featured in films have been linked at festivals to goals of economic empowerment, social development, and capacity building in the region. Theoretical formulations of Pan-African or Dhow culture could thus mark and promote films that would be approached as practical efforts to support local filmmaking and advance the development of local and regional cultural industries. One consequence has been the linkage of West, East or Pan-African countries with the rest of the Global

South through the screening of films from around the world and in confronting issues such as migration, sustainable social and economic development, HIV/AIDS, and the legacies of slavery and colonialism.

The imagination of Pan-African or Dhow culture draws together these economic and deliberative elements and relates them to the variegated yet homogenising tendencies understood as globalisation. Those tendencies have been employed by festival organisers in Zanzibar, Ouagadougou and elsewhere in the Global South to suggest that the histories of their respective cultures offer alternatives to the prevailing Western engagement of diversity and change in the contemporary world. At the same time, and especially through the production of local or regional festivals themselves, globalisation is invoked as a backdrop to underscore how the regions can retain their own complex integrity.

Community Resource and Public Ritual

Film festivals in the Global South can be seen to recapitulate a problematic at the heart of debates about cultural production and diversity: namely, is culture chiefly an expressive realm of shared beliefs, meanings and understandings or a commodifiable activity based in products and markets? This tension between the common-interest and economic values of culture needs to be unpacked further to address the experiences at individual festivals. To do so, it is useful to consider the *public* value of festivals.

'The theming of public consumer space is an invitation to inscribe a context with distinctiveness and difference from the private', Charles Acland writes. 'Generally speaking, such appeals are opportunities to reconstruct distinctions between private and public locations, even as they borrow presumptions about each realm for their own' (2003: 154-5). Such a distinction is complicated, as Acland acknowledges, despite the apparently public essence and technological basis of festivals (Acland 2003: 154). We might even consider 'events' here in locationally as well as temporally specific terms. Film or cultural festivals, in particular, may be public events that rely on cinema as a social medium to build on the ephemeral engagement of social communities with cinema.

Acland goes on, 'modifications in a commodity's life cycle and the associated fracturing of audiences reignites efforts to reconstitute and stabilise cinemagoing's place and particularity' (153). So it may be that the public/private opposition is less useful in mapping the more global cartography of contemporary cinema. Emmanuel Ethis offers alternative axes, 'distance' and 'ultra-proximity', to juxtapose the proliferating international circuit of specialised and, especially, urban film festivals with the continuing technological evolution of 'home theatres' (2006: 52). While the public-private formulation remains useful to a degree in comprehending festival dynamics, the evolution of technologies, distribution networks, and exhibition practices also urges consideration of others, including distance-proximity.

For FESPACO, the emergence of a worldwide film festival circuit from the 1990s, particularly in the Global South, remade what had been a more limited festival economy in which it held a privileged status. During the 1970s-1980s, the Burkinabé festival had shared the African stage only with events in Carthage and Cape Town. The former festival, Les Journées Cinématographiques de Carthage, founded by the Tunisian Minister of Cultural Affairs in 1966 and also biannual, features films of the Maghreb, Africa and the Middle East. Recognising potential conflicts, the organisers agreed with FESPACO in the early 1970s to hold their respective events in alternating years. The latter, started in 1977 as the Cape Town Film Festival, grew slowly during the apartheid era before expanding in the 1990s as both a film showcase and a marketplace (SITHENGI). Beyond the continent's shores, festivals from New York to Milan arose or dedicated programming to celebrate and promote cinemas of Africa and the diaspora.

These festivals tend to operate, as Stringer observed of European events, 'in two directions at once' and 'market both conceptual similarity and cultural difference' – presumably both to each other in the region and to the rest of the world, particularly the Global North (139). At ZIFF, besides efforts to provide resources to burgeoning film industries, the role of the event in determining and shaping Dhow cultural identity or community relies precisely on the articulation of historical commonalities and differences. The production of the festival lends a rootedness to circuits of exchange and flows of cultural production by identifying, growing and producing shared understandings. The festival may well also illuminate how de-nationalisation is succeeded less by open-ended globalism or the complete de-territorialisation of the nation than by regionalisms and hybrid solidarities. Like other festivals around the world (and as Lucy Mazdon has written about Cannes), ZIFF might usefully 'be positioned within a regional/national/global nexus' of audiences and industries (2006: 19-30).

Such a nexus grows complicated when considering FESPACO. During the late 1990s-2000s, the Burkinabé festival experienced tremendous pressures to adapt to shifting cinematic, technological and economic environments. Geopolitically, globalisation provoked stock-taking about the contemporary meaning of Pan-Africanism. At the same time, the continent was experiencing a growing regionalisation. As Neils Buch-Jepsen asserts symptomatically, the 'deceptive aura of cultural homogeny [posited by the African festival] will dissipate over time' (2003). A noteworthy break at the time was linguistic: the longstanding predominance of Francophone productions as the mainstays and vanguard of African cinema was giving way to the expansion and improved quality of Arab and Anglophone productions and audiences.

An illustrative moment occurred in 2007. At the 20th anniversary festival, at what should have been a triumphal expression of historical success and future prospects, *Cahiers du Cinéma* published a special supplement to mark the occasion. Following a laudatory piece on the festival's 'birthday', separate articles focused on Africa's three most vibrant contemporary national cinemas – South Africa, Morocco and Egypt (2007). When the publication appeared at the FESPACO press centre, and notwithstanding the frequent use of French language in Moroccan productions or French government subsidies to filmmakers in Egypt, the recognition of a shift from the great Francophone filmmakers of the past to innovative Anglophone and Arab-language industries gave pause. That sobriety was only underscored at the end of the same festival when a Nigerian film (Newton I. Aduaka's *Ezra* [2007]), made in English, earned the coveted top prize. While on one hand seeming to affirm the festival's commitment to cinema as cultural form for all Africa, showcasing such films reflected a shift away from the longtime privileging of a certain type of Francophone cinema associated with West Africa.

Such a shift returns our attention to the multidimensional idea of culture. Writing at the 2004 Zanzibar festival, his last as director there, Imruh Bakari observed, 'the Festival and its associated programmes are a gateway for the articulation and expression of Dhow Culture, the interrogation of its relevance, and its comments on the contemporary world space' (2004b: 3). ZIFF itself becomes here more than a facilitator of research on cultural forms or practices of the past or even a venue for showcasing film to regional audiences. Instead, Bakari suggests that the festival was positioned to be a laboratory for refining understandings of Dhow culture and then a platform for communicating those understandings. The discourse of Dhow culture, he would later say, is 'a means to express our location and perceptions thus making a contribution to the meaning of our own life [sic]' (2004a: 2).

ZIFF was therefore positioned as a resource for both the ongoing intellectual exploration of the concept of 'Dhow culture' and the practical support of productions representing that culture. Together, the efforts constituted not only a specific regional focus cast in terms other than those of 'Dhow culture', but also a more pragmatic shift from analyses of the concept to active service and resource provision, networking and capacity-building. While informed by understandings of the region's past, these activities assumed heretofore acknowledged but undertheorised linkages between the development of culture and that of society and the economy.

Relevant here is the proliferation of festivals during the late 1990s and early 2000s in the East African region. Events in Nairobi, Kampala, Kigali and elsewhere served, like in Zanzibar, not only as opportunities for public screenings and related programming but as platforms for production training, distribution negotiations, forums about regional politics, culture and cinema, and markets for film and television.[5] Analyses of cultural geographies of these festivals grounded, variously, in transnational, regional, national, and/or urban contexts paralleled the debates at ZIFF about Dhow culture (Acland: 291 n. 136; Stringer: 138). While lived social experience, especially in cities, is increasingly hybridised, plural and, finally, de-nationalised, in other words, films and many of the festivals that exhibit them also continue to showcase aspirations involving democratic governance and freedom of expression that necessarily proceed from a revivified nation-state system – and, as Harvey suggests, possibly supported by regional cooperation (3).

Even as they imagine and seek to constitute particular cultural formations, festivals themselves are also shaped through the construction of their own history and memory. For a film festival, the visual character and emphases of these constructions and reworkings of the past are vital to understandings of the cultures they engage and advance. With cinema as centerpiece, a festival serves as an expressive and economic base for the preservation and reconstruction of the self-understanding and representation of a given culture and its people. In Africa, as elsewhere in the South, where few film archives exist, festivals serve an additional role in preserving those histories and sharing them with audiences.

To speak of multiple aspects of festivals is to suggest a range of overlapping purposes to the events: the strengthening of social bonds and affiliations; the celebration of certain constructions of history and belonging; a demonstration of respect for given values, beliefs or practices; and, sometimes, the fulfilment of the emotional needs of practitioners and the intrinsic pleasure of the activities themselves. In other words, film festivals function as rituals for imagined communities and cultures (Bell 1997). Such a notion has been explored in analyses of the Cannes Film Festival[6] (Ethis 2001: 68). As well, Martin Mhando has affirmed that mounting a 'ritual' event, with cinema at its heart, is one aim of ZIFF planning (Slocum 2007).

Festivals might be seen as celebratory deliberations of the constitutive ideas, texts and practices of regional culture(s). Adopting Marijke de Valck's resonant phrase, the events are 'sites of passage' in which local and regional cultural forms and practices are re-framed and advanced (2008). As a result, the forms and practices are made comprehensible and marketable in film festival and general tourist economies. The re-framing also does important work for imagined and actual publics locally. The events both commodify and serve as a survival strategy for their respective cultural imaginaries. These mutually reinforcing aspects of festivals parallel two persistent lines of thinking at FESPACO and ZIFF, namely the reconstruction and revitalisation of histories and memories of Pan-African or Dhow cultures *and* the act of transformative deliberation and resource-provision for present-day conditions and future possibilities.

Markets and Development

Nowhere is the need for material resources addressed more directly than at the film (and television) marketplaces instituted at many festivals. Oftentimes, as happened at FESPACO and ZIFF, markets emerge years after the founding of the festivals proper, once producer and distribution networks were consolidated. MICA was thus established in 1983 and is a major site for exchange of film and video productions, packaged programmes and even audio-visual equipment. The Soko-Filam film market in Zanzibar was launched in 2007 and provides exhibits and displays of film and video productions as well as networking opportunities and forums on improving the regional industry. While potentially encouraging in their operation or volume, these markets demand many of the same decisions about prioritising content by geography or medium or aesthetics faced by festival programmers (Barlet 2007). That said, at both events, as at many other festivals, little coordination occurs between festival programmes and screenings in the marketplace; MICA consequently offers its own screenings separate from FESPACO official offerings.

During the 2005 festival there, the United Nations Development Program (UNDP) sponsored a debate on 'Cinema and Cultural Diversity' that called for cultural policies that 'give priority to dialogue, the sharing of responsibilities and resources, a respect for difference and permanent quest for tolerance' (Sawadago 2005: 6).[7] In 2007, the festival theme was 'African Cinema and Cultural Diversity', and a conference convened to explore the theme's significance produced rather more pointed results. Especially as the two-day gathering came to an end, debates erupted between cultural organisations and producers over the terms of the closing statement. The former group, comprising formal conference presenters, was drawn from UNESCO, the French and Burkinabé governments, and the Organisation Internationale de la Francophonie (OIF). The latter group of producers, speaking mostly from the audience, included filmmakers, who pressed to clarify how 'cultural diversity' could be enabled at the level of resources for production, access to distribution, and provisions for exhibition. It was a discussion that was less about the idea of 'cultural diversity' and more about how, materially, the idea could inform the actually existing conditions of cultural producers.

In Zanzibar, the lag between the establishment of the festival and creation of the market coincided with international debates over cultural policy and the importance of cultural activity as a contributor to social and economic development.[8] ZIFF had from its beginnings demonstrated a commitment in programming to the complicated linkages between cultural production and the social and economic conditions in which they operate. Among other activities, including regular production workshops, the years 2003-2004 saw major efforts to build a technical production infrastructure that would allow ZIFF more effectively to produce its own events and better support other regional cultural producers. By 2006, culture came to be seen squarely as 'an opportunity to engage with the pressing task of rationalizing the role of creativity and innovation in the interest of economic empowerment and social well-being' ('2007-2010 Strategic Plan' 2007: 2).

The festivals pursue institutional alignments in several ways. Organisations increasingly position themselves as regional resource centres by sponsoring production and distribution workshops, providing other technical and capital support, and creating institutional networks and marketplaces. Besides corporate sponsorships, which are often local and take the form of in-kind aid, the most prominent ties have involved funding from NGOs and governmental entities. At FESPACO, longtime festival patrons include the OIF, various UN agencies, like UNESCO and UNDP, and the European Union as well as the Embassies of Denmark, Finland, France, Germany, the Netherlands, Sweden and even Taiwan. ZIFF likewise relies on the Ford Foundation, Hivos and the Prince Claus Fund as well as the Embassies of Sweden, Finland and France. For independent festival organisations like ZIFF, without an endowment or other proprietary holdings (like equipment or real estate), the challenge of raising new funding for each successive festival grows more pressing with the passing of time.

As noted, FESPACO is unusual in being an office of the Ministry of Culture of Burkina Faso. The support of home governments for other festivals, including ZIFF, is more varied. Generally speaking, they promote local creative industries, local or regional film and media trade, and tourism. In Zanzibar, local government agencies and officials have been regularly represented, both on the festival board and ceremonially at the event, though the organisation has suffered from what Martin Mhando cites as 'the minimal [financial] support of the governments of Zanzibar and Tanzania towards culture' (2007: 51). To whatever degree, government involvement in festivals is often linked to the events' complex articulations of collective values and cultural claims. That these events imagine and promote cultural ideas that may or may not correspond to those favoured by politicians is therefore a potential conflict of interest. Put simply, the very exploration and fostering of specific cultural formations, like Pan-Africanism or the Dhow, may not correspond to government positions or priorities.

A further potential conflict between festivals and governments is the link that many organisers seek to develop between the institutionalisation of cinematic and media activities and more overtly social, economic and political agendas. Cast under the rubric of development, the much-discussed issues of shared Pan-African or Dhow identity and community are thus brought to bear on the establishment of open, locally centred and accessible markets and similarly open, self-determined and participatory politics. This broader vision of development becomes a basis for the exploration of advancement of democracy in the region. It accords with turn-of-the-century models of public life and politics that yoke together elements from different theories of cultural production and, specifically, the media in what has been called 'complex democracy' (Habermas 1996; Crossley and Roberts 2004). The communicative and participatory activities of the festivals mobilise, in ways both informal and institutional, what Nicholas Garnham terms 'a perspective from which to think about the problem of democracy in the modern world' (2007: 203).

The two African festivals have used film as the basis for interrogating and developing a culturally-based perspective on the problem of democracy. In other words, they have propounded ideas of local or regional culture – grounded in film but embracing other cultural forms and practices as well as social and political values – as the basis of a socially organised, discursive and communicative realm. Moreover, the festivals can be seen as part of a process of thinking about the relationship between cultural production and democracy. If the geographical dimensions of this enterprise have been subject to particular scrutiny, so has the debate about its institutional or structural bases. How individual film programmes, other festival events, or organisers participate in culture is one question that has been variously addressed; as important but often less directly engaged is how festival activities relate to economic and political conditions. This latter question turns on the roles of film and related media productions, diverse voices and social institutions, and local and regional markets in the ongoing development of democracy in the host countries and surrounding regions.

The cohesion of a given culture, as the conceptual basis for imagining a regional formation and taking social action, is consequently not just a matter of festival self-definition but of the social relations, economic and political institutions, and mediating structures that sustain the events. In Ouagadougou and Zanzibar, using film to represent culture, both on-screen and as a public event, has occurred with uneven success. Yet by persistently employing cinema as the basis of re-shaping regional cultural formations, the festivals do important political work. Particularly through the ongoing formulation of actual and imagined communities and markets, they not only aid cultural production but engage the meaning of democracy at home and throughout the world.

Notes

[1] This essay reworks material previously published in 'Ten Years of 'Dhow culture': The Evolution of an Idea at the Zanzibar International Film Festival, 1998-2007', *ZIFF Journal*, 4 (2008).

[2] The festival was made an organ of the Ministry of Culture of Upper Volta in 1972.

[3] ZIFF was chartered, as a non-governmental and non-profit organisation, in March 1998. The first Zanzibar International Film Festival event was held from 11-18 July.

[4] Participants included Salaam, DK (Denmark); Mexican Embassy, Nairobi; ZIFF Slavery Films (with UNESCO); M-NET (South Africa); Buster/DFI (Denmark); SABC (South Africa); Film Resource Unit (FRU)/SACOD (South Africa Communications for Development).

[5] A partial list would include the first Kenyan International Film Festival (KIFF), held in Nairobi, 9-14 October 2006; the 4th Amakula Kampala International Film Festival, 1-13 May 2007 (http://www.amakula.com); the 1st Amani Great Lakes Film Festival launched in Kigali, 20-27 July 2007 (http://www.amanifilmfestival.org); the second edition of Lola Kenya Screen, presented in Nairobi, 6-11 August 2007 (http://www.lolakenyascreen.or.ke);

and the 3rd Rwanda International Film Festival, 16-30 March 2008 (www.rwandafilmfestival.org). Also worth mentioning is the parallel emergence of film festivals in other Dhow countries, such as the four Muscat Film Festivals held in Oman since 2001 (www.omanfilm.org).

[6] Among relevant possibilities cited in discussions of Cannes is that film festivals are 'enactment[s] of a funerary ritual which celebrates the disappearance of cinema in favour of other means of disseminating images' and, presumably, cultural materials and memories, more generally [my translation] (Ethis 2001: 68).

[7] 'Cinema and Cultural Diversity' took place on 2 March 2005, in Ouagadougou.

[8] A shift occurred at the time in Dhow culture discourse toward 'producing frameworks of cultural industry'; as Martin Mhando wrote, 'cultural diversity is the theory and the cultural industries is the product' (2007: 48).

Works Cited

Acland, Charles (2003) *Screen Traffic: Movies, Multiplexes, and Global Culture.* Durham: Duke University Press.

Adewara, Bola (1999) 'We Are not Interested in FESPACO Now', *Vanguard*, 30 May, 30.

Apter, Andrew (2005) *The Pan-African Nation: Oil and the Spectacle of Culture in Nigeria.* Chicago: University of Chicago Press.

Bakari, Imruh (2004a) 'Opening', 'Dhow Culture and the Visual Imagination', A Report of the Symposium, Mazsons Hotel, Stone Town – Zanzibar, 25-26 September. ZIFF Archives, AA/219.

____ (2004b) 'ZIFF Festival of the Dhow Countries 2004: Exploring the Currents, Feeling the Winds', *ZIFF Journal*, 1, 1.

Barlet, Olivier (2003) 'FESPACO 2003: The Onus of Cinematic Creation', *Africultures*, 1 May. On-line. Available. HTTP: http://www.africultures.com/php/index.php?nav=article&no=5672 (15 Feb 2009).

____ (2007) 'Cinema: An Audience but No Market,' *Africultures*, 23 February. On-line. Available. HTTP: http://www.africultures.com/php/index.php?nav=article&no=5851 (15 Feb 2009).

Bell, Catherine (1997) *Ritual: Perspectives and Dimensions.* New York: Oxford University Press.

Buch-Jepsen, Neils (2003) 'Fespaco and the Transformation of Pan-African Film Promotion,' *Senses of Cinema*, 26. On-line. Available. HTTP: http://archive.sensesofcinema.com/contents/festivals/03/26/fespaco.html (15 Feb 2009).

Two African Film Festivals

'Cinéma africain aujourd'hui' [Special Supplement] (2007), *Cahiers du cinéma*, 620.

Crossley, Nick and John Michael Roberts (eds) (2004) *After Habermas: New Perspectives on the Public Sphere*. Oxford: Blackwell.

de Valck, Marijke (2007) *Film Festivals: From European Geopolitics to Global Cinephilia*. Amsterdam: University of Amsterdam Press.

Deckard, Sharae (2006) '"Dhow Aesthetics": Negotiating the Global and the Local; The 9th Zanzibar International Film Festival, 14-25 July, 2006', *Senses of Cinema*, 41. On-line. Available.
HTTP: http://www.sensesofcinema.com/contents/festivals/06/41/zanzibar-iff-2006.html (15 Feb 2009).

Deutsch, Jan-Georg (2008) 'Imaginaries of the Past: Nostalgia and Social Conflict in Zanzibar, c.1950-2000', *ZIFF Journal*, 4.

Diawara, Manthia (1992) *African Cinema: Politics and Culture*. Bloomington: Indiana University Press.

____ (1993) 'Report from FESPACO: Recovery vs. Nostalgia', *Black Film Review*, 7, 1, 22-5.

Ethis, Emmanuel (2006) *Sociologie du cinéma et de ses publics*. Paris: Armand Colin.

____ (ed.) (2001) *Aux Marches du palais: le Festival de Cannes sous le regard des sciences sociales*. Paris: La Documentation française.

'Festival Overview' (1999) Festival of the Dhow Countries, 2-10 July, Zanzibar.

Garnham, Nicholas (2007) 'Habermas and the Public Sphere', *Global Media and Communication* 3, 2.

Habermas, Jürgen (1996) *Between Facts and Norms*, trans. William Rehg. Cambridge, MA: The MIT Press.

Harvey, Sylvia (2006) 'Introduction: Trading Culture in the Age of Cultural Industries', in Sylvia Harvey (ed.) *Trading Culture: Global Traffic and Local Cultures in Film and Television*. Eastliegh: John Libbey.

Mazdon, Lucy (2006) 'The Cannes Film Festival as Transnational Space,' *Post-Script*, 25, 2, 19-30. On-line. Available.
HTTP: http://galenet.galegroup.com (15 Feb 2009).

Mhando, Martin (2007) 'Zanzibar International Film Festival: A History, A Vision', in Fatma Aloo (ed.) *10 Years of ZIFF*. Zanzibar: Gallery Publications-ZIFF.

Roberts, Martin (1999) '*Baraka*: World Cinema and the Global Culture Industry', *Cinema Journal*, 22, 1.

Sawadago, Poussi (2005) 'Cultural Diversity Explained', *FESPACO News*, 6, 3 March, 6.

Slocum, J. David (2007) Interview with Martin Mhando, Zanzibar, 14 March.

Stenou, Katerina (ed.) (2004) *UNESCO and the Issue of Cultural Diversity: Review and Strategy, 1946-2004*, rev. version. Paris: UNESCO.

Stringer, Julian (2001) 'Global Cities and the International Film Festival Economy', in Mark Shiel and Tony Fitzmaurice (eds) *Cinema and the City: Film and Urban Societies in a Global Context*. London: Blackwell.

Ukadike, Nwachukwu Frank (1994) *Black African Cinema.* Indianapolis: Indiana University Press.

'Zanzibar International Film Festival: 2007-2010 Strategic Plan' (2007) ZIFF Archives; electronic file, no locator.

'ZIFF Jury Report' (1998). ZIFF Archives.

Part 3

Dispatches from the Festival World

Chapter Ten

Widescreen on Film Festivals[1]

Mark Cousins

The London Film Festival has just celebrated its fiftieth year. The Edinburgh International Film Festival was 60 this summer. Cannes in 60 next May. Venice was 63 this year. The film festival regulation body FIAPF (Federation Internationale des Associations de Producteurs de Film) reckons there are 700 of them in total, the *New York Times* claims there are over 1,000. The numbers have rocketed in the last decade.

Film festivals have caught on like never before. They are a cultural idea that is spreading like a Richard Dawkins meme. Venice, Edinburgh, Cannes and London are right to celebrate their longevity but as the elite of the festival circuit clink another glass of champagne at another party to salute a venerable old festival or the launch of a new one, it would be no surprise if their smiles were a little strained. Masked by glamour and ubiquity, the world of film festivals is, in fact, in crisis. There are too many of them, they are too political, and too colluding.

At least 3,000 films are made each year. Film festivals are the shop windows for such production – visible and glamorous but powerless in that they (mostly) only *respond* to it. Since, at most, only 150 of the annual 3,000 films are of real artistic merit, this means that the thousand shop windows need to fight tooth and claw to showcase the best. This is what happens. When I was director of Edinburgh, I'd frequently lock horns with the then director of London. Cannes tends its relationship with Pedro Almodovar with great care but if he doesn't win the Palm d'Or there soon, might he switch allegiances to Venice? Venice has, for years, been the festival of choice for Woody Allen but might Toronto or Berlin be making approaches behind the scenes?

To make things worse, FIAPF operates a pointless 'A List' of the 12 festivals it thinks deserve top ranking: Berlin, Mar Del Plata, Cannes, Shanghai, Moscow, Karlovy Vary, Locarno, Montreal, Venice, San Sebastian, Tokyo and Cairo. Two of these are inferior festivals and the omissions are glaring – no Sundance, London, Rotterdam or Toronto, for example – but to qualify, each of the 12 must have a competition section containing at least 14 *world-premiered* films. So, each year, the A listers alone have at least 168 slots for new films to fill which means, in theory, swallowing up all 150 of the good movies of the year, and some. This really makes the gloves come off.

That the film festival circuit is political with a big P, as well as crowded, will surprise no-one. The Italian fascist government meddled with the programming of the Venice film festival (launched in 1934) way back in 1938. Such interference was the reason why Cannes was founded, in 1939. In 1995 and 1996 a major start-up festival in Prague tried to replace Karlovy Vary (established in 1946 in the province of Bohemia) as the main film event in the region. Karlovy Vary, the challengers contended, was too tainted by its past as the main showcase for Soviet era cinema. Also it was argued, as scholar Dina Iordanova has shown, that the newly blossoming Czech capital would, symbolically, be a better location and would deliver bigger audiences (2008). Centre-provincial political tension also explains the recent spats between Montreal's Festival of World Cinema, and that of Toronto; the edginess between the Mexican festivals in Mexico City, Guadalajara and Morelia; and the friction between the start up Roman festival and Venice.

Such cat-fights are exacerbated by the fact that lots of public money is at stake. Few film festivals raise more than 20 per cent of their income from box office, most much less than this. Most of the funding comes from the public sector or sponsorship. Of the thousand festivals, a handful of the biggest have budgets upwards of £10m, two of the UK's festivals cost over £1 million and the smallest are in the £10,000 bracket. If we guess that the average budget is, say, £400,000, then the total cost of the circuit is £400 million. This figure excludes the costs of the trips of the professionals (PR people, journalists, etc), who attend. Perhaps 40 per cent of this £400,000 comes from the private sector, which leaves £240 million from the public purse.

How is this spend justified? The festivals argue that they are net contributors to their local economies (mostly in the service sectors), that they raise the international profile of their cities, that they enhance the cultural life of their citizens, and that they develop audiences' taste for non-mainstream cinema. All true, but in the spread of the film festival meme in the last decade, the first two reasons – the economic and PR ones – have taken precedent and come to define what a film festival is. They exist now, and are everywhere, because economic development departments and tourism honchos understand them. That's fine, but the implications are significant.

Film festivals grew out of the film society movement in the 1920s. The founders of these, and the first film festivals, wanted, in the words of Marco Müller, the current director of Venice, to 'reveal what the markets hide' (2000). I have argued before that the international film industry is a market boosted, as if by steroids, by Hollywood's massive advertising spend on its own product. The film festival circuit is, then, a counter market, itself boosted by a steroid injection of £240 million annually. Toronto Film Festival's Piers Handling called this counter-market an 'alternative distribution network' (in Turan 2002: 8). In his book *European Cinema: Face to Face with Hollywood*,

Thomas Elsaesser says that this network has created 'symbolic agoras of a new democracy' (2005: 104).

Müller, Handling and Elsaesser each think that the purpose of a film festival is to act counter to the mainstream, cookie-cutter cinema that prevails in most parts of the world but is this really how festivals now operate? When the latest Star Wars film premiered at Cannes, and the latest in the Matrix franchise, too, and Troy and The DaVinci Code, for example, it was clear that the festival was spending some of its (public) money to subsidise Hollywood publicity budgets. 'You fly over Tom/Brad/Keanu and we'll pick up his hotel bill and host the media circus'. That's the way festivals work and, to an extent, have always done so. If that's what has to happen to create the buzz, to draw the world's media which will then, because they are there, cover the alternative films on offer and, so, reveal not only the market but what it hides, its counter, then fine. But festivals collude too much these days. They seem to have forgotten that their primary function must be discovery and revelation. Yes, they will say, but how do we do so when there are so many of us fighting over so few exciting films? The answer is that festivals have never only been about recent films. They have always, also, had retrospectives, masterclasses, tributes, etc. What is infuriating, and where they aren't warranting their public sector subventions, is that so many of them present retrospectives of, or tributes to, filmmakers, genres or themes that are already well established, part of the canon. Another Cocteau season? Another Bergman or Kurosawa retrospective? This conservative, blinkered programming is the heart of the contemporary film festival problem. They all do retrospectives of first world directors but almost none is looking at, for example, African filmmakers, or the great Indian directors beyond the obvious one – Satyajit Ray. If film festivals work with, and enjoy the glitter of, the cinematic mainstream they should also, as a matter of principle and to justify their existence, look at the past of film culture in the broadest geographical terms. Only then will they reveal what the market hides.

Note

[1] This essay was originally printed in *Prospect,* issue 129 (December, 2006). It is reprinted with permission from the author and *Prospect.*

Works Cited

Elsaesser, Thomas (2005) 'Film Festival Networks: The New Topographies of Cinema in Europe', *European Cinema: Face to Face with Hollywood.* Amsterdam: Amsterdam University Press, 82-108.

Iordanova, Dina (2008) 'Showdown of the Festivals: Clashing Entrepreneurships and Post-Communist Management of Culture', *Film International*, 4, 5, 23, 25-38.

Müller, Marco (2000) On the Role of Festivals', *Kerala International Film Festival.* On-line. Available
HTTP: http://www.keralafilm.com/iffk5/chatmuller.html (2 October 2005).

Turan, Kenneth (2002) *Sundance to Sarajevo: Film Festivals and the World They Made.* Berkeley: University of California Press.

Chapter Eleven

Coming to a Server near You: The Film Festival in the Age of Digital Reproduction[1]

Nick Roddick a.k.a. Sight & Sound's Mr. Busy

The following piece is made up mainly of excerpts from a column which I have been writing in *Sight & Sound* for almost 20 years. It is called 'The Business' and is based on the belief that *Sight & Sound* readers need to know about the business of film as well as the art of cinema. Given its genesis, what follows is not so much a sustained argument as a series of apercus which, while straining for the dubious status of generalised truth, belong pretty much to the time at which they were written. The columns quoted all come from the past half-decade and I have included them, in an edited form, in the order in which they were written, occasionally clarifying points left unclear by the pressure of monthly deadlines.

The excerpts all have to do with film festivals and the way in which they have become an integral part of the film business. I have not tried to reshape them – columns have a structure of their own – but a through-argument does emerge: broadly, that the role played by festivals in showcasing non-studio films and hopefully shepherding them into distribution is under threat from the digital technology which will soon come to dominate the film distribution process.

Not so long ago, I had lunch with the Editor of *Sight & Sound*, who has never tried to influence what I write. But if he could, I asked, what would he do? Well, he said, you might occasionally be a little more optimistic. Looking through the five columns that follow – dating from April 2005 to February 2009 – I see what he means. But then those four years have been largely downhill when it comes to the adaptability of the film business and the standing of film festivals.

Let's start with some thoughts following the Berlin Film Festival in 2005.

Trapped in a Taxi (April 2005)

Film festivals are like freebies: the people who would really benefit from them don't often get the chance to go, while those of us who do go seem to become increasingly jaded about the whole experience. I know this because, whenever I have written a piece in a festival daily about some glitch in the system, some inexplicable failure on the part of the festival organisers to pick the right films, serve the right kind of wine or prevent the rain from falling, people stop me and say, 'How true!'. If, on the other hand, I write a piece about how great the films are and how smoothly the event seems to be functioning, the silence is deafening.

Since festivals are now an essential part of the world's film distribution system, they increasingly raise the question of why this system works so badly. Anywhere other than in the Latin Quarter of Paris, the amount of cinema on offer is minimal compared with the selection of books you can find in your local supermarket. We seem to accept as normal that there should be, in most major towns (like my own, which is not London), two multi-screen cinemas where the only competition is between the decor (sixties modern versus eighties modern) and the prices on the concession stands (post-post-modern, in terms of both money and nutritional value). The films they show are, meanwhile, the same, with variations so slight as to be imperceptible.

Maybe, as *The Jam* memorably pointed out in a song called 'That's Entertainment', 'the public wants what the public gets'. But the public is more diverse than we realise: we generalise about its taste at our peril. Take the two taxi drivers I encountered, arriving at and leaving the Berlin Film Festival last month. The first, who picked me up from the airport, had heard that Jerry Lewis was coming to Berlin. I expressed some doubt about this. 'No, no'. He insisted. 'Jerry is coming. Don't you think he's a genius?' Sure enough, a few days later, there was the old droll, gurning his way up the red carpet as though it was still 1955. But my surprise was no so much that the Berlinale would disinter this dubious Hollywood icon, but that the taxi driver, who must have been in his 40s, not only remembered but idolised him.

Then, on the way home, I was delivered a long lecture by a quite different taxi driver on just how limited the choice of films was in German cinemas, how all you could see was the big studio pictures which were about nothing and certainly had nothing to do with Germany and how he had a 15-year-old son who hated those films, too. It was a refreshing change from the xenophobic diatribes, which pass for conversation in a London taxi. And the driver certainly had a point: for a Berlin cinemagoer no longer of student age and habits, it is often hard, sometimes uncomfortable and occasionally impossible to connect with anything much beyond a dubbed version of *Miss Congeniality 2* (John Pasquin, Australia/USA, 2005).

Festivals, meanwhile, are overflowing with adventurous and demanding new works, often made with generous helpings of public money and thus intended, one assumes, for the public. There certainly appears to be a demand for this kind of film in Berlin, to judge by the two- and three-hour queues at the public ticket offices (though what taxi driver could afford three hours out of his day to queue for a movie ticket?). But if this demand is there, why cannot it be met on a regular basis? After all, against all the laws of supply, demand and price sensitivity, organic produce is one of the fastest growing areas in the supermarket business. Might the same not happen to art cinema, running a similar gamut from the macrobiotic (the films of Alexander Sokurov) via exotically tasty items (the films, say, of Wong Kar-wai) through to misleadingly labelled junk food like much off-Hollywood product?

Well maybe. Except the picture has recently grown muddy. A decade and a half ago, there was arthouse (cheap, challenging and with a decent chance of earning its limited investment back from small cinema circuits and adventurous TV programmers); and there was mainstream, which was expensive, reassuring and mass-marketed.

Then came crossover: films with arthouse potential that could appeal to a larger audience - like, say, *Wo Hu Cang Long* (*Crouching Tiger, Hidden Dragon*, Ang Lee, China/Hong Kong/Taiwan /USA, 2000). With larger audiences came money to make bigger films, and a whole new network of producers and sales agents whose behaviour became more and more like the big boys at the studios (who often paid their salaries). And the resulting films, often introduced to the world at Sundance, look more and more like studio films. To look at the Market in Berlin this year [this was 2005, remember: it's no longer true in 2009] was to be confronted with something akin to the Milan Fashion Week for films: a launch pad for ambitious new talents who could (albeit not in quite the same way) also feed the mainstream. Those producers – like, say, Anatole Dauman and Pierre Braunberger, who were midwives to the talent of the French New Wave – have been replaced by middlemen who trade in non-mainstream product.

This may be no bad thing for the film business qua business. But it is effectively closing the door on the kinds of film-making that reinvigorated European cinema in the 1940s (in Italy), the 1950s (UK), the 1960s (France) and the 1970s (Germany). There was a cinema which did not need – and, more importantly, could not afford – the middleman.

I'm far from seeing a solution to all this. But I think I really do begin to see a problem.

Meanwhile, a couple of years down the track...

A Walk on the Wild Side (April 2007)

There is a narrow line of cobblestones set into the streets and pavements between the Potsdamer Platz, headquarters of the Berlin International Film Festival, and the Martin-Gropius-Bau (MGB), home to the Festival's fast-growing European Film Market.

Chapter Eleven

A lot of people attending the Berlinale have probably never noticed the cobblestones, which retrace the line of the Wall, during whose 28-year existence the Potsdamer Platz was a weed-strewn wasteland and the MGB a boarded-up ruin. It is now almost a generation since the Wall came down and, after the public relations triumph of the 2006 World Cup, history is no longer a skeleton in the closet: it's just part of the overall tapestry of modern Germany. The Wall – the longest remaining section of which still stands just east of the MGB – was unmissable. Nowadays, however, it is woven discreetly into the landscape.

But, if it was easy to overlook the line of cobblestones, it was, last month, much harder to miss a more temporary reminder of changing times erected on a piece of wasteground half-way between the Potsdamer Platz and the MGB: a brightly lit Portacabin housing French production and sales company Wild Bunch. Even the huge, brightly lit billboard at the corner of the site, which a week earlier had carried an ad for the imminent erection of an architecturally challenging if functionally dubious apartment block, had been replaced by a poster for Wild Bunch's big title of spring 2007, *Molière* (Laurent Tirard, France, 2007). The Portacabin was the company's 'office' for the duration of the Berlinale.

It wasn't always going to be thus. Up until three weeks before the Festival started, Wild Bunch were all set to be housed along with their fellow sales companies in a spacious, elegantly designed stand in the MGB, confident that their big film – a colourful romp charting the life and loves of the playwright before he actually 'became' *Molière* – would screen in competition in Berlin. It didn't, and the sequence of events which led Wild Bunch to opt for the Portacabin provides a more than usually public illustration of the fractious interdependency between the European film business and the continent's larger film festivals, which regular readers of this column will recognise as a recurrent theme.

Wild Bunch was originally an offshoot of French cable TV giant Canal+, but broke free a few years back. As the name implies, the company likes to think of itself as a maverick – 'often controversial, always provocative, our line-up stands as our statement of intent', declares its website. But, in truth, it is well on its way to becoming a fully integrated, solidly financed movie company on the scale of, say, Pathé. Its line-up encompasses such films as *Panj é Asr* (*At Five in the Afternoon*, Samira Makhmalbaf, France/Iran, 2003), *Irréversible* (*Irreversible*, Gaspar Noé, France, 2002) and *Laberinto del Fauno, El* (*Pan's Labyrinth*, Guillermo del Toro, Mexico/Spain/USA, 2006) but also *Molière*, Steven Soderbergh's *Che* (France/Spain/USA, 2008) and the latest Chabrol film. As the slate – and the budgets – grow larger, the 'maverick' stance has of necessity given way to a more business-like approach.

Molière, a successor to *Cyrano de Bergerac* (Jean-Paul Rappeneau, France, 1990) (or perhaps as a French *Shakespeare in Love* [John Madden, UK/USA, 1998]), did OK at home but was always going to need a leg-up from a major festival if it was to achieve international success. And Berlin was always going to be its shop-window of choice. All this began to unravel when the Berlinale turned the film down. To make matters worse, Wild Bunch got the news not directly but through government-backed promotional agency Unifrance, which is the cinematic equivalent of being dumped by text message. Unifrance pulled whatever strings were available, but could only get an invitation for *Molière* to open the Festival's Panorama section – to play, that is, in the Coca-Cola League when it was expecting the Premiership. Much miffed, Wild Bunch withdrew the film, cancelled its Market stand, declared a total embargo on its titles being shown in any Berlin festival section and generally threw whatever other toys it could find out of the pram.

Sales chief Vincent Maraval told *Screen International* that, while he remained in contact with Cannes programme chief Thierry Frémaux and his Venice equivalent, Marco Müller, 'all year', he had had no real contact with Berlinale director Dieter Kosslick: hell, he didn't even have Kosslick's mobile number. In other words, it wasn't that the old boys network had broken down: it was that Kosslick – normally gregariousness incarnate – wasn't part of it. Or not part of the French one, anyway.

'When we go to a festival', added Maraval, getting down to the real point, 'it is part of our promotional strategy'. Yes, Vincent, I'm sure it is, but that's not really what festivals are there for. Except, of course, that festivals have been supping with the devil for years: trade-offs of one kind or another are part and parcel of being a festival. Was *The Da Vinci Code* (Ron Howard, USA, 2006) really the peak of cinematic achievement that its opening slot at Cannes last year might suggest? Of course not. But it got Tom Hanks on the red carpet – and alongside a rising French star (Audrey Tautou) to boot.

Festivals, remember, need films in just the same way that films need festivals. Each exploits the other, but it's a relationship that, like the cobblestones in the street, should be a discreet part of the mesh that links the business and the event – a truth that rarely dares to speak its name. It took a pissed-off Frenchman to out it.

Top Down or Up from the Roots? (October 2007)

The UK's film distribution system is a bit like the British railway network – a highly ambitious and brilliantly engineered infrastructure developed a long time ago to serve a world which no longer exists. The big difference between the two is that film distribution didn't need a Beeching to axe its unprofitable but socially useful branch-lines: economics achieved the same result, with regional and suburban cinemas beginning the long, slow slide from Bingo hall to carpet warehouse in the 1960s. Ever since, the distribution set-up in the UK has struggled to cope with the organisational equivalent of point failures, leaves on the line and signals stuck on red.

No matter: shit happens. The train replaced the stage-coach much as cinema replaced theatre and television edged out cinema. Now, each is struggling to compete in a world where the private is replacing the public.

Much as the car has taken over from the train, so home entertainment in all its multiple-delivery formats is threatening the existence of cinemas and the hegemony of broadcast television. More and more, we want to be one-to-one with our entertainment.

From the consumer's point of view – that is to say, yours and mine – this may not be such a bad thing. But one thing is certain: digital distribution will drastically reduce one element in any film's P&A costs – the 'P' part, which stands for prints (the 'A – do I have to tell you this? – stands for advertising). A 35 mm print costs around a grand; a digital one costs virtually nothing. 35 mm prints have to be shipped physically around the country in great big heavy metal boxes that take a good 24 hours to arrive. Digital copies can be sent for nothing by fibre optic or satellite (giving them a much reduced carbon footprint) and are delivered immediately.

The industry could react to this in two ways: it could take advantage of the new delivery platforms to cash in on the profile of blockbusters in their first week, when all the press and TV coverage happens; or it could use the new technology to offer a much more diverse viewing experience. It's either *Transformers* (Michael Bay, USA, 2007) starting every 10 minutes in Screens 1-10; or it's *Transformers* in Screen 1 and nine different films in Screens 2-10. Chances are, it will be the former. I say that not because I'm cynical, but because that's the way it's always gone before – and because the '*Transformers* every 10 minutes' model is actually a direct quote from a U.S. exhibitor passing on what his audiences told him they wanted.

But there is another kind of evidence, not recorded with the slavish attention to detail the studios devote to weekend gross reports, but compelling nonetheless. My experience at a string of film festivals over the summer – three in Eastern Europe (Cluj, Karlovy Vary and Motovun), one in Scotland (go on, guess), one in Canada (Toronto) – is that there is a vast young audience with a very healthy appetite for the kinds of films that don't get shown in multiplexes.

In the case of Motovun, an idyllic, boutiquey kind of festival held in a tiny Croatian hilltop town, some 10,000 young people from all over the region camp at the foot of the hill and pack out the afternoon and evening screenings (they also party all night, but that doesn't stop them from turning up for the next day's screenings). Festivals, as Bill Clinton might have said, are about the films, stupid. Multiplexes increasingly strike me as being about something else.

Digital Dreams (February 2008)

I seemed to go to an awful lot of film festivals last year. I don't 'do' as many as some of my colleagues, for whom it has become a lifestyle choice. But I go often enough to upset the dog, who does a passable impersonation of Little Orphan Annie every time a suitcase appears.

The Film Festival in the Age of Digital Reproduction

Some of the trips were undoubtedly worthwhile, artistically speaking: Cannes had a vintage year and Toronto revealed hints of a new golden age. Some festivals were fun, especially the inimitable Motovun on its Croatian hilltop, and Bergen, which has a student audience big enough to make much bigger events jealous. And then there was Cairo, a shambling fiasco of an event that has no trouble coming up with a fleet of black Mercedes to ferry guests through the city's entertaining traffic, but can't seem to get the right film on screen at the right time. Cairo's 'A' status is the scandal of the Festival circuit – and one that everyone seems too scared to address.

Film festivals may not register much on the average *Sight & Sound* reader's radar. But they are certainly a growth industry. There are already over 700 of them, at least 50 of which are important outside the place they happen. New, high-profile events with budgets in the $10 million range have kicked off in the last two or three years in Rome, Dubai and Abu Dhabi, each eagerly attended by senior film-industry executives whose flights and hotel rooms are paid under the belief that their presence will generate business. And the film industry, already over-populated with flight-and-hotel-room junkies, plays happily along, its execs sometimes putting in an appearance on a hastily convened panel to discuss the burning issues *du jour*.

Right now this issue seems to be digital distribution (I've been on four such panels in the past three months). That film festivals should be so interested in digital distribution is not surprising, since they see it as a key part of their future – a development that will justify their overtures to 'the business' by making them ever more central to its strategy. I'm not so sure.

As cinema moves into its long-tail era, it's likely that cinephiles will directly access the titles they have read about in magazines or heard praised on speciality websites, while bigscreen outlets (i.e. cinemas) will restrict themselves to 'event' movies. In this process, festivals reckon they will become the initial platform necessary to set all of this in motion – that, at any rate, was the accepted wisdom on the festival circuit last year. Festivals clearly regard the whole digital business as an opportunity rather than a threat, because they believe they will be the place where the buzz begins.

Hollywood, meanwhile, is still largely in denial: the Motion Picture Association of America, which represents the major studios, is so fixated on catching and locking up those who illegally download its movies that it hasn't even started thinking about how it could help its members profit from the new technology. A defensive strategy rules, and it will be a long time yet before Hollywood switches over to seeing the technology of digital distribution as an opportunity rather than a threat.

But are the festivals going too far the other way? Makers of short films have already embraced the net as the prime outlet for their work, preferring to be downloaded for free, even pirated, rather than ignored. The only barrier to this process spreading to non-mainstream feature films is technological, and even there it is a question of the development of existing technology rather than a whole new breakthrough. As soon as a download box is developed that can link the web direct to your TV (or wall-mounted flat screen) and speakers; as soon as it becomes possible to download a feature film in three minutes without excessive compression and at a reasonable price; and as soon as doing all this becomes no more difficult than operating a normal remote, then most of our entertainment needs, audio or visual, are likely to be met online.

Festivals are kidding themselves if they think they will remain the key to this process. The current arthouse pantheon – Almodóvar, Wong Kar-wai, Haneke – was certainly consecrated by the festival circuit. But the next generation's pantheon could well by-pass festivals altogether, using social-networking sites for awareness-creation, and relying on broadband technology for distribution. When that happens, all the free flights and hotel rooms in Rome are not going to persuade any serious executive to spend one week in another town. They will be too busy trying to monetise the product flow.

Digital Nightmares (February 2009)

A couple of months ago in this column, I quoted an example of how a sharp decline in house-building had knock-on effects in brick-making, clay-production and clay-mining. Here's a more recent example, but this time from the entertainment business. As you probably know, cross-ownership between film and television companies is labyrinthine and widespread; Rupert Murdoch owns Fox along with a string of TV stations and newspapers. The American TV network ABC and Disney are joined at the hip. So are Paramount and Viacom (BET Networks, MTV Networks). And so on. Well, TV viewer numbers – and therefore TV advertising revenue – in the U.S. are shrinking on an almost daily basis. While almost 50 per cent of all U.S. households watched 1954's highest-rated show, *I Love Lucy*, a mere 12.7 per cent tuned into 2008's top show, CSI.

And then there's there the little problem of Detroit. The U.S. car industry, as you've probably heard, is in deep trouble. Now, automobile advertising has been the mainstay of U.S. television since the late 1940s: indeed, the very notion of a new television 'season' starting in September can be traced to the fact that September was when Detroit launched its new models. Take away car advertising, add a depression and you have a close to perfect storm, not just for U.S. television but for the worldwide filmed entertainment business in general. Few are the countries whose multiplexes are not kept full, whose technicians are not kept in employment and whose facilities companies are not kept equipped by major Hollywood movies. And few are the Hollywood companies not impacted by the problems of television.

All of which suggests that the entertainment industry is currently poised like Eddie the Eagle at the top of the slope, nervously surveying the tips of its skis while wondering whether it still knows what to do – and indeed whether there is a landing area at the end of the ramp.

The Film Festival in the Age of Digital Reproduction

In this turbulent conjuncture what, I wonder, will happen to the industry's posh relation: film festivals? Already, one small but respected U.S. regional event – the Jackson's Hole Film Festival – has thrown in the towel, citing the increasingly ubiquitous trend of vanishing sponsors. How much this matters to people outside Wyoming is a moot point. But a bit of a ring-round among people who don't want to be quoted suggests that a 30 per cent drop in film festivals' sponsorship revenue next year is as good as it's going to get. And that means either more public funding (yeah, right) or cutbacks.

But let's go back for a moment to Jackson's Hole. In the wildly optimistic atmosphere of just a few months ago, Wyoming's loss would have been given scant attention. But, even without what has happened since, surely it's time to start asking ourselves just what all these film festivals are for if not, in that particular instance, the people of Wyoming?

Well, film festivals are sexy, which is what attracts city, regional and national tourist promotion agencies: come to our town, see some films, spot some stars, spend some money. But the international film industry also has a lot to do with the insane proliferation of overlapping events that has characterised the past decade. Like everything else in the (hopefully now defunct) free market era, film festivals have become commodified, their success measured, not just by the quality of the films they show, nor even the number of tickets they sell (in Cannes, public tickets are not even available), but by the amount of business they generate, the film sales they rack up and the industry executives they attract.

In realistic terms, there are between six and 10 film festivals around the world (I'd say Sundance, Rotterdam, Berlin, Cannes, Venice, Telluride, Toronto and Pusan) which really do 'matter' to the film business. And yet a couple of dozen others (at least) aspire to such significance, often to the detriment of what should be their primary aim: providing local audiences, from Jackson's Hole to Jihlava, with a chance to see and celebrate the kind of cinema that falls outside the everyday fare of the multiplex.

That's why they're called festivals. Surely it's about time we got back on track and stopped pretending they are cornerstones of the film business. Not, I suspect, that there's going to be much choice.

Note

[1]   This essay contains column entries originally printed in *Sight & Sound*. They are reprinted with permission from the author and *Sight & Sound*.

Chapter Twelve

Programming Balkan Films at the Thessaloniki International Film Festival

Dimitris Kerkinos

Thessaloniki International Film Festival in the Context of the Festival Circuit

The Thessaloniki International Film Festival (TIFF), like most other film festivals, functions as an alternative network of distribution, screening films that otherwise wouldn't have been seen outside their country of origin. Although some films manage to find distribution after their presentation in a festival, most art-house films don't, due to the dominance of American and European mainstream films. This is definitely a very important reason for the existence of a film festival, especially in a country that belongs to the periphery of the worldwide cinematic industry.

In this sense, the proliferation of festivals around the world is a positive phenomenon, as they give the opportunity to people around the world to see films that would not find theatrical distribution in their country. Another positive aspect of this is that nowadays, a lot of festivals are specialising their programming to accommodate films that address very special audiences and which would not normally be screened in 'mainstream' festivals. Such 'specialised' festivals are very interesting and useful, working independently and, at the same time, complementarily to the 'official' festivals.

On the other hand, with such a proliferation it's inevitable that the competition between festivals has increased dramatically, especially between those which share similar profiles. This is the case with TIFF's discovery competition section, which focuses on first and second films, something common nowadays to a lot of festivals. Such festivals have a more difficult task, as they have to find good films which have not been presented outside their country or screened in the official sections of other international festivals. In this respect, you could say that 'discovery festivals' also give another opportunity to films that weren't selected by the major festivals and, as a result, they fit into the festival network. When it comes to programming a tribute, success depends more on a combination of taste, insight and good timing rather than on the Festival classification, which means that any programmer at any festival has the opportunity to make interesting and relatively original propositions.

Another important aspect is that all festivals are very important to the city and the region where they are organised as, aside from the importance of hosting a cultural event, the economy of the city also benefits. TIFF is held in Thessaloniki. As the second most important Greek city, both culturally and economically, Thessaloniki lies in the north of the country, very close to the borders of Albania, F.Y.R.O.M., Bulgaria and Turkey. It has had a long tradition of a multi-ethnic population, consisting mainly of Greeks, Turks, Jews and Armenians, something that gradually changed after the city's incorporation into the Greek state in 1912. It once again attracted a multi-ethnic population after the fall of the socialist block in 1989, with a new influx of immigrants from the Balkans and Eastern Europe. As a result, it is often said that Thessaloniki is a crossroads of cultures.

In 1992 the Thessaloniki Festival became international. Since 1960 it had been a festival dedicated to Greek films, and for some years it had an international programme consisting of foreign films that had found distribution in Greece as well. But now, as an international event, it had two major aims. The first is to place cinema in the centre of cultural activities in Greece and bring to the Greek audience new trends, new directors and new national film. Consequently, through the screening of films but also through the organised round tables, master classes, conferences, seminars and publications, the audience has the opportunity to come into direct contact with important directors, giving TIFF a major educational role for film.

This educational mandate has become obvious with the passing of time, as the audience, hesitant at first with some of the new cinematic propositions, gradually became accustomed to them and now supports them through steady attendance, year after year. It should be also noted that TIFF has parallel activities throughout the year, including activities such as the Thessaloniki International Documentary Festival and Images of the 21st Century, which is its second most important event (the 11th edition will take place in March 2009), as well as educational programmes, continuous programming with tributes to directors, national cinemas and thematic units in Thessaloniki and Athens. All these activities highlight TIFF's pedagogical role and its effort to form an audience capable of supporting a cinematic culture.

The festival's second goal is to help Greek cinema come out from its isolation and become part of the international cinematic circuit, giving Greek filmmakers the opportunity not only to present their films to the representatives of the international press but also to come in contact with directors and film professionals from all over the world, to exchange opinions and experiences, as well as to be systematically informed about the developments in film production and the possibilities of international co-operations that various European programmes are offering.

In 1994, TIFF took another important step in shaping its identity. In a time of political and social flux, during which the Balkans were suffering the civil war in Yugoslavia and the economic crisis brought about by the collapse of the communist regimes, TIFF established the 'Balkan Survey' section, turning its gaze to the creativity of the Balkan countries. Its major aim was to present to the Festival's Greek and foreign audience with a review of the annual film production and the latest cinematic developments through a selection of the most important films to come out of the Balkan countries. This would enable it to create a bridge of communication and connect with the wider area of Northeastern Europe and connecting Balkan cinema to that of Europe.

The TIFF 'Balkan Survey' initiative stemmed not only from the interest generated by living in the same part of the world and seeking our common roots but, mainly, from the fact that the Greek audience was essentially ignorant of Balkan cinema. As a result, this cinema had for a long time been 'anonymous' to the Greek audience. Aside from a few exceptions, such as Dušan Makavejev, Yilmaz Güney and Emir Kusturica, most Balkan directors and their work were completely unknown to most Greeks. Consequently, through the films of the new generation of Balkan directors (Srdjan Dragojevic, Srdan Golubovic, Milcho Manchevski, Zeki Demirkubuz, Yesim Ustaoğlu, Derviş Zaim, Fatmir Koçi, to mention just a few), TIFF gave the audience the opportunity to enjoy an artistically inspired regional cinema.

While it is committed to programming the work of new directors, the festival is also committed to showing the work of past masters. As a result, a number of tributes to veteran directors have been organised, such as the Romanian Lucian Pintilie (1996), the Yugoslavians Zivojin Pavlovic (1997) and Srdjan Karanovic (1999), the Bulgarian Eduard Zahariev (1997), and the Turk Ömer Kavur (1997). Tributes to new directors are also held, such as to the Turks Kutluğ Ataman (2006), Nuri Bilğe Ceylan (2007), and the Romanian Nae Caranfil (2008).

Other tributes that have been held by TIFF and TDF (Thessaloniki Documentary Festival), focusing on the new Turkish cinema (1999, 2008), and the Yugoslavian civil war (2001), respectively. The idea of these tributes is not only to introduce the audience to the work of renowned and emerging directors but also to fill important gaps in the development of a national cinema. The tribute to Caranfil is characteristic: having presented the films of all the new Romanian directors since 2001 (Cristi Puiu, Cristian Mungiu, Radu Muntean, Corneliu Porumboiu, Cristi Nemescu) in the competition or the Balkan Survey sections, the idea behind the tribute to Caranfil, a director who belongs to the generation of the transitional period of Romanian cinema, was to link the pre-revolutionary period to the so-called 'New Wave' that emerged at the dawn of the twenty-first century.

If the timing is right, any tribute to a national cinema naturally highlights its contemporary state or the emergence of a new current. That was the case with last year (2008)'s Balkan Survey spotlight on Romanian shorts and the tribute to contemporary Turkish cinema. This not only celebrated an extremely successful year for Turkish films (forming an integral part of the official programme in major festivals) but also presented the new films of two

The Thessaloniki International Film Festival

different 'generations' of filmmakers: the one that rejuvenated Turkish cinema in the mid-1990s, garnering international acclaim and winning numerous distinctions at major festivals, and a new generation of filmmakers taking its first hope-filled steps.

Taking into account Thessaloniki' s geographical location as well the cultural and financial role that it has traditionally played in the Balkans, the importance of this section for the festival is more than obvious. Its international significance became evident very soon, as it attracted the interest of film professionals who were given the opportunity to see a selection of the year's most important films from the region. In the following years, the promotion of Balkan cinema was further reinforced, with the Balkan Script Development Fund (established in 2003 by the festival director at the time, Michel Demopoulos), the Crossroads Co-production Forum, which aims to support the producers of feature-length fiction film projects linked to the Mediterranean and Balkan regions (founded in 2005 by the new and current festival director Ms. Despina Mouzaki), the Balkan Works in Progress, and the special Agora (Market) screening programme, which gives film professionals the opportunity to be the first to discover selected projects from the entire Balkan region shortly before their completion (established in 2006 by Despina Mouzaki).

In this context, a number of Balkan film projects have started their international career with the support of TIFF's Balkan Fund, such as *Uglasevanje* (*The Tuning*, Slovenia, 2005) by Igor Sterk, or *Guca!* (*Gucha-Distant Trumpet*, Austria/Bulgaria/Germany/Serbia and Montenegro, 2006) by Dusan Milic. Others have premiered internationally in the Balkan Survey, including *Edinstvenata Lubovna Istoria Koiato Hemingway ne Opisa* (*A Farewell to Hemingway*, Bulgaria, 2008) by Svetoslav Ovcharov, and *Sakli Yüzler* (*Hidden Faces,* Turkey, 2007) by Handan Ipekci. Others, such as *Grbavica* (Austria/Bosnia and Herzegovina/Croatia/Germany, 2006) by Jasmila Zbanic, or *Snijeg* (*Snow,* Bosnia and Herzegovina/Germany/France/Iran, 2008) by Aida Begic were premiered in Berlin and Cannes respectively, where they won the Golden Bear Award in 2006 and the Critics' Week Grand Prix in 2008. At the same time, there are a number of anticipated projects in the pipeline, such as: *Welcome Aboard* by Constantine Giannaris, *Palto* (*The Coat)* by Kutluğ Ataman, *Odbrana I Poslednji Dani* (*Kingdom Cum*) by Srdjan Dragojevic, *Un Balon în Formă de Inimă* (*A Heart Shaped Balloon*) by Catalin Mitulescu and *Felicia Înainte de Toate* (*First of All, Felicia*) by Razvan Radulescu. Films that were presented as Balkan works-in-progress in TIFF before they were selected by major festivals include: *California Dreamin'* (*nesîrşit*) (*California Dreamin'* (*endless*), Romania, 2007) by Cristian Nemescu (Camera D' Or, 2007), *Iki Çizgi* (*Two Lines*, Turkey, 2008) by Selim Evci (selected by Venice), *Nokta* (*Dot*, 2008) by Derviş Zaim (selected by Sarajevo, Montreal), and *Tatil Kitabi* (*Summer Book*, Turkey, 2008) by Seyfi Teoman (selected by Berlin). This is also the case with some Greek works-in-progress, such as *Istoria 52* (*Tale 52*, 2008) by Alexis

Alexiou or *Ecce Momo!* (2008) by Anestis Charalambidis (both selected by Rotterdam).

At the same time, the establishment of Thessaloniki as a significant platform for the promotion of Balkan national cinemas has been reinforced by the systematic selection of films from the region in the festival's competition section (up to now, 14 Balkan films have been screened), with some of them winning the major prizes – Fatmir Koçi's *Tirana, Année Zéro* (*Tirana Year Zero*, Albania/France, 2001) was awarded the Golden Alexander at the 42nd edition in 2001, and Derviş Zaim's *Tabutta Rövaşata* (*Somersault in a Coffin*, Turkey, 1996) was awarded the Silver Alexander at the 38th edition in 1997. Last year's Silver Alexander went to Adrian Sitaru's *Pescuit Sportiv* (*Hooked*, France/Romania, 2008) in the 49th edition of 2008. Moreover, five films have been presented in the out of competition section. Together, these prizes and entries have not only resulted in the promotion of Balkan cinema; they have also made it one of TIFF's major attractions.

Programming Balkan Films

The TIFF is a discovery festival. All programmers in our festival are trying to discover new talent and new trends, to catch the pulse of what's happening in cinema at the moment. The competition programme, which consists of 14 films, is the festival's showcase and is run by the festival's director. All first and second films are considered for the competition section, with the exception of those that have competed in a major festival. Because they include films that interest other sections too (Independence Days, Balkan Survey, Focus), all the programmers work together, holding meetings to discuss the most interesting work and schedule its screening in line with the programme's needs.

The TIFF presents festival-goers with films that have been made in the last 18 months. None of the works will have been screened anywhere else in Greece, except those that are part of a retrospective. Retrospectives on important directors and a focus on national cinema form part of the TIFF programme every year. Other than that, there is not any other particular mandate regarding foreign films. As far as Greek films are concerned, they should be in 35 mm format and must have applied for the State Quality Awards, which are presented by the Ministry of Culture in a ceremony organised by TIFF after the festival is over. These films must have been produced/screened during the past year. Greek films shot in video are selected to compete in the Digital Wave part of the Greek section of the festival. As there is a special section for Greek films every year, Greek films are not included in the Balkan Survey Section. However, two Greek films are selected for the international competition section.

Film selection is a very subjective procedure which depends on 'cultural' sensitivities, ideas about cinema, and work philosophy. A film can be chosen because it is moving or important (aesthetically or thematically), or because

The Thessaloniki International Film Festival

the programmer feels it must be presented (even though the audience might not like it). A film can also be chosen because it suits the programmer's specific approach. The programmers express their ideas on the aesthetics as well as the intellectual value of the film through the programme, which ultimately resembles a completed puzzle, each film combining with the others to produce a certain picture and statement. The programmers' philosophy is expressed by the way the selected films are grouped and presented, thus developing a certain logic rather than being a mere presentation of films or a showcase of premieres.

First and foremost, a programmer is an investigator who uses all possible means and sources to find films for the programme. In the search for what's happening in cinema right now, the programmer follows the work of selected directors, looks for new talents, and seeks to find films that are in development or post production through personal contacts, festival workshops, industry magazines or other research. Then the programmer must attend festivals, some of them on a regular basis (in my case Sofia, Istanbul, Sarajevo, Cannes, NexT) and some occasionally (such as Cluz, Zagreb, Novi Sad, Varna). Attending Balkan festivals is very important, as it offers the opportunity not only to see the latest local films but also to make useful contacts with producers and directors, to find out about the films that are about to emerge, and to obtain screeners. Exchanging information and opinions with other festival programmers or film journalists is also essential, as it is impossible to visit all the festivals. But you find out about their programmes by asking other festivals for their catalogue, from which you find films and contacts in order to ask for screeners. And of course, there are the screeners that you receive from independent filmmakers and production companies, which can often be the source of wonderful, unknown discoveries.

When I started programming the Balkan Survey section in 2002, my aim was not only to present films that were characterised by cinematic and thematic originality or to discover new talents and trends, but also to try to bridge the cultural gap with our neighbours through cinema, highlighting our similarities along with our differences, and thus familiarising the local audience with the region's contemporary social reality which otherwise would have been largely unknown. As a result, my programming could also be characterised by an effort to understand and communicate the complex historical and contemporary Balkan reality through the cinematic representations of the native (and sometimes non-Balkan) directors. In addition, through these images of life in our neighbouring countries, I wanted to contribute to the overcoming of the prejudice with which a great part of the Greek population faced anything from Eastern Europe (unless someone was sympathetic to socialistic ideals), something that has also affected the reception of films from the area.

In short, it could be said that my programming embodies an anthropological approach, as I am interested in presenting films that examine contemporary Balkan reality and the social factors that determine today's state of affairs in the area, such as society's economic and social transition after the fall of the socialist regimes, the traumas of civil war in Yugoslavia or other political unrest, and the preoccupation with historical memory. Such an initiative is greatly facilitated by today's Balkan cinema as it is inseparable from the historical reality of the peninsula.

Whether referring to the past or the present, Balkan narratives are heavy with historical memories and contemporary socio-political issues. Most of the personal stories told by today's Balkan filmmakers are permeated by the wounds of the past or the fluidity and insecurity of modern-day social changes that spring precisely from this historical process. Thus, the different viewpoints through which filmmakers tackle such issues do not merely signal a need for artistic expression; they provide themselves, as well as the filmgoers, with the opportunity to better understand the region's complexities, endowing Balkan cinema with such functions as cultural criticism, the healing of historical wounds and the negotiation of contemporary social dynamics.

In effect, my idea of programming Balkan films is an effort to complete the puzzle of every year's production as efficiently as possible, as it is one thing to like a film and another to actually include it in your selection, due to parameters that are often beyond your power, such as the sales agents' strategy for the film or the timing of the film's release in relation with the dates of the festival, etc. As a result, such an attempt is not always 100 per cent successful and I do not always screen all the films that I would have liked. However, I consider that my programme's profile is not affected dramatically by such gaps, since through screening most of the films that I consider important, the general picture is there.

As there are not many festivals which focus on the Balkan region, the major difficulty in presenting Balkan films comes from the producers' and sales agents' wish to participate in 'A Festivals', such as Rotterdam, Berlin, Cannes, Karlovy Vary, Locarno, Venice, and San Sebastian (listed chronologically). As these festivals want their films to be premieres, the most interesting films prefer to wait to be selected by them rather than to apply to TIFF's Balkan Survey section. Once they have been screened there, it is easier – although not without complications – to get a print of a film that seems appropriate. Balkan films that have been awarded a major prize in an A festival are often bought by local distributors whose strategy may not include screening the film at our festival. Print availability, especially now that Balkan cinema is on the rise and every festival wants to include a film from the area, can also be a problem, especially when these festivals take place around the same period of time (such as Mannheim, Cottbus, Ljubljana, Festival on Wheels). This is usually solved by the festivals themselves, which share prints and schedule films by taking the dates of the other festivals into consideration. So, all in all, I think that sales agents are among the greatest obstacles in screening a film in TIFF's Balkan Survey.

As far as competition among the festivals is concerned, it is obvious that a 'B Festival' such as TIFF cannot compete with the 'A Festivals', especially when it comes to premieres, which reinforce a festival's prestige and are much sought after. When it comes to the festivals that showcase Balkan films, the fact that TIFF takes place at the end of the year gives it an advantage over others in that it presents a more complete picture of the annual Balkan production. On the other hand, Sarajevo IFF, which takes place three months before TIFF, gets to screen some Balkan films first, introducing them as 'regional premieres'. However, Sarajevo's 'regional' competition programme is not purely Balkan, as it also includes countries such as Austria, Hungary or Malta. In any case, I consider that festivals striving for premieres are disorienting, as quite often programmers make concessions in an effort to secure premieres by choosing films that are not that strong. So, I think that in the end what matters is the effort to have the best possible selection, in order for the local audience to enjoy regional cinema, especially when the distribution of Balkan films in Greece is minimal. After all, films are made for people to watch, and in a traditionally audience-oriented festival such as TIFF, what is more essential is the quality of the films. In my opinion, that is where reputations are built, and once a good reputation is established premieres are bound to follow – as they have done at TIFF in recent years.

Taking the festival's major aims into consideration, as well as the natural development of the promotion of Balkan cinema, TIFF is one of the 'Festivals with Geopolitical Agendas', as described by Turan in his categorisation of festivals (2002). It is therefore significant on a regional, national and international level. On a regional level, it provides the people of Thessaloniki and northern Greece (those who attend the festival itself and those who attend the regional screenings organised by the festival in various cities around Thessaloniki) with an opportunity to watch films, see the directors presenting their films, ask them questions, or follow master classes held by the filmmakers themselves. The festive atmosphere is not restricted to the festival venue but spreads throughout Thessaloniki during these 10 days, as parallel activities such as concerts, exhibitions and parties take place.

At the same time, the festival brings visitors to the city. Foreign guests get to know the city and its lifestyle and visit its museums and archeological sites. On a national level, it promotes Greek cinema, connecting it to the World Cinema circuit/ system and, as already mentioned, it gives Greek professionals – for whom the festival is an intense working period – the opportunity to be part of that circuit. On an international level, TIFF works as a meeting place for new and veteran directors as well as film professionals from all over the world. The fact that TIFF has become a renowned annual meeting point for the international film community, attracting a great deal of international interest, signifies its importance in the world festival circuit.

Work Cited

Turan, Kenneth (2002) *Sundance to Sarajevo: Film Festivals and the World They Made*. Berkeley: University of California Press.

Part 4

The Field of Festival Studies

Chapter Thirteen

Film Festival Studies:
An Overview of a Burgeoning Field

Marijke de Valck and Skadi Loist

Film festivals have been a blank spot of cinema scholarship for many years. Although plenty of individual festival histories and anniversary books have been published and the topic of film festivals has occasionally been addressed in academic studies – (focusing, for example, on art or national cinemas), the phenomenon of film festivals was, until recently, rarely the main focus of scholarly study. In the last few years, academics have turned to study the broad range of film festival constituencies. Their work aims to explain, theorise and historicise film festivals and, in doing so, point to the emergence of a new academic field in which knowledge of festivals is considered essential for our understanding of cinema and media cultures: film festival studies.

This article aims to give an account of the current state of film festival research. First, we will briefly sketch out the tasks and potentials of film festival studies. Second, we will describe how scholars have approached film festivals as research objects, suggesting we should understand festivals as sites of intersecting discourses and practices. Adding to this perspective is the slightly different categorisation of existing film festival research into ten themed clusters (some of which are divided into subsections).[1] For this, we have set out to collect the most important existing film festival publications and compiled them into the first themed bibliography on film festival research, which is included in the third section of this article.[2] In conclusion, we will point to research opportunities and topics that have not yet been dealt with or need further elaboration, and which we feel are of particular relevance to the burgeoning field of film festival studies.

I. What is 'Film Festival Studies'? Tasks and Potentials

While film festivals have long been neglected by scholars, they have generated countless pages of non-academic writing, ranging from brief festival reports in newspapers to glossy coffee table anniversary books. An obvious difference between journalistic or pop-cultural accounts of film festivals and academic film festival research is that the latter by definition goes beyond the glamour, stars and gossip of one specific festival. Festival research, however, also differs from serious film criticism. If it is the task of film critics to visit festivals in order to report on recent trends, point the public to great new films and write thoughtful reviews, film festival scholars instead work *out-of-sync* with the imposing festival rhythm and offer meta-views and frameworks for understanding festivals in broader *and* more specific contexts. Bringing to bear different approaches and methods – such as network theory, film analysis, discourse analysis, history of institutions, film history of industry and distribution, national cinema etc. – academics have a key part to play in clarifying the formative yet complex role of film festivals in our cultures, industries and societies.

Drawing on different research traditions and methodologies, film festival studies is an inherently interdisciplinary field. In this way the new field is emblematic for the move made by film studies towards the much more broadly defined media studies in the last two decades. Film festival studies, then, sits somewhere halfway between these institutionalised fields. In a clear departure from film studies, the field of film festival research takes a cultural studies approach, reframing interests in film aesthetics, art and the role of national and festivals as sites of self-identification and community building. It acknowledges above all the political and economic context of film production and distribution and understands film festivals both as players in the film industry and, conversely, as events in which various stakeholders are involved. Not surprisingly, film festival research is conducted in the humanities as well as social sciences, most notably by film and media scholars but also as part of organisational studies and business schools, gender studies, history, anthropology, urban and tourism studies and various regional studies (e.g. Asian studies). As the diversity of these researchers bring their own toolbox to the study of film festivals, the field boasts a remarkable variety of resources – from speech-act theory to system theory, from historical archive material to hard business data. Depending on one's audacity, the present organisation of the field as a loose collection of lateral efforts can be embraced as a fertile base for chance discoveries and out-of-the-box thinking. On the other hand, one might also make a strong case arguing that the current fragmentation of the field stands in the way of it coming to full bloom. Dina Iordanova, for example, writes: 'The study of festivals ... remains scattered and is in need of a more systematic and focused approach,' (2008: 4–5, section 1).[3] A first step in developing such approaches is to map what has been done in film festival research so far.

Categorising the existing film festival research is not an easy task. One way to tackle the problem of film festivals as elusive and hard-to-define objects for academic study is to see them as *sites of intersecting discourses and practices*. Within the realm of a film festival different axes intersect. First, there is the aesthetic discourse, which treats film as an art work; second, there is the economic continuum from production to distribution, which is organised along flows of capital; third, there is the very heart of a festival which, rather than being an empty space for the display of films (cf. Hope and Dickerson 2006a, section 10), represents the institution of the festival itself, which is operated by people, in need of funding, and functioning according to certain mechanisms; fourth comes the axis of reception, which includes audiences, exhibitions, and the construction of specialised public spheres; and fifth, there is the politics of place, in which the festival's meaningful and often strategic relation to local or national parties is defined. Each separate axis as well as the complex entity they constitute provides objects for film festival researchers.

Beyond the individual festival, there is another level of analysis, which we will call the sixth axis (see below). This covers a) the way they are connected with each other in the network of festivals that is the international film festival circuit with its constant flow of culture and capital (cf. de Valck 2007, section 1.1); and b) the timeframe of historical development and change taking place in the festivals and the festival circuit.

Any categorisation or mapping of film festivals is bound to be contestable. Likewise, festival research cannot easily be packed into neat boxes; the different research foci often overlap and can hardly be separated if one is interested in contextualised findings rather than broad generalised assertions. For the bibliography in section three of this article we have taken the idea of festivals as sites of intersecting discourses and practices as our conceptual starting point and reworked it to fit the demands of a user-friendly reference tool. Here we have chosen to work, bottom-up, with a straightforward thematic ordering that follows from the topics addressed by contemporary festival research. The bibliography, thus, is a thematic list of literature references grouped under ten clusters that are easily recognisable: 1) Film Festivals: The Long View; 2) Festival Time: Awards, Juries and Critics; 3) Festival Space: Cities, Tourism and Public Spheres; 4) On the Red Carpet: Spectacle, Stars and Glamour; 5) Business Matters: Industries, Distribution and Markets; 6) Trans/National Cinemas; 7) Programming; 8) Reception: Audiences, Communities and Cinephiles; 9) Specialised Film Festivals; and 10) Publications Dedicated to Individual Film Festivals. Where needed sections are further divided into subsections. Many references, however, fit into more than one cluster and our cross-referencing will attest to this.

Our clustering might seem to sit squarely to the six axes – film, economics, institution, reception, place, and the extra level of the network and history – mentioned above. The intention, however, is not to present a definitive mapping, which is arguably both an impossible and undesirable goal, but to offer practical and hopefully illuminating guides to contemporary research on film festivals. Thus, while the original on-line bibliography is meant to disclose publications, be consulted as reference tool, and get (new) researchers started, the overview presented below aims to give a (meta) introduction to the newly emerging field and is meant to be read in one piece. For the latter objective we feel the idea of festivals as sites of intersecting discourses and practices is more suitable. So, instead of summarising the arguments of the pieces gathered under the ten rubrics of the online version of the bibliography, we will try here to bring the two levels of axes and rubrics together in a preliminary perspective on the new field.

II. How to Approach Film Festival Studies

Axis One – Film as Work of Art

The first axis, or first way to approach film festival research, is using a film as the focus lens. Highlighting the film as the element that guides the study of film festivals reveals a variety of processes taking place around film festivals that not only occur during the festival time but also before and after.

Before the festival the film is already subjected to rigid agenda-setting processes. The first stage the film must pass through is entrance to the festival. The film can be submitted by filmmakers or producers according to the festival regulations, or be solicited by programmers (see the service guides for professionals, section 5.3). Next, it has to pass the first selection process, i.e. pass through screening committees, previewers or programmers (cf. Krach 2003, Thomson 2003; section 7). If it fits the profile and programming criteria of the festival, it will be placed in the programme. Its placement – itself created in an intricate process subject to different agendas – has an effect on reception, reviewing and the future of the film after the festival.

The way a festival programme is curated depends on the programmer and his/her ideas and ideals (for several accounts of individual programming concepts of curators see section 7). Equally, programming depends on the kind of festival in question. For instance, queer film festivals need to consider more identity-based criteria such as 'a film made by, for, about, or of interest to' the queer community (cf. June 2004, section 9.1.1), whereas a 'universal survey festival' will look for world premieres and other criteria (cf. Klippel 2008, section 7).

Apart from describing the creative aspect, the analysis of programming concepts gives insights into (economic) exploitation strategies by industry and festivals, such as presenting Hollywood classics in a retrospective in corollary with a DVD release or the transnational cross-over marketing of blockbusters (Stringer 2003a, b; section 7). Another aspect for consideration is the degree to which festival programming influences film criticism, scholarship, canons and genre formations (Stringer 2003, section 1.1; June 2004, section 9.1.1).

The last selection process a film might pass at a festival is the competition. The festival audience or a jury of film professionals will bestow prestige on it by awarding a prize. Film festival studies have started to point out some of the concerns regarding awards and juries, such as the subjective nature of evaluations (Helmke 2005; Pride 2002), the effects of awards on distribution (Dodds and Holbrook 1998), and the correlation between taste and mediation in high art (Shrum 1996, all section 2).

Axis Two – Economic Continuum: From Production to Distribution

While the first axis of festival analysis focuses on film as art and the festival's core task of screening them, the second axis focuses on film as product and the way festivals facilitate 'the business' of cinema. The spotlight is on the direct economic context of the film.

Film festivals are a platform for and of the film industry. This becomes very obvious when considering one of the organisations with a very strong influence on the festival circuit: the International Federation of Film Producers Associations (FIAPF). Since 1933, the FIAPF has represented the economic, legal and regulatory interests of film and TV production industries who are part of the organisation. It also regulates (accredited) film festivals and the business conducted there and decides the status of major festivals, keeping the number of so-called A-level festivals limited to assure the hierarchy on the circuit (cf. Fehrenbach 1995, section 1.2; de Valck 2007, section 1.1). The business conducted at their adjoined markets is a significant part of A-festivals (Berlin: European Film Market; Cannes: Marché du Film). Thus, on the business side, festivals are measured by their industry attendants at the market, their sales rates, and the production deals closed (see section 5).

When attempting to answer the question as to why film festivals exist, discussions tend to gravitate toward the problem of distribution. Film festivals provide several 'answers' to this problem. Gideon Bachmann (2000, section 5.2) distinguishes between 'wholesale' and 'retail' events: the former act primarily as markets where sales agents sell films, the latter are essentially exhibitors (correspondingly Mark Peranson distinguishes two models: 'business festivals' and 'audience festivals' [Peranson 2008, section 1.1]). With the increasing pressure on art-house exhibition and a simultaneous boom in mid-size and smaller film festivals, the events themselves have become an alternative distribution method.

While festivals function as an alternative distribution circuit, they are also part of the marketing strategies for traditional distribution. In the era of the 'attention economy', film festivals are increasingly used by the industry as platforms to create a buzz (i.e. media discourse), around films which helps their box office in theatrical release. Daniel Dayan pointed out that film festivals exist in at least two versions: the visual festival of films and the 'written festival' created by print material produced by and about the festival (Dayan 2000, section 1.1). The strategy of creating attention is, for instance, used for blockbuster premieres at big festivals, serving both the festival and the (Hollywood) producer: the festival gets attention for premiering the film, preferably in attendance of stars (see section 4), while the film gets a stamp of artistic approval for being shown at a festival – often out of competition and thus without running the risk of bad reviews (Stringer 2003a, section 7).

Smaller films without theatrical release lined up can raise their cultural capital through the value-adding process at festivals (cf. de Valck 2007). Each selection process (mentioned above) adds value to a film. This way a small film might be able to cross over from the alternative (yet closed) distribution network that is the festival circuit into (theatrical) distribution. If one festival is not enough, a chain of screenings at festivals might be used to build up momentum slowly (depending on marketing strategy and regional market characteristics).

Festivals have been expanding their operations constantly from exhibition to distribution, facilitating sales and networking. In the last decades, festivals have moved even further into the film business; now they also provide training for filmmakers (e.g. Berlinale Talent Campus) and production funds (e.g. Frameline's Completion Fund wants to 'bring new work to under-served audiences' in the LGBT community and 'especially encourage[s] applications by women, people of color and transgender persons'; Rotterdam's Hubert Bals Fund for young filmmakers in disadvantaged countries [cf. Loist 2008, section 9.1.1.; Steinhart 2006, section 5.1]). This way festivals stop being mere exhibitors of current productions and instead become active players in the film industry.

Axis Three – Festival as Institution

While axis two considered the film industry as a part of the festival (business), axis three looks at the festival as an institution. As the business side has already made clear, the festival is not an empty space for the display of films but rather an organisation with its own (business) agenda. At the same time, there are a number of interest groups (e.g. film professionals, sponsors, politicians) whose various demands and expectations the festival has to meet. Thus, in axis three the festival is approached on the level of people/actors.

On a personal level, festivals are special meeting spaces: different groups – e.g. film professionals, stars and everyday cineastes – can meet and talk about film in a way that is not possible anywhere else. Focusing on the interest groups or attendees of a festival, one can distinguish groups involved with and interested in the festival: 1) industry representatives of various fields such as a) film production, b) press, c) distribution, d) unions and professional associations, e) exhibition, f) training and education; 2) festival guests; 3) event and festival organisers; 4) regular audience members (cf. Reichel-Heldt 2007: 55-65, section 1.1). These groups already represent a wide range of interests and demands toward the festival.

A different group from the people attending a festival are the people working in various positions for the festival(s) in question: festival directors, programmers, selection committee members, events managers and development and press people are 'specialised intermediaries', to borrow a term from museum studies (cf. Stringer 2003: 19; section 1.1). Analysis of long-term developments and movements of people between festivals shows the significance of individual careers as well as historical shifts in the professional history of the circuit, such as the rise of the programmer in the 1960s (cf. de Valck 2007, section 1.1).

While the development of major festivals is often closely linked to geopolitics (cf. Turan 2002, section 1), one should not forget that only a very small fraction of the approximately 1,000 festivals are FIAPF-accredited A-festivals. Thus, the analysis of festivals as institution needs to consider a variety of festivals and their specific contexts (cf. Evans 2007, section 1.1). The founding strategy, for instance, of the Berlinale as a cultural bastion and market hub of the West in the Cold War climate is quite different from the engagement of cineclubs and adult education centres (*Volkshochschule*), which resulted in festivals such as the Northern German regional festival Emden-Aurich-Norderney (with a small team of part-time staff). Similarly, the gay liberation movement resulted in an all-volunteer structure of the Hamburg Lesbian and Gay Film Festival (cf. Reichel-Heldt 2007, section 1.1).

The variety of organisational structures (volunteer, for-profit and hybrids) and cultural/political contexts also results in different expectations from players in the field (industry, state/city funders, etc.) and a variety of funding strategies in a climate of declining resources (state-funding of arts or regional economics, private sponsorship, community-funding) (e.g. Reichel-Heldt 2007, section 1.1; Gamson 1996, Rhyne 2007, both section 9.1.1)

Axis Four – Reception: Audiences and Exhibition

The approach of the fourth axis centres on reception. Although various actors have already been mentioned in axis three (understanding festivals as meeting places for various stakeholders and interest groups), the primary activity and function of film festivals is to screen films. These are targeted specifically at professionals in press screenings and private video booths as well as to the general public, which effectively means that *all* festival visitors are constituted as members of an audience.

Several important issues are foregrounded when we approach the international film festival circuit as a network of exhibition.

Firstly, the specific reception environment created by film festivals is largely defined by the event nature of the festival. While cinema attendance is often bemoaned as declining, festival attendances across-the-board are reported as going up. The opportunity to see something first, or something that cannot be seen elsewhere, something unexpected – and maybe even the added possibility of seeing a film star – brings people to the festival (cf. Reichel-Heldt 2007, section 1.1; cf. de Valck 2005, section 8). Likewise, the spectacular setting of the festival is believed to be beneficial to the buying-

and-selling of films and festival buzz is a key ingredient in the production of festival hits and the discovery of noteworthy films (see axis two).

Secondly, for specialised festivals, the general feeling of belonging to a group, a cinephile community, is heightened by identity cues. Audience members of horror genre festivals (cf. Stringer 2008, section 8) or queer film festivals, to name just two examples, share a common interest that goes beyond film (or even a genre of film) in general. They meet with like-minded viewers, sometimes the sub-cultural community, when congregating at a festival screening. Such a specific context adds to the special nature of the reception setting. In a queer film festival, this might even result in critical, communal counter-readings of films (cf. Searle 1996, section 9.1.1). In a general sense, setting and programming structure of the event can induce a focused form of reception ('discovering form, inferring meaning') which brings about 'new cinemas' (Nichols 1994, section 8). In film festival research, specialised festivals are often used to narrow a research focus and select case studies. There are different categories according to which festivals can be grouped, and it is important to be aware that our choices of categorisation inform the writing of festival history.

Thirdly, the issue of programming, already discussed under axis one, is also intimately connected to the issue of reception. Curators imagine a certain programme and by doing so envision a way to highlight, promote and contextualise a film. The programme, however, is also dependent on the audience and its actual reception. Film festivals offer a framework which generates certain audience expectations; with their programme festival curators (often) try to encourage the active reception of the audience (cf. Klippel 2008: 10, section 8). Some scholars and curators would even go so far as to say that programming means not (only) programming films but 'programming the public' (Fung 1999, section 9.1.1). They point to the fact that programming directly influences the constituency of the audience – although no one can foresee what audience reaction and outcome a certain programme will have (see bibliography section 8 on reception, e.g. Stringer 2008).

Finally, a whole different angle on reception issues concerns the analysis of the spatial aspects of film reception at festivals. What are we to make of exhibition practices at festivals that move beyond the traditional cinema and expand to include installations and online 'screenings'?

Axis Five – Politics of Place

Related to the spatial configuration of exhibition contexts is the broader range of spatial aspects of film festivals. Space and place are so important in festivals' functioning that they form a separate axis of the academic framing of festivals. This approach borrows from work done in social geography and follows the 'spatial turn' in the humanities. Janet Harbord, for example, looks at festivals as 'spaces of flow' and asserts that 'the film festival is a particular manifestation of the way that space is produced as practice'. She goes on to explain that 'film festivals have since their inception ... entwined film culture within the organisation and materialisation of national and regional space' (Harbord 2002: 61; section 3). More specifically, we should understand festival space as being made up of complex dynamics of local and global forces, always defined by the physical place in which the event is organised but at the same time embedded in an international circuit. Building on insights from globalisation theory, this interplay is understood as a public arena in which uneven power relations are acted out (Stringer 2001, section 3). For example, international film festivals in developing countries are criticised for marketing (exotic) national cinemas to Western audiences while neglecting to support local industries (cf. Diawara 1993, section 6.3).

Another research focus that follows from globalisation theory in general and tourism/urban studies in particular is festivals' relation to the city. Spatial aspects such as city planning and city policies concerned with tourism-related sponsorship are scrutinised in relation to festivals (cf. Stringer 2001, section 3; Elsaesser 2005, section 1.1). The city, much more than the nation, is the spatial entity that has come to define festivals' identity and functional logics, in particular since the 1980s. A question that is often posed in relation to festivals' contemporary spatial configuration is whether it is possible to strengthen community cultural development and cultural tourism simultaneously (cf. Derrett 2000, 2003; section 3). In other words, can festivals be tailored to local community interests while at the same time stimulating urban development? At the large film festivals in particular, programmes tend to have a strong international character and therefore attract cosmopolitan visitors who want to celebrate and consume world/art cinema rather than screen programmes that express regional distinctiveness and cater to the local population.

Finally, looking at how space is used at the lowest level of festival organisation can shed light on the ways film festivals foster an atmosphere of exclusivity and staged rituals that add value to films and filmmakers.

Axis Six – The Film Festival Circuit and History

Moving beyond the level of individual festivals, the phenomenon of film festivals at a more general level can be approached as an interconnected network with specific historical developments. If one wants to understand any single festival organisation or edition, it is essential to frame its functioning in connection to the logics of the international film festival circuit, since no festival can exist outside the influence sphere of the festival network and this network is more than the sum of its parts. Topics that come to the fore when looking at festivals from the angle of a cultural network/system include the existence of a festival calendar, the flows of capital and culture through the circuit, the task division between different (types of) festivals, mutual relations of competition and emulations as well as rankings of prestige and influence (see bibliography section 1 on film festival theory).

Finally, any theorisation of film festivals needs to be contextualised. The international film festival circuit is in constant transformation, responding and adapting to developments in aligned areas, such as the film industry, as well as to larger trends, like globalisation, digitisation and commercialisation today.

III. Film Festival Research: Thematic, Annotated Bibliography

1. Film Festivals: The Long View

The books, dissertations and articles in this category are characterised by an interdisciplinary orientation and, in this way, contest the inherent complexity of the film festival 'object', which is in fact multiple objects in one. Taking a meta-perspective on film festivals, these studies frame and discuss the various festival constituencies (on which separate studies are included under categories 2-10 below). Some do so by presenting one or more case studies. Questions that are addressed include: How do festivals function? Can festivals' historical development be divided into phases? Which 'models' drive their institutionalisation? What is their *raison d'être*? Which actors are involved? What relations with Hollywood exist? And what critical perspectives can help us understand the diverse range of festival practices? Also included in this category, directly below, are important early publications that approach the film festival phenomenon from a more anecdotal or journalistic angle.

Bachmann, Gideon (1976) 'Confessions of a Festival Goer', *Film Quarterly*, 29, 14-17.
Gregor, Ulrich (2001) 'Filmfestivals: Letzte Bastionen der Filmkultur?', in Jacobi Reinhold (ed.) *Medien, Markt, Moral: Vom ganz wirklichen, fiktiven und virtuellen Leben*. Freiburg im Breisgau: Herder, 61-65.
Turan, Kenneth (2002) *Sundance to Sarajevo: Film Festivals and the World They Made*. Berkeley: University of California Press.

1.1 Film Festival Theory

As one of the first critical studies of film festivals, Bill Nichols' article 'Global Image Consumption in the Age of Late Capitalism' takes up a central concern of film festival research: the local/global dynamics. 'Never only or purely local, festival films nonetheless circulate, in large part, with a cachet of locally inscribed difference and globally ascribed commonality. They both attest to the uniqueness of different cultures and specific filmmakers and affirm the underlying qualities of an "international cinema"' (Nichols 1994: 68). Media anthropologist Daniel Dayan introduced a second recurring theme in his study of the Sundance Film Festival: the engagement of distinctive groups with diverse interests. He described the festival as a set of divergent performances (by filmmakers, distributors, festival organisers, journalists, the audience etc.) and argues that it is not limited to visual display but that it is above all a 'verbal architecture ... made up of different versions, relaying different voices, relying on different sources of legitimacy' (Dayan 2000: 52). Several studies have attempted to make festivals' versatility understandable. Julian Stringer (2003) explored film festivals as institutions, festival nations, festival cities, festival films and festival communities in his dissertation, developing theoretical approaches to fit each new angle. Kenneth Turan (2002, section 1) and Marijke de Valck (2007) tackled the diverse festival phenomenon with case studies that respectively take geopolitical, business and cultural/aesthetic perspectives. Thomas Elsaesser (2005) and Janet Harbord (2002, section 3) offer valuable insights into festivals' temporal and spatial dimensions. Other threads running through all festival theories include the festival network as alternative distribution system, core-periphery relations, festival programming as agenda setting, value addition and distinction, spectacle, and the festival as media event.

Dayan, Daniel (2000) 'Looking for Sundance: The Social Construction of a Film Festival', in Ib Bondebjerg (ed.) *Moving Images, Culture and the Mind*. Luton: University of Luton Press, 43-52.

de Valck, Marijke (2003) 'Nové objevení Evropy. Historický přehled fenoménu filmvých festivalů [The Reappearance of Europe. A Historical Overview of the Film Festival Phenomenon]', *Iluminace*, 15, 1, 31-51.

_____ (2007a) 'As Vária Faces dos Festivais de Cinema Europeus [The Multiple Faces of European Film Festivals]', in Allessandra Meleiro (ed.) *A Indústria Cinematográfica Internacional: Europa*. São Paulo: Escrituras Editora, 213-41.

_____ (2007b) *Film Festivals: From European Geopolitics to Global Cinephilia*. Amsterdam: Amsterdam University Press.

Elsaesser, Thomas (2005) 'Film Festival Networks: The New Topographies of Cinema in Europe', in *European Cinema: Face to Face with Hollywood*. Amsterdam: Amsterdam University Press, 82-107.

Ethis, Emmanuel (2001) *Aux Marches du Palais: Le Festival de Cannes sous le Regard des Sciences Sociales*. Paris: La Documentation Française.

_____ (2002) *Avignon, le Public Réinventé: le Festival sous le Regard des Sciences Sociales*. Paris: La Documentation Française.

Evans, Owen (2007) 'Border Exchanges: The Role of the European Film Festival', *Journal of Contemporary European Studies*, 15, 1, 23-33.

Iordanova, Dina (2008) 'Editorial (Special Issue on Film Festivals)', *Film International*, 6, 4, 4-7.

Chapter Thirteen

Lutkehaus, Nancy C. (1995) 'The Sundance Film Festival', *Visual Anthropology Review*, 11, 2, 121-29.

Nichols, Bill (1994) 'Global Image Consumption in the Age of Late Capitalism', *East-West Film Journal*, 8, 1, 68-85.

Peranson, Mark (2008) 'First You Get the Power, Then You Get the Money: Two Models of Film Festivals', *Cineaste*, 33, 3, 37-43.

Porton, Richard (ed.) (2009) *Dekalog 3: On Film Festivals*. London: Wallflower Press.

Reichel-Heldt, Kai (2007) *Filmfestivals in Deutschland: Zwischen kulturpolitischen Idealen und wirtschaftspolitischen Realitäten*. Frankfurt am Main: Lang.

Stringer, Julian (2003) 'Regarding Film Festivals', unpublished PhD thesis, University of Indiana.

1.2 Political Aspects of Film Festivals (History)

Our understanding of today's film festivals and the contemporary international film festival circuit is tied to our knowledge of festival histories. Geopolitical interests held the first wave of (European) film festivals in a tight grip until the mid-1960s. The articles and books in this subcategory analyse certain parts of festival history in detail, such as the Fascist influence over the Venice Film Festival in the late 1930s (de Valck 2007, section 1.1), the Cold War agenda of the Berlin Film Festival (Fehrenbach 1995) and politically informed (programming) practices in Eastern Europe (Iordanova 2006; Karl 2007; Kötzing 2007a, b; Moine 2007).

Fehrenbach, Heidi (1995) 'Mass Culture and Cold War Politics: The Berlin Film Festival of the 1950s', in *Cinema in Democratizing Germany: Reconstructing National Identity after Hitler*. Chapel Hill/London: University of North Carolina Press, 234-59.

Iordanova, Dina (2006) 'Showdown of the Festivals: Clashing Entrepreneurships and Post-Communist Management of Culture', *Film International*, 4, 5, 25-37.

Karl, Lars (2007) 'Zwischen politischem Ritual und kulturellem Dialog: Die Moskauer Internationalen Filmfestspiele im Kalten Krieg 1959-1971', in Lars Karl (ed.) *Leinwand zwischen Tauwetter und Frost: Der osteuropäische Spiel- und Dokumentarfilm im Kalten Krieg*. Berlin: Metropol, 279-98.

Kötzing, Andreas (2007a) 'Filmfestivals als historische Quelle', *Deutschland Archiv: Zeitschrift für das vereinigte Deutschland*, 40, 4, 693-99.

____ (2007b) 'Zeigen oder nicht zeigen? Das "Prinzip der Selbstnominierung" sozialistischer Filme auf der Leipziger Dokumentarfilmwoche', in Lars Karl (ed.) *Leinwand zwischen Tauwetter und Frost: Der osteuropäische Spiel- und Dokumentarfilm im Kalten Krieg*. Berlin: Metropol, 299-316.

Film Festival Studies

Moine, Caroline (2007) 'Blicke über den Eisernen Vorhang: Die internationalen Filmfestivals im Kalten Krieg 1945-1968', in Lars Karl (ed.) *Leinwand zwischen Tauwetter und Frost: Der osteuropäische Spiel- und Dokumentarfilm im Kalten Krieg.* Berlin: Metropol, 255-78.

Stein, Gabby (1997) 'Censorship and the Film Festival', *Cinema Papers*, 118, 58-9.

1.3 General Academic Studies on Festivals (Not only *Film* Festivals)

Of great value to the study of film festivals is the extensive body of literature on festivals that has been produced from an anthropological and sociological perspective. A small selection is included below. Festivals were first studied to gain an understanding of so-called primitive people. Jean Duvignaud (1976) argues that the classic analysis of festivals goes back to Émile Durkheim, who distinguished between the sacred and profane and wrote about 'collective effervescence' as the supreme moment of the solidarity of collective consciousness (Duvignaud 1976: 13). In the overview below, Alessandro Falassi presents a morphology of festivals with 10 ritual acts (rites) as building blocks for actual festivals (1987: 3-6). However, there is not one 'essence of the festival' common to all civilisations, as Duvignaud argues, save, perhaps, that all are in a way antagonistic (1976: 18-19). Particularly relevant to film festival research is his observation that some festivals revolve around prestige and competition rather than tribal disorganisation and are related to economic activity rather than mythical fascinations with nature. When we turn to studies of modern festivals then, recent work specifically addresses the effects of commercialisation and globalisation. Montserrat Crespi-Valbona and Greg Richards, for example, argue that the 'focus [in recent studies on festivalisation] has often been on the replacement of local, traditional culture by globalised, popular culture, and the transition from "ritual" to "spectacle"' (2007: 106).

Allen, Johnny, William O'Toole, Ian McDonnell and Robert Harris (2005) *Festival and Special Event Management.* Milton: Wiley.

Crespi-Valbona, Montserrat and Greg Richards (2007) 'The Meaning of Cultural Festivals: Stakeholder Perspectives in Catalunya', *International Journal of Cultural Policy*, 13, 1, 103-22.

Duvignaud, Jean (1976) 'Festivals: A Sociological Approach', *Cultures*, 3, 1, 13-28.

Falassi, Alessandro (1987) *Time Out of Time: Essays on the Festival.* Albuquerque: University of New Mexico Press.

Harris, Neil (2007) 'Festival Culture, American Style', in Casey N. Blake (ed.) *The Arts of Democracy: Art, Public Culture, and the State.* Philadelphia: University of Pennsylvania Press, 11-29.

MacAloon, John J. (ed.) (1984) *Rite, Drama, Festival, Spectacle: Rehearsals toward a Theory of Cultural Performance*. Philadelphia: Institute for the Study of Human Issues.

2. Festival Time: Awards, Juries and Critics

The exceptional temporal frame of festivals has been theorised extensively from an anthropological and sociological perspective. In the introduction to *Time Out of Time: Essays on the Festival*, Alessandro Falassi describes how 'festival time imposes itself as an autonomous duration, not so much to be perceived and measured in days or hours, but to be divided internally by what happens within it from its beginning to its end' (Falassi 1987: 4; section 1.3). In addition, film festival research has addressed the defining temporal characteristics that are more specific to *film* festivals, such as festivals' use of exceptional temporality to add value and set agendas (Elsaesser 2005, de Valck 2007, both section 1.1), as well as the festival calendar, which defines the relation of festivals to one another, positions them in the circuit, and sets the expiration date at a one-year maximum. More specifically, our understanding of the way these characteristics shape film festivals needs to be advanced with close analyses of festival prizes, festival juries and the role of critics. The articles in this category flesh out some of the main concerns, such as the subjective nature of evaluations (Helmke 2005, Pride 2002), the effects of awards on distribution (Dodds and Holbrook 1998), and the correlation between taste and mediation in high art (Shrum 1996).

Dodds, John C. and Morris B. Holbrook (1998) 'What's an Oscar Worth? An Empirical Estimation of the Effects of Nominations and Awards on Movie Distribution and Revenues', *Current Research in Film: Audiences, Economics and Law*, 4, 72-88.

Helmke, Julia (2005) *Kirche, Film und Festivals: Geschichte sowie Bewertungskriterien evangelischer und ökumenischer Juryarbeit in den Jahren 1948 bis 1988*. Erlangen: CPV Christliche-Publizistik-Verlag.

Nuchelmans, André (2004) 'De Loden Last van het Gouden Kalf: Het belang van filmprijzen voor regisseur en acteur', *Boekman*, 60, 115-20.

Pride, Ray (2002) 'The Prize Patrol: The Inexact Science of Festival Juries and Critics Awards', *The Independent: Film and Video Monthly*, 25, 1, 26-9.

Ranvaud, Don (1985) 'Don Ranvaud and Festivals', *Filmnews*, 15, 9, 10-11.

Rosenbaum, Jonathan (2000) 'Trafficking in Movies: Festival-hopping in the Nineties', in *Movie Wars, How Hollywood and the Media Limit What Films We Can See*. London: Wallflower, 143-73.

Scott, Robert Dawson (1999) 'Bridging the Cultural Gap: How Arts Journalists Decide What Gets onto the Arts and Entertainment Page', *Critical Quarterly*, 41, 1, 46-56.

Shrum, Wesley Monroe Jr. (1996) *Fringe and Fortune: The Role of Critics in High and Popular Art.* Princeton: Princeton University Press.

3. Festival Space: Cities, Tourism and Public Spheres

In recent years, research on tourism has contributed significantly to spatial analyses of cultural festivals. There are two perspectives: the 'arts and urban development' perspective sees festivals 'as a catalyst for urban renewal, attracting tourists and capital investments, enhancing a city's image and creating new jobs' (Crespi-Valbona and Richards 2007: 106; section 1.3), the 'liveable cities' perspective stresses how communities can appropriate commoditised festival events for their own purposes, such as self-identification and developing a local sense of community and place. Julian Stringer argues that festivals market both global similarity and conceptual difference, often using local attractions to compete in the contemporary global space economy. Taking the unevenly differentiated power relations between nations and regions into consideration, he regards the international film festival circuit as 'a series of diverse, sometimes competing, sometimes cooperating public spheres' (Stringer 2001: 138).

Derrett, Ros (2000) 'Can Festivals Brand Community Cultural Development and Cultural Tourism simultaneously?', in John Allen, Robert Harris, Leo K. Jago and A. J. Veal (eds) *Events Beyond 2000: Setting the Agenda: Proceedings of Conference on Event Evaluation, Research and Education Sydney July 2000.* Sydney: Australian Centre for Event Management, 120-29. On-line. Available HTTP: http://www.utsydney.cn/business/acem/pdfs/Events2000_finalversion.pdf (18 February 2009).

___ (2003) 'Festivals & Regional Destinations: How Festivals Demonstrate a Sense of Community & Place', *Rural Society*, 13, 1, 35-53.

___ (2004) 'Festivals, Events and the Destination', in Ian Yeoman, Martin Robertson, Jane Ali-Knight, Siobhan Drummond and Una McMahon-Beattie (eds) *Festival and Events Management: An International Arts and Culture Perspective.* Amsterdam: Elsevier Butterworth-Heinemann, 32-51.

Gold, John Robert and Margaret M. Gold (2004) *Cities of Culture: Staging International Festivals and the Urban Agenda, 1851-2000.* Aldershot: Ashgate Publishers.

Harbord, Janet (2002) 'Film Festivals: Media Events and the Spaces of Flow', in *Film Cultures.* London: Sage, 59-75.

Prentice, Richard and Vivien Andersen (2003) 'Festivals as Creative Destination', *Annals of Tourism Research*, 30, 1, 7-30.

Shapiro, Michael J. (2007) 'The New Violent Cartography', *Security Dialogue*, 38, 3, 291-313.

Stringer, Julian (2001) 'Global Cities and International Film Festival Economy', Mark Shiel and Tony Fitzmaurice (eds) *Cinema and the City: Film and Urban Societies in a Global Context.* Oxford: Blackwell, 134-44.

4. On the Red Carpet: Spectacle, Stars and Glamour

Many critics have written about the glamour of film festivals. Often they denounce the 'hoopla' as distracting from the cultural significance of the festival's programming (Sklar 1996). On the other hand, many try to weaken the persistent myth of festival folly set in Cannes in the 1950s by focusing on the mundane realities of attending film festivals (Stapleton and Robinson 1983). As media events, film festivals are of great interest to different people: young girls longing to become famous (starlets), Hollywood companies looking to launch their next blockbuster (Jungen 2005, 2008), and filmmakers in search of an audience and (international) career. International film festivals contribute to the creation of a transnational and cosmopolitan film culture, and to achieve this end they use spectacle, stars and glamour (Schwartz 2007).

Jungen, Christian (2005) 'Der Journalist, ein Geschäftspartner der Studios: Starinterviews als Mittel der Filmpromotion', Vinzenz Hediger and Patrick Vonderau (es.) *Demnächst in Ihrem Kino: Grundlagen der Filmwerbung und Filmvermarktung.* Marburg: Schüren, 297-312.

___ (2008) *Hollywood in Canne\$: Die Geschichte einer Hassliebe, 1939-2008.* Marburg: Schüren.

Marshall, William (2005) *Film Festival Confidential.* Toronto: McArthur & Co.

Schwartz, Vanessa (2007) 'The Cannes Film Festival and the Marketing of Cosmopolitanism', in *It's So French! Hollywood, Paris and the Making of Cosmopolitan Film Culture.* Chicago/London: University of Chicago Press, 56-99.

Sklar, Robert (1996) 'Beyond Hoopla: The Cannes Film Festival and Cultural Significance', *Cineaste*, 22, 3, 18-20.

Stapleton, John and David Robinson (1983) 'All the Fun of the Festivals', *Films & Filming*, 345, 14-16.

5. Business Matters: Industries, Distribution and Markets

Although film festivals' core business is screening films, many festivals also facilitate 'the business' of cinema. Arguably, the big international film festivals – Cannes, Berlin, Toronto etc. – owe a great deal of their prestigious and influential position in the festival network to the success of their market activities and their services to the industry. Art cinema, world cinema and independent cinema increasingly depend on the nodes of the festival network for financing, sales, promotion and traffic (Biskind 2004, Perren 2001).

In the subcategories listed below a variety of publications is collected. The diversity of audiences addressed by these works – academic, professional and institutional/governmental – points at a widespread recognition of the vital role film festivals play in media industries worldwide.

Biskind, Peter (2004) *Down and Dirty Pictures: Miramax, Sundance, and the Rise of the Independent Film*. New York: Simon & Schuster.
Perren, Alisa (2001) 'Sex, Lies and Marketing: Miramax and the Development of the Quality Indie Blockbuster', *Film Quarterly*, 55, 2, 30-9.

5.1 Markets and Funds

The writings in this subcategory look at film festival markets and funds from a predominantly cultural perspective. Cultural diversity (instead of economic productivity and efficiency) is therefore at the heart of these reflections and analyses of the business side of festivals. Most authors display a concern for an inclusive cinema culture: stretching from first world national cinemas to cinema in developing countries, keeping standards of artistic quality high, and offering space for aesthetic experiments, adversary views or lifestyles, and marginal voices.

Chin, Daryl (1997) 'Festivals, Markets, Critics: Notes on the State of the Art Film', *Performing Arts Journal*, 19, 1, 61-75.
Chin, Daryl and Larry Qualls (1998) 'To Market, to Market', *Performing Arts Journal*, 20, 1, 38-43.
___ (2001) 'Open Circuits, Closed Markets: Festivals and Expositions of Film and Video', *Performing Arts Journal*, 23, 1, 33-47.
Creton, Laurent (1997) *Cinéma et Marché*. Paris: Armand Colin/Masson.
Fallaux, Emile, Malu Halasa and Nupu Press (eds) (2003) *True Variety: Funding the Art of World Cinema*. Rotterdam: International Film Festival Rotterdam.
Perry, Simon (1981) 'Cannes, Festivals and the Movie Business', *Sight & Sound*, 50, 4, 226-32.
Qualls, Larry and Daryl Chin (2004) 'Three Blind Mice: Fairs, Festivals, Expositions', *Performing Arts Journal*, 78, 62-71.
Scharres, Barbara (1990) 'Still Number One? The Cannes International Film Festival and Market', *The Independent: Film and Video Monthly*, 13, 8, 16-19.
Steinhart, Daniel (2006) 'Fostering International Cinema: The Rotterdam Film Festival, CineMart, and Hubert Bals Fund', *Mediascape*, 2, 1-13. On-line. Available HTTP: http://www.tft.ucla.edu/mediascape/Spring06_FosteringInternationalCinema.pdf (18 February 2009).

5.2 Distribution

When attempting to answer the question as to why film festivals exist, discussions tend to gravitate to the problem of distribution. In a competitive market driven by commercial objectives and moulded by the aggressive strategies of major film companies, it is difficult for non-mainstream films to find theatrical distribution. Film festivals provide several 'answers' to this problem.

Bachmann, Gideon (2000) 'Insight into the Growing Festival Influence: Fest Vet Discusses "Wholesale" and "Retail" Events', *Variety*, 28 August. On-line. Available
HTTP: http://www.variety.com/article/VR1117785609.html
(18 February 2009).
Burgos, Sergi Mesonero (2008) 'A Festival Epidemic in Spain', *Film International*, 6, 4, 8-14.
Gaines, Christian (2008a) 'State of the Fest – Part One: Do Festivals Matter?', *The Circuit – Blog on Variety.com*. On-line. Available
HTTP: http://www.variety.com/blog/1390000339/post/1980031998.html
(18 February 2009 [20 August 2008]).
____ (2008b) 'State of the Fest – Part Two: Things Gotta Change', *The Circuit – Blog on Variety.com*. On-line. Available
HTTP: http://www.variety.com/blog/1390000339/post/50032005.html (18 February 2009 [21 August 2008]).
Iordanova, Dina (2008) 'The Festival Circuit', in *Budding Channels of Peripheral Cinema: The Long Tail of Global Film Distribution*. Blurb.com, 25-32.

5.3 Service Guides for Professionals

For newcomers to the international film festival circuit, festivals are notoriously difficult places to find your way around. For these 'virgin' professionals, service guides are published that offer 'strategies for survival' or disclose 'festival secrets'. For those aiming to set up their own film festival, there are also several guides on the market.

BFI (2001) *How to Set Up a Film Festival*. Eldridge, Pippa and Julia Voss. London: BFI. On-line. Available
HTTP: http://www.bfi.org.uk/filmtvinfo/publications/pub-rep-brief/pdf/how-filmfest.pdf (18 February 2009).
____ (2002) *At a Cinema Near You: Strategies for Sustainable Local Cinema Development*. Baker, Robin, J. Ron Inglis and Julia Voss. London: BFI. On-line. Available
HTTP: http://www.bfi.org.uk/filmtvinfo/publications/pub-rep-brief/pdf/acny_all.pdf (18 February 2009).

Craig, Benjamin (2004) *Sundance: A Festival Virgin's Guide – Surviving and Thriving in Park City at America's Most Important Film Festival*. London: Cinemagine Media.

___ (2006) *Cannes: A Festival Virgin's Guide – Attending the Cannes Film Festival for Filmmakers and Film Industry Professionals*. London: Cinemagine Media.

Falco, Sidney (1988) 'Everything You Always Wanted to Know about Film Festivals (But Were Afraid to Ask)', *Films & Filming*, 406, 22-3.

Gaydos, Steven (ed.) (1998) *The Variety Guide to Film Festivals: The Ultimate Insider's Guide to Film Festivals around the World*. New York: Berkley Publishers Group.

Gore, Chris (1999) *The Ultimate Film Festival Survival Guide*. Los Angeles: Lone Eagle.

Greuling, Matthias (2004) *Cannes, Venedig, Berlin: Die großen Filmfestivals: Ein Servicebuch für Filmer und Medienvertreter*. Norderstedt: Books on Demand.

Holland, Christopher (2009) *Film Festival Secrets: A Handbook for Independent Filmmakers*. Austin: Stomp Tokyo. On-line. Available HTTP: http://www.filmfestivalsecrets.com/dddownload (18 February 2009).

Langer, Adam (2000) *The Film Festival Guide: For Filmmakers, Film Buffs, and Industry Professionals*. Chicago: Chicago Review Press.

Nowlan, Robert A. and Gwendolyn Wright Nowlan (1988) *An Encyclopedia of Film Festivals*. Greenwich: JAI Press.

Stolberg, Shael (1998) *International Film Festival Guide*. Toronto: Festival Products.

Tanner, Laurie Rose (2005) *Creating Film Festivals: Everything You Wanted to Know but Didn't Know Who to Ask*. San Francisco: Big Horse Inc.

5.4 Studies / Reports Related to Film Festival Research

This final subcategory in the business section contains institutional reports, overviews and directories of national or pan-national (EU) organisations that may be relevant to film festival research. The publications are predominantly quantitative in nature, listing numbers of festival admissions, accredited festivals and other data.

Aas, Nils Klevjer (1997) 'Flickering Shadow: Quantifying the European Film Festival Phenomenon', On-line. Available HTTP: http://www.obs.coe.int/online_publication/expert/00001262.html.en (18 February 2009 [3 January 2003]).

AG Kurzfilm e.V. – Bundesverband Deutscher Kurzfilm (2006) *Kurzfilm in Deutschland: Studie zur Situation des kurzen Films*. Michael Jahn, Christina Kaminski and Reinhard W. Wolf (eds). Dresden: AG Kurzfilm e.V. On-line. Available

HTTP: http://www.ag-kurzfilm.de/shared/doc/upload/page/212/page_de_212.pdf
(18 February 2009).

British Council (ed.) (1998) *Directory of international film and video festivals 1999 and 2000.* London: British Council.

FIAPF (2008) *FIAPF Accredited Festivals Directory / L'Annuaire des Festivals Accrédités par la FIAPF: 2008.* International Federation of Film Producers Associations (FIAPF). On-line. Available HTTP: http://www.fiapf.org/pdf/2008FIAPFDirectory.pdf (18 February 2009).

Internationale Kurzfilmtage Oberhausen (1997) *Die Zukunft der Filmfestivals – neue Bedingungen in der Informationsgesellschaft: Ideen, Vorschläge, Diskussionen.* Protokoll und Dokumentation der Konferenz 27-28 April 1997. Angela Haardt (ed.) Oberhausen.

Samlowski, Wolfgang (ed.) (2008) *International Guide Film-Video-Festivals 2009.* Berlin: Vistas.

6. Trans/National Cinemas

As the concept of the nation state has increasingly come under attack, cinema studies have slowly adopted the approach and strive to think through the concept and different possibilities of the trans/national in cinema. Thomas Elsaesser (2005, section 1.1) emphasises the different ways in which film production as well as film reception transcend borders and, thus, calls for an account of the transnational in film.

Film festivals are the platforms where new national waves can be discovered (cf. Nichols 1994, section 8). Or as Owen Evans suggests, film festivals (in Europe) are 'loci of cultural dialogue between Hollywood and the rest of the world's cinema' (2007: 24; section 1.1). What needs to be taken into account when stating this is the power difference that exists between the (Western) film festival circuit and national cinema/'world cinema' (Stringer 2001, section 3). In the last few years, scholars have started to analyse how film festivals (in the West) have served as cultural taste-makers for global cinema and had a significant influence on global film markets. This influence continues until today.

We have subdivided section 6 Trans/National Cinema in order to map out the different regions that have been studied in this context and try to account for the differences that have been highlighted in the respective pieces.

6.1 Europe

As the cradle of film festivals, Europe's encounter with trans/national relations between film and their showcases for (inter)national competition is as old as the festival phenomenon. Lucy Mazdon investigates the role of the Cannes festival as a transnational space (2006) and its relationship to French cinema (2007). The meaning of Cannes for German film (Fründt and Lepel 1987) or Hollywood (Jungen 2008, section 4) has also been scrutinised. Several historical studies with a focus on film history during the Cold War era give insight into the history (of the study) of European film. They examine the way it was discussed across borders at certain international film festivals which did not conform to the general division of Western and Eastern bloc politics/art (Karl 2007, Kötzing 2007, Moine 2007, all in section 1.2). A special focus in this history is the analysis of trans- or intra-national discussions of German film on either side of the Wall.

Felsmann, Klaus-Dieter (2002) 'Eine feste Bank: DEFA-Kinderfilme in 25 Berlinale-Jahren', in DEFA-Stiftung (ed.) *apropos Film 2002: Das Jahrbuch der DEFA-Stiftung*. Berlin: Bertz, 190-98.

Hofstede, Bart (2000a) 'Hoofdstuk 4: Filmfestivals en het Succes van Nederlandse films in het Buitenland', in *De Nederlandse Cinema Wereldwijd: De Internationale Positie van de Nederlandse Film*. Amsterdam: Boekmanstudies, 101-29.

____ (2000b) *In het Wereldfilmstelsel: Identiteit en Organisatie van de Nederlandse film sedert 1945*. PhD thesis. Delft: Eburon.

Fründt, Bodo and Bernd Lepel (1987) *Träume unter goldenen Palmen / Dreams beneath the Golden Palms: Der deutsche Film auf dem Internationalen Filmfestival in Cannes / German Films at the International Film Festival in Cannes*. (Biligual edition), in Eberhard Junkersdorf and Deutsche Export-Union des Deutschen Films e.V. München (eds). Ebersberg: Ed. Achteinhalb.

Kuhlbrodt, Dietrich (2005) 'DEFA-Filme in Oberhausen: Rückblick auf fünfzig Jahre', in DEFA-Stiftung (ed.) *apropos Film 2005: Das Jahrbuch der DEFA-Stiftung*. Berlin: Bertz+Fischer, 106-18.

Mazdon, Lucy (2006) 'The Cannes Film Festival as Transnational Space', *Post Script*, 25, 2, 19-30.

____ (2007) 'Transnational "French" Cinema: The Cannes Film Festival', *Modern and Contemporary France*, 15, 1, 9-20.

6.2 Asia

The pieces in this section look at several aspects of the transnational nature of the film festival circuit in relation to Asia and Asian cinema. Soyoung Kim highlights the political and cultural context of the emergence of several film festivals in South Korea in the 1990s. Kim's piece offers a great contextualisation for further analyses by SooJeong Ahn who looks at the development of PIFF and its strategic moves to establish a hub for Korean cinema, as well as Asian cinema in general and what it has undertaken to enter a global market (Kim 1998: 183, section 9.1; Ahn 2008a, b; Ahn forthcoming). Several other scholars have taken a look at the impact the international film festival circuit has had on the acknowledgement, praise and economic exploitation of Asian film (cf. Stringer 2001, section 3), with perspectives on Chinese Cinema (Zhang 2002), Hong Kong Cinema (Wong 2007), and Taiwan Cinema (Wu 2007).

Ahn, SooJeong (2008a) 'Re-imagining the Past: Programming South Korean Retrospectives at the Pusan International Film Festival', *Film International*, 6, 4, 24-33.

____ (2008b) 'The Pusan International Film Festival 1996-2005: South Korean Cinema in Local, Regional, and Global Context', unpublished PhD thesis, University of Nottingham. On-line. Available HTTP: http://etheses.nottingham.ac.uk/archive/00000513/01/AHN_etheses_all.pdf (18 February 2009).

____ (2009) 'Building up Asian Identity: The Pusan International Film Festival in South Korea', in Ruby Cheung with D. H. Fleming (eds) *Cinemas, Identities and Beyond*. Newcastle upon Tyne: Cambridge Scholars Publishing.

____ (forthcoming) 'Placing South Korean Cinema into Pusan International Film Festival: Programming Strategy in the Global/Local Context', in Chris Berry, Darren Aoki and Nicola Liscutin (eds) *What a Difference a Region Makes: Cultural Studies and Cultural Industries in North-East Asia*. Hong Kong: Hong Kong University Press.

Tan, Ye and Zhang Yimou (2000) 'From the Fifth to the Sixth Generation: Interview with Zhang Yimou', *Film Quarterly*, 53, 2, 2-13.

Wong, Cindy Hing-Yuk (2007) 'Distant Screens: Film Festivals and the Global Projection of Hong Kong Cinema', in Gina Marchetti and Tan See Kam (eds) *Hong Kong Film, Hollywood and New Global Cinema: No Film is an Island*. London/New York: Routledge, 177-92.

Wu, Chia-chi (2007) 'Festivals, Criticism and International Reputation of Taiwan New Cinema', in Darrell William Davis and Ru-shou Robert Chen (eds) *Cinema Taiwan: Politics, Popularity, and State of the Arts*. Abingdon: Routledge, 75-91.

Zhang, Yingjin (2002) 'Chinese Cinema and Transnational Cultural Politics: Reflections on Film Festivals, Film Productions, and Film Studies', in *Screening China: Critical Interventions, Cinematic Reconfigurations, and the Transnational Imaginary in Contemporary Chinese Cinema*. Ann Arbor: Center for Chinese Studies, 15-42.

6.3 Africa

This section assembles articles focusing on African cinema and African film festivals and their place within the international film festival circuit. The publications listed here focus on the two oldest film festivals on the African continent: Les Journées Cinématographiques de Carthage (JCC) and Festival

Panafricain du Cinéma et de la Télévision de Ouagadougou (FESPACO). These two festivals, both taking place biannually in alternating years, have showcased and promoted African film regionally and internationally. This seemingly positive outcome, however, also has a drawback for the African film market, which lacks an infrastructure, argues Manthia Diawara (1993). With the raised profile of African cinema, the marketing of these films became the dominant purpose of the larger (i.e. mostly Western) festival system. With better connections to established (Western) film markets, African (and other) film festivals held in Europe and North America provide filmmakers with a more important/effective film production and distribution infrastructure than that of their home countries in Africa. This in, turn, leaves the former spokes-festivals for African film, Carthage and Ouagadougou, in a dilemma: they are unable to feature prestigious new African productions (Diawara 1993, 1994; Ruoff 2008; cf. Turan 2002: 65-80; section 1).

Bachmann, Gideon (1973) 'In Search of Self-Definition: Arab and African Film at the Carthage Film Festival (Tunis)', *Film Quarterly*, 26, 3, 48-51.

Diawara, Manthia (1993) 'New York and Ouagadougou: The Homes of African Cinema', *Sight & Sound*, 3, 11, 24-6.

___ (1994) 'On Tracking World Cinema: African Cinema at Film Festivals', *Public Culture*, 6, 2, 385-96.

Ruoff, Jeffrey (2008) 'Ten Nights in Tunisia: Les Journées Cinématographiques de Carthage', *Film International*, 6, 4, 43-51.

6.4 The Middle East

The relationship between the film festival circuit and cinema from/in the Middle East has seldom been studied. Bill Nichols developed his study of reception patterns at film festivals and the 'discovery' of new cinemas using the example of Iranian cinema (Nichols 1994, section 1.1; Nichols 1994, section 8). Jeffrey Ruoff has described the Carthage Film Festival as a festival focused on the promotion of Arab (and African) film (Ruoff 2008, section 6.3). Azadeh Farahmand (2002, 2006) has presented a very detailed analysis. Farahmand takes the increasing attention paid to Iranian cinema since the 1990s as a starting point to examine how socio-economic factors and institutional politics, especially those facilitated through international film festivals contribute to the production and elevation of films and national cinema. Key issues she touches on are the problem of censorship, (inter)national financing of film productions through the film festival circuit, and political negotiations via cultural exchange (Farahmand 2002).

Farahmand, Azadeh (2002) 'Perspectives on Recent (International Acclaim for) Iranian Cinema', in Richard Tapper (ed.) *The New Iranian Cinema: Politics, Representation and Identity*. London: I.B. Tauris, 86-108.

_____ (2006) 'At the Crossroads: International Film Festivals and the Constitution of the New Iranian Cinema', unpublished PhD thesis, University of California, Los Angeles.

6.5 South America

We found only one article explicitly dealing with the transnational quality of film festivals in relation to South America. Julianne Burton stresses the impact of the political, left wing Italian film festival in Pesaro on the circulation of South American cinema in Europe and North America in her 1975 festival report.

Burton, Julianne (1975) 'The Old and the New: Latin American Cinema at the (Last?) Pesaro Festival', *Jump Cut: A Review of Contemporary Media*, 9, 33-5. On-line. Available HTTP: http://www.ejumpcut.org/archive/onlinessays/JC09folder/PesaroR eport.html (18 February 2009).

7. Programming

The vast majority of the pieces addressing the issue of programming assembled here are written from a practical point of view. Some aim to explain the decision-making processes at work during the act of programming behind the scenes of film festivals (Krach 2003; Thomson 2003). Others, often written by curators themselves, explicate the ideas and ideals of curators (Czach 2004; Givanni 2004; Haslam 2004; Marks 2004; Sandlos 2004; Schulte-Strathaus 2004, 2008; Straayer and Waugh 2005; section 9.1.1). Further pieces are interviews with curators (Gramann 2008; Gregor and Gregor 2008; Han and Morohoshi 2004; Noll Brinkmann 1990) or biographies (Heijs and Westra 1996). Beyond the specifics of the act of programming, other, more general concerns are addressed. The context of film programming and film reception plays an important role for programmers (Lehrer 1999).

Armatage, Kay (forthcoming) 'Fashions in Feminist Programming', in Corinn Columpar and Sophie Mayer (eds) *(Un)Making the Cut: Feminism, Filmmaking, Fluidity*. Detroit: Wayne State University Press.
Czach, Liz (2004) 'Film Festivals, Programming, and the Building of a National Cinema', *The Moving Image*, 4, 1, 76-88.
Givanni, June (2004) 'A Curator's Conundrum: Programming "Black Film" in 1980s-1990s Britain', *The Moving Image*, 4, 1, 60-75.
Gramann, Karola (2008) '"Man nehme ...": Ein Gespräch mit Heide Schlüpmann', in Heike Klippel (ed.) *'The Art of Programming': Film, Programm und Kontext*. Münster: LIT, 127-40.

Gregor, Erika and Ulrich Gregor (2008) 'Every Time the Curtain is Going Up, We are Hoping and Longing ... Talking to Dina Iordanova', *Film International*, 6, 4, 72-6.

Han, Ju Hui Judy and Marie K. Morohoshi (1998) 'Creating, Curating, and Consuming Queer Asian American Cinema', David L. Eng and Alice Y. Hom (eds) *Q & A: Queer in Asian America*. Philadelphia: Temple University Press, 81-94.

Haslam, Mark (2004) 'Vision, Authority, Context: Cornerstones of Curation and Programming', *The Moving Image*, 4, 1, 48-59.

Heijs, Jan and Frans Westra (1996) *Que Le Tigre Danse: Huub Bals een Biografie*. Amsterdam: Otto Cramwinckel.

Klippel, Heike (ed.) (2008) *'The Art of Programming': Film, Programm und Kontext*. Münster: LIT.

Krach, Aaron (2003) 'Unlocking the Secret of the Screening Committee', *The Independent: Film and Video Monthly*, 26, 3, 44-6.

Lehrer, Jeremy (1999) 'But Will It Play in Peoria: Two Festival Curators Assess the Audience for Experimental Media Today', *The Independent: Film and Video Monthly*, 22, 6, 28-31.

Marks, Laura U. (2004) 'The Ethical Presenter: Or How to Have Good Arguments over Dinner', *The Moving Image*, 4, 1, 35-47.

Noll Brinkmann, Christine (1990) 'The Art of Programming: An Interview with Alf Bold, July 1989', *Millennium Film Journal*, 23/24, 86-100.

Sandlos, Karyn (2004) 'Curating and Pedagogy in the Strange Time of Short Film and Video Exhibition', *The Moving Image*, 4, 1, 17-33.

Schager, Nick (2006) 'The Short Story at Sundance: Behind the Scenes with the Short Film Programmers', *The Independent: Film and Video Monthly*, 29, 1, 32-5.

Schulte-Strathaus, Stefanie (2004) 'Showing Different Films Differently: Cinema as a Result of Cinematic Thinking', *The Moving Image*, 4, 1, 1-16.

____ (2008) 'Andere Filme anders zeigen: Kino als Resultat filmischen Denkens', in Heike Klippel (ed.) *'The Art of Programming': Film, Programm und Kontext*. Münster: LIT, 89-103.

Stringer, Julian (2003a) 'Neither One Thing nor the Other: Blockbusters at Film Festivals', in Julian Stringer (ed.) *Movie Blockbusters*. London/New York: Routledge, 202-13.

____ (2003b). 'Raiding the Archive: Film Festivals and the Revival of Classic Hollywood', in Paul Grainge (ed.) *Memory and Popular Film*. Manchester: Manchester University Press, 81-96.

Thomson, Patricia (2003) 'Clutterbusters: Programmers at Five Leading Festivals Expound on Heady Process of Selecting Films', *Variety*, 18 August. On-line. Available HTTP: http://www.variety.com/article/VR1117891042.html (18 February 2009).

Chapter Thirteen

8. Reception: Audiences, Communities and Cinephiles

Curators imagine a certain programme and by doing so envision a way to highlight, promote and contextualise a film. The programme, however, is also dependent on the audience and its actual reception. Film festivals offer a framework which generates certain audience expectations; with their programme festival programmers (often) try to encourage the active reception of the audience (cf. Klippel 2008: 10). Some scholars and curators would even go so far as to say that programming means not (only) programming films but 'programming the public' (Fung 1999, section 9.1.1). They point to the fact that programming directly influences the constituency of the audience – although no one can foresee what audience reaction and outcome a certain programme will have (Stringer 2008).

Armatage, Kay (2008a) 'Screenings by Moonlight', *Film International*, 6, 4, 34-40.
____ (2008b) 'Sidebar: Traveling Projectionist Films', *Film International*, 6, 4, 41-2.
de Valck, Marijke (2005) 'Drowning in Popcorn at the International Film Festival Rotterdam? The Festival as a Multiplex of Cinephilia', in Marijke de Valck and Malte Hagener (eds) *Cinephilia: Movies, Love and Memory*. Amsterdam: Amsterdam University Press, 97-109.
Frohlick, Susan (2005) '"That Playfulness of White Masculinity": Mediating Masculinities and Adventure at Mountain Film Festivals', *Tourist Studies*, 5, 2, 175-93.
Nichols, Bill (1994) 'Discovering Form, Inferring Meaning: New Cinemas and the Film Festival Circuit', *Film Quarterly*, 47, 3, 16-30.
Rosenbaum, Jonathan (2003) 'Sampling in Rotterdam', in Jonathan Rosenbaum and Adrian Martin (eds) *Movie Mutations: The Changing Face of World Cinephilia*. London: British Film Institute, 52-60.
Stringer, Julian (2008) 'Genre Films and Festival Communities: Lessons from Nottingham, 1991-2000', *Film International*, 6, 4, 53-9.

9. Specialised Film Festivals

The vast proliferation of film festivals and the differentiation of film markets contribute to the development of specialised film festivals. There are a number of categories according to which these festivals can be grouped. The choice of our categories here is founded on basic elements which differentiate films and thus their showcase festivals as such. There are, for instance, festivals for long or short films, for features or documentaries, for animation or experimental films. Yet there are also other qualities that cluster films by way of a special programming profile of a festival: there are festivals that choose films not only according to their length, format or style, but rather according to a theme or context. Furthermore, not all specialised festivals have been studied yet. Thus, our categorisation is influenced by the texts available.

9.1 Identity-Based Festivals

The largest group of available research on specialised film festivals is dedicated to identity-based film festivals. Thus, this is the group located at the top of the list. As becomes visible in this list, there has been great interest in queer film festivals as well as women's film festivals. It is not surprising that this is the case considering the identity debates in feminist and queer activism and theory. Many of the pieces on queer film festivals are not only interesting to researchers of the queer theories or sub-cultural fields. Rather, these pieces can contribute to general discussions of the relationships between film festivals and their cinephile communities, between reception contexts and programming.

Apart from women's and queer film festivals, there exists a wide range of other identity-based film festivals – which have not (often) been specifically studied as such. There are pieces, however, that deal with examples such as the Jewish film festival (Galliner 2004, section 10), Black American film festivals, Asian (American) film festivals etc.

Kim, Soyoung (1998) '"Cine-Mania" or Cinephilia: Film Festivals and the Identity Question', *UTS Review: Cultural Studies und New Writing*, 4, 2, 174-87.
___ (2003) 'The Birth of the Local Feminist Sphere in the Global Era: "Trans-Cinema" and *Yosongjang*', *Inter-Asia Cultural Studies*, 4, 1, 10-24.

9.1.1 LGBT/Queer Film Festivals

As identity-based festivals, queer film festivals have a specific relationship to the audience they are catering to. More specifically, most of these festivals have had a strong connection to the political and social movement behind the lesbian and gay/queer agenda and try to maintain this relationship between cultural event and political framework (Jusick 2004; Stryker 1996; Ommert and Loist 2008). Because of this history, queer film festivals have a strong tradition of a nuanced critical inquiry into the interconnections of cultural event management, community politics, nation state politics, funding and marketing strategies, organisational structures (cf. Rhyne 2007, Zielinski 2008).

Resulting from this is a cluster of pieces that deal with the relationship between film festivals and communities, focusing on the mutual formative processes between the two actors (festival and community/audience) (Gamson 1996; Rich 1993, 1999), and constantly updating the question of necessity (Schulman 1994). A strongly connected issue is the representation

Chapter Thirteen

of the group/subculture in films of the so-called (New) Queer Cinema and at the LGBT/queer film festivals (Rich 1993, 1999; Hohenberger and Jurschik 1994; Stryker 1996; Siegel 1998; Woitschig 2001; Loist 2008).

In the general film festival discussion, a neglected field (except for the attempt by Stringer 2008) is the concept of the (counter) public sphere. This has been discussed in much detail in relation to LGBT film festivals (Rich 1993; S. Kim 1998; dossier ed. by Patricia White 1999; S. Kim 2003; Perspex 2006; Gorfinkel 2006; J. Kim 2007; Ommert and Loist 2008). As an extension of this discussion, special aspects such as spatial elements of queer film festival have been scrutinised (Brooke 1998, Zielinski 2008).

Becker, Edith (1992) 'The New York Lesbian and Gay Experimental Film Festival', *Jump Cut: A Review of Contemporary Media*, 37. On-line. Available HTTP: http://www.ejumpcut.org/archive/onlinessays/JC37folder/NYexptl GayLesFest.html (18 February 2009).

Berry, Chris (1999a) 'Bangkok's Alternative Love Film Festival Raided: Chris Berry interviews Sopawan Boonimitra', in *Intersections: Gender, History and Culture in the Asian Context*, 2. On-line. Available HTTP: http://intersections.anu.edu.au/issue2/Sidebar.html (18 February 2009).

___ (1999b) 'My Queer Korea: Identity, Space, and the 1998 Seoul Queer Film & Video Festival', *Intersections: Gender, History and Culture in the Asian Context*, 2. On-line. Available HTTP: http://intersections.anu.edu.au/issue2/Berry.html (18 February 2009).

Brooke, Kaucyila (1998) 'Dividers and Doorways: How to (De)Personalize Your Lifestyle with Architectural Details', *Jump Cut: A Review of Contemporary Media*, 42, 50-7. On-line. Available HTTP: http://www.ejumpcut.org/archive/onlinessays/JC42folder/Dividers Doorways.html (18 February 2009).

Clarke, Eric O. (1999) 'Queer Publicity at the Limits of Inclusion', *GLQ: A Journal of Lesbian and Gay Studies*, 5, 1, 84-9.

Fung, Richard (1999) 'Programming the Public', *GLQ: A Journal of Lesbian and Gay Studies*, 5, 1, 89-93.

Gamson, Joshua (1996) 'The Organizational Shaping of Collective Identity: The Case of Lesbian and Gay Film Festivals in New York', *Sociological Forum*, 11, 2, 231-61.

Gorfinkel, Elena (2006) 'Wet Dreams: Erotic Film Festivals of the Early 1970s and the Utopian Sexual Public Sphere', *Framework*, 47, 2, 59-86.

Grundmann, Roy (1992) 'Politics Esthetics Sex: Queer Films and Their Festivals', *Cineaste*, 19, 1, 50-52, 62.

Hohenberger, Eva and Karin Jurschick (1994) '*As Women, as People of Color, as Lesbians* ... : Diskussionen und Filme über *race* und *gender* bei den Gay and Lesbian Film Festivals in New York und San Francisco 1993', *Frauen und Film*, 54/55, 149-64.

June, Jamie L. (2004) 'Defining Queer: The Criteria and Selection Process for Programming Queer Film Festivals', *CultureWork*, 8, 2. On-line. Available HTTP: http://aad.uoregon.edu/culturework/culturework26.html (18 February 2009).

Jusick, Stephen Kent (2004) 'Gay Art Guerrillas: Interview with Jim Hubbard and Sarah Schulman', in Matt Bernstein [Mattilda] Sycamore (ed.) *That's Revolting! Queer Strategies for Resisting Assimilation*. Brooklyn: Soft Skull Press, 39-58.

Kim, Jeongmin (2007) 'Queer Cultural Movements and Local Counterpublics of Sexuality: A Case of Seoul Queer Films and Videos Festival', trans. Sunghee Hong, *Inter-Asia Cultural Studies*, 8, 4, 617-33.

Loist, Skadi (2008) 'Frameline XXX: Thirty Years of Revolutionary Film: Der Kampf um queere Repräsentationen in der Geschichte des San Francisco International LGBT Film Festival', in Ulla Wischermann and Tanja Thomas (eds.) *Medien – Diversität – Ungleichheit: Zur medialen Konstruktion sozialer Differenz*. Wiesbaden: VS Verlag für Sozialwissenschaften, 163-81.

McWilliam, Kelly (2007) '"We're Here All Week": Public Formation and the Brisbane Queer Film Festival', *Queensland Review*, 14, 2, 79-91.

Olson, Jenni (2002) 'Film Festivals', *glbtq: An Encyclopedia of Gay, Lesbian, Bisexual, Transgender, and Queer Culture*. On-line. Available HTTP: http://www.glbtq.com/arts/film_festivals.html (18 February 2009 [19 November 2004]).

Ommert, Alek and Skadi Loist (2008) *'Featuring interventions*: Zu queer-feministischen Repräsentationspraxen und Öffentlichkeiten', in Celine Camus, Annabelle Hornung, Fabienne Imlinger, Milena Noll and Isabelle Stauffer (eds) *Im Zeichen des Geschlechts: Repräsentationen – Konstruktionen– Interventionen*. Königstein/Taunus: Ulrike Helmer, 124-40.

Peach, Ricardo (2005) 'Queer Cinema as a Fifth Cinema in South Africa and Australia', unpublished PhD thesis, Sydney University of Technology.

Perspex (2006) 'The First Asian Lesbian Film and Video Festival in Taipei Celebrates a New Form of Social Activism', *Inter-Asia Cultural Studies*, 7, 3, 527-32.

Rhyne, Ragan (2007) 'Pink Dollars: Gay and Lesbian Film Festivals and the Economy of Visibility', unpublished PhD thesis, New York University.

Rich, B. Ruby (1993) 'Reflections on a Queer Screen', *GLQ: A Journal of Lesbian and Gay Studies,* 1, 1, 83-91.

____ (1999) 'Collision Catastrophe Celebration: The Relationship between Gay and Lesbian Film Festivals and Their Publics', *GLQ: A Journal of Lesbian and Gay Studies*, 5, 1, 79-84.

Said, Roiya Zahara (forthcoming 2009) 'The De-Fusion of Good Intentions: Notes on Outfest's Queer of Color Film Festival', *GLQ: A Journal of Lesbian and Gay Studies*, 15, 3.

Schulman, Sarah (1994) 'What is the Role of Gay Film Festivals?', in *My American History: Lesbian and Gay Life during the Reagan/Bush Years.* New York: Routledge, 253-55.

Searle, Samantha (1996) 'Film and Video Festivals: Queer Politics and Exhibition', *Meanjin*, 55, 1, 47-59.

___ (1997) *Queer-ing the Screen: Sexuality and Australian Film and Television.* St. Kilda: Australian Teachers of Media (ATOM).

Siegel, Marc (1997) 'Spilling out onto Castro Street', *Jump Cut: A Review of Contemporary Media*, 41, 131-36. On-line. Available HTTP: http://www.ejumpcut.org/archive/onlinessays/JC41folder/OnCastr oStreet.html (18 February 2009).

Straayer, Chris and Thomas Waugh (eds) (2005) 'Queer Film and Video Festival Forum, Take One: Curators Speak Out', [Contributions by Michael Barrett, Charlie Bourdeau, Suzy Capo, Stephen Gutwilig, Nanna Heidenreich, Liza Johnson, Giampaolo Marzi, Dean Otto, Brian Robinson, and Katharine Setzer] *GLQ: A Journal of Lesbian and Gay Studies*, 11, 4, 579-603.

___ (eds) (2006) 'Queer Film and Video Festival Forum, Take Two: Critics Speak Out', [Contributions by Juan A. Suárez, Yves Lafontaine, Yau Ching, M. R. Daniel, José Gatti, Joel David, Ragan Rhyne, and B. Ruby Rich] *GLQ: A Journal of Lesbian and Gay Studies*, 12, 4, 599-625.

___ (eds) (2008) 'Queer Film and Video Festival Forum, Take Three: Artists Speak Out', [Contributions by Bill Basquin, Maureen Bradley, Q. Allan Brocka, Olivier Ducastel, Su Friedrich, Barbara Hammer, Jacques Martineau, and Onir] *GLQ: A Journal of Lesbian and Gay Studies,* 14, 1, 121-37.

Stryker, Susan (1996) 'A Cinema of One's Own: A Brief History of the San Francisco International Lesbian & Gay Film Festival', in Jenni Olson (ed.) *The Ultimate Guide to Lesbian & Gay Film and Video.* New York: Serpent's Tail, 364-70.

White, Patricia (ed.) (1999) 'Queer Publicity: A Dossier on Lesbian and Gay Film Festivals', *GLQ: A Journal of Lesbian and Gay Studies,* 5, 1, 73-93.

Woitschig, Britta Madeleine (2001) 'Raus aus dem Klischee: Transgender-Filmfestivals seit 1996 als selbstbestimmte Darstellung trans- und intersexueller Lebensformen', in Paul M. Hahlbohm and Till Hurlin (eds) *Querschnitt – Gender Studies: Ein interdisziplinärer Blick nicht nur auf Homosexualität.* Kiel: Ludwig, 182-201.

Zielinski, Ger (2008) 'Furtive, Steady Glances: On the Cultural Politics of Lesbian and Gay Film Festivals', unpublished PhD thesis, McGill University, Montreal.

9.1.2 Women's Film Festivals

Considering the impact feminist activism and theory has had on film theory, it is surprising that women's film festivals have not been analysed as much as, say, queer film festivals. The pieces listed here focus on different issues related to women's film festivals. As is true for festival journalism in general, several articles provide a review of the films shown at these festivals. They are interspersed with descriptions and analyses of the structures, concepts and practices of the festivals (Brauerhoch 1987, Hammer 1998, Hiller and Holy 1976, Huang 2003). Beyond these historical snapshots of the women's film festival landscape, a few articles look at the historical contexts which informed and necessitated the establishing of women's film festivals (Barlow 2003, Hohenberger and Jurschick 1994, Quetting 2007).

Soyoung Kim and Yu Shan Huang provide insight into the concept of (women's) film festivals as alternative public spheres in the Asian context, South Korea and Taiwan respectively (Kim, S. 1998, 2003, section 9.1; Huang 2003).

Barlow, Melinda (2003) 'Feminism 101: The New York Women's Video Festival, 1972-1980', *Camera Obscura*, 18, 3, 3-38.

Brauerhoch, Annette (1987) 'Jenseits der Metropolen: Frauenfilmfestivals in Créteil und Dortmund', *Frauen und Film*, 42, 94-100.

Hammer, Barbara (1998) 'Turning 20: The Festival International de Films de Femmes de Créteil', *The Independent: Film and Video Monthly*, 21, 7, 18-19.

Hiller, Eva and Renate Holy (1976) 'Festival of Women's Films New York 1976', *Frauen und Film*, 10, 49.

Hohenberger, Eva and Karin Jurschick (1994) 'Zehn Jahre *Feminale*: Zehn Jahre feministischer Film', in Eva Hohenberger (ed.) *Blaue Wunder: Neue Filme und Videos von Frauen 1984 bis 1994*. Hamburg: Argument-Verlag, 7-17.

Huang, Yu Shan (2003) '"Creating and Distributing Films Openly": On the Relationship between Women's Film Festivals and the Women's Rights Movement in Taiwan', *Inter-Asia Cultural Studies*, 4, 1, 157-58.

Hüchtker, Ingrid (1992) 'Die verfluchte, die geliebte Öffentlichkeit: Pressearbeit für ein Frauen-Film-Festival (Ein Fallbeispiel mit Conclusio)', in Gruppe Feministische Öffentlichkeit (ed.) *Femina Publica: Frauen – Öffentlichkeit – Feminismus*. Köln: PapyRossa, 203-18.

Quetting, Esther (ed.) (2007) *Kino Frauen Experimente*. Marburg: Schüren.

9.2 Genre-Based Festivals

The festivals under this category select their films according to what can be called 'genre' distinctions in the broadest sense.
a) film genre: fantasy, science fiction, horror, crime (cf. Stringer 2008, section 8).
b) stylistic or narrative character: animation, experimental (Becker 1992, section 9.1.1), fiction, documentary (Kötzing 2004, Martini 2007, both section 10), silent film (Sørenssen 2008) or

c) length: short film (Kelly 2000; AG Kurzfilm 2006, section 5.4; cf. Reichel-Heldt 2007, section 1.1; Hedling 2008, section 9.3)

Kelly, Andrew (2000) 'Briefly Encountering Short Films: Reflections on Running a Film Festival 1994-99', *Journal of Media Practice*, 1, 2, 108-13.

Pócsik, Andrea (2008) 'Their Life and Our Vicarious Experiences: On Human Rights Films and Festivals', *Politics and Culture*, 2. On-line. Available HTTP: http://aspen.conncoll.edu/politicsandculture/page.cfm?key=623 (18 February 2009).

Sørenssen, Bjørn (2008) 'Le giornate del cinema muto: Pordenone', *Film International*, 6, 4, 77-81.

9.3 National or Regional Showcases

Traditionally film festivals have been influenced by, or only exist due to, geopolitics. Festivals do not only showcase films an audience would otherwise not have a chance to see. The film festival circuit as an alternative distribution network has a strong influence on the status of a film, the attention it receives and potentially the commercial life it has. Thus, many regional festivals – financed by the regional municipalities – are expected to weigh in their influence to highlight national and regional works and further the region's (film) economy (cf. Reichel-Heldt 2007, section 1.1)

Hedling, Olof (2008) '"Detta dåliga samvete": om kortfilmen, regionerna och filmfestivalerna ["This Bad Conscience": On Short Film, Regions and Film Festivals]', in Mats Jönsson and Erik Hedling (eds) *Välfärdsbilder: svensk film utanför biografen*. Stockholm: Statens ljud- och bildarkiv, 261-81.

9.4 Online Film Festivals

In a time when 'media convergence' is a general buzz phrase and when cinema operators fear that the wave of digitalisation might extinguish cinephilia as we know it, there has been a proliferation of hybrid forms, where film festivals make use of or altogether migrate to the Internet. The label 'online film festival' is not an easy one to define. Many major festivals also show a selection of (short) films online (*Sundance, Berlinale*). Some festivals only exist in the virtual world (e.g. *Babelgum Online Film Festival*). Others let audiences vote online while screening the winning films in a conventional cinema (*Bitfilm*, Hamburg). The pieces collected under this rubric provide different views on this issue.

Castle, Scott (2000) 'What's in a Name? Does the Term "Online Film Festival" Mean Anything at all?', *The Independent: Film and Video Monthly*, 23, 6, 18-20.

de Valck, Marijke (2008) '"Screening" the Future of Film Festivals: A Long Tale of Convergence and Digitization', *Film International*, 6, 4, 15-23.

Hernandez, Eugene (1999) 'The Point of No Return: On-Line Film Festivals, Showcases & Distributors', *The Independent: Film and Video Monthly*, 22, 9, 26-8.

Kurtzke, Simone (2007) 'Webfilm Theory', unpublished PhD thesis, Queen Margaret University.

10. Publications Dedicated to Individual Film Festivals

The last section of our annotated film festival bibliography collects articles, book chapters and books that have been created with varying purposes. There are several books that have been edited to celebrate major anniversaries of festivals; some of those focus on the glamour and highlights (e.g. Baecque 2007, Toubiana 1997 etc.), while others strive for a contextualisation and critical remembrance (e.g. Behnken 2004, Schenk 2007). Among the books, chapters, and articles are pieces collecting and describing a festival history (Stanfield 2008), or analysing specific discourses and issues using a specific case study (e.g. Hope and Dickerson 2006a, b, c; Martini 2007).

Bart, Peter (1997) *Cannes: Fifty Years of Sun, Sex & Celluloid: Behind the Scenes at the World's Most Famous Film Festival.* New York: Hyperion.

Beauchamp, Cari and Henri Béhar (1992) *Hollywood on the Riviera: The Inside Story of the Cannes Film Festival.* New York: W. Morrow and Co.

Behnken, Klaus (ed.) (2004) *Kurz und klein: 50 Jahre Internationale Kurzfilmtage Oberhausen.* Ostfildern-Ruit: Hatje Cantz.

Billard, Pierre (1997) *Festival de Cannes: d'Or et de Palmes.* Paris: Gallimard.

Bono, Francesco (1991) 'La Mostra del Cinema di Venezia: Nascita e Sviluppo nell'Anteguerra (1932-1939)', *Storia Contemporanea*, 22, 3, 513-49.

____ (1992) 'Venezia 1932: Il Cinema Diverta Arte', in *Biennale*. Venezia: Fabbri Editori, 91-109.

____ (2001) 'EXTASE am Lido: Chronik eines Skanals', in Armin Loacker (ed.) *Ekstase.* Wien: Filmarchive Austria, 115-45.

Corless, Kieron and Chris Darke (2007) *Cannes: Inside the World's Premier Film Festival.* London: Faber and Faber.

De Baecque, Antoine (ed.) (2007) *Les leçons de cinéma du Festival de Cannes.* Paris: Panama.

Deleau, Pierre-Henri (ed.) (1993) *La Quinzaine des Réalisateurs à Cannes: Cinéma en Liberté (1969-1993).* Paris: Èditions de la Martinière.

Chapter Thirteen

Friers, Pamela (ed.) (1998) *Abgezoomt – das Buch zum Festival: Filme, MacherInnen und Entwürfe*. München: KoPäd-Verlag.

Galliner, Nicola (ed.) (2004) *Jewish Film Festival Berlin: Filme, Bilder, Geschichten. Die ersten 10 Jahre*. Berlin: be.bra-Verlag.

Hope, Cathy and Adam Dickerson (2006a) '"Films for the Intelligent Layman": The Origins of the Sydney and Melbourne Film Festivals (1952-1958)', *Screening the Past*, 19. On-line. Available HTTP: http://www.latrobe.edu.au/screeningthepast/19/sydney-melbourne-film-festivals.html (18 February 2009).

___ (2006b) '"Ill-Will with the Trade": The Sydney and Melbourne Film Festivals (1959-1964)', *Screening the Past*, 20. On-line. Available HTTP: http://www.latrobe.edu.au/screeningthepast/20/sydney-melbourne-film-festivals-1959-1964.html (18 February 2009).

___ (2006c) '"Separating the Sheep from the Goats": The Sydney and Melbourne Film Festivals (1965-1972)', *Screening the Past*, 20. On-line. Available HTTP: http://www.latrobe.edu.au/screeningthepast/20/sydney-melbourne-film-festivals-1965-1972.html (18 February 2009).

Jacobsen, Wolfgang (1990) *Berlinale: Berlin International Film Festival*. Berlin: Deutsche Kinemathek.

___ (ed.) (2000) *50 Jahre Berlinale: Internationale Filmfestspiele Berlin; [1951–2000]*. Berlin: Nicolai.

Kötzing, Andreas (2004) *Die Internationale Leipziger Dokumentar- und Kurzfilmwoche in den 1970er Jahren*. Leipzig: Leipziger Universitäts-Verlag

KurzFilmAgentur (ed.) (2002) *Festschrift 10 Jahre KurzFilmAgentur Hamburg*. Hamburg 2002. On-line. Available HTTP: http://agentur.shortfilm.com/uploads/media/festschrift_KFA.pdf (18 February 2009).

Latil, Loredana (2005) *Le festival de Cannes sur la scène internationale*. Paris: Nouveau Monde.

Manciet, Yves and Jean-Claude Carrière (2004) *Cannes: Premières années du Festival*. Roanne: Thoba's.

Martini, Heidi (2007) *Dokumentarfilm-Festival Leipzig: Filme und Politik im Blick und Gegenblick*. Berlin: DEFA-Stiftung.

McArthur, Colin (1990) 'The Rises and Falls of the Edinburgh International Film Festival', in Eddie Dick (ed.) *From Limelight to Satellite: A Scottish Film Book*. Edinburgh: Scottish Film Council and British Film Institute, 91-102.

Mitterrand, Frédéric (2007) *Le Festival de Cannes*. Paris: Robert Laffont.

Museum of Modern Art (ed.) (1992) *Cannes 45 Years: Festival International du Film*. Published on occasion of the exhibition. New York: Museum of Modern Art.

Pascal, Michel (1997) *Cannes: Cris et Chuchotements*. Paris: N.I.L éditions.

Philippe, Claude-Jean (1987) *Cannes, le festival*. Paris: Nathan Sipa.

Quin, Élisabeth and Noël Simsolo (eds) (2007) *Cannes: Elles/Ils ont Fait le Festival*. Paris: Cahiers du cinéma.

Reinhardt, Thomas (1998) *20 Jahre Filmfestival Max-Ophüls-Preis*. Sulzbach: Moviestore-Co.-Verlag.

Roddolo, Enrica (2003) *La Biennale: Arte, Scandali e Storie in Laguna*. Venezia: Marsilio.

Romer, Jean-Claude (2002) *Cannes Memories 1932-2002: La Grande Histoire du Festival*. Montreuil: Media Business & Partners.

Schenk, Ralf (2007) *Bilder einer gespaltenen Welt: 50 Jahre Leipziger Dokumentar- und Animationsfilmfestival*. Berlin: Bertz+Fischer.

Schröder, Nicholaus (ed.) (2000). *Zwischen Barrikade und Elfenbeinturm: Zur Geschichte des unabhängigen Kinos. 30 Jahre Internationales Forum des Jungen Films*. Freunde der Deutschen Kinemathek. Berlin: Henschel.

Servat, Henry-Jean (2007) *Si le festival de Cannes m'était conté ...* Paris: Filipacchi.

Smith, Lory (1999) *Party in a Box: The Story of the Sundance Film Festival*. Salt Lake City, UT: Gibbs Smith.

Stanfield, Peter (2008) 'Notes Toward a History of the Edinburgh International Film Festival, 1969-77', *Film International*, 6, 4, 62-71.

Toubiana, Serge (1997) *Cannes Cinéma: 50 ans de festival vus par Traverso*. Editions du Seuil.

Uféras, Gérard and Marc Bessou (2005) *Les coulisses du festival: Cannes*. Carlton: Flammarion.

IV. Looking Forward: Research Opportunities

While it is true that film festivals need to be studied in greater detail and with more systematic rigour, it is no longer possible to maintain that there are no comprehensive studies of film festivals available. Our overview and bibliography point to a refreshing and rich academic research practice (albeit a somewhat scattered one) that includes the development of what we may tentatively call film festival theory. However, now that we have a rough understanding of how festivals work (as multifaceted networks, different festivals for various stakeholders etc.), we need to push for the next level: refine our theoretical models, develop more systematic methodologies, try and achieve synergy between disciplines, and reflect on the role of the researcher within the film festival network, especially vis-à-vis and in cooperation with festival professionals.

When we consider the framing of complex phenomena using interdisciplinary approaches as one of the major academic challenges faced in the humanities and social sciences today, the young field of film festival studies looks particularly promising as both vantage point and practice. Located on the nexus of several discourses and practices, current research on film festivals is manifesting itself as a productive path to expand the classical cinema studies agenda and as a fresh ground from which to formulate answers to new (interdisciplinary) questions. In conclusion to this article and our overview of the field of film festival studies we would like to briefly draw attention to four important topics that demand our joint attention and which ought to be the concerns of film festival scholars in the (near) future.

1) Digitisation and Distribution Flows

Over the decades film festivals have been described as an alternative distribution system with different agendas: early European festivals emerged as solution to and in cooperation with hegemonic Hollywood; in the 1960s festivals became safe havens for World Cinema with artistic and political agendas; later festivals were increasingly used as stepping stones for the circulation of (independent) quality films. Time and again, the festival network has adjusted to the demands of the new age. Today, digitisation is posing new challenges to existing festival formats. Research is much needed to assess the effects of emerging digital media platforms on distribution flows. How will festivals reposition themselves? What new relationships will be formed with (commercial) stakeholders? How will this affect festivals' ability to set agendas and add value? Specific research projects could include the tracking of films that travel the festival circuit: How do they accumulate value and attract attention? What are the patterns in the 'paths' that films and filmmakers follow? And what are the effects of awards on distribution and revenues?

2) Festivals as Popular Exhibition Sites

A second important topic for future film festival research concerns exhibition. The number of film festivals worldwide is still expanding and the events have become objects of popular attention. Contrary to the situation of only two decades ago, film festivals attract mass audiences, while regular cinema-going is in decline. Can we understand festivals as a counterweight to the 'death of cinema'? How does the festival exhibition style relate to the larger trend of 'eventisation'? Do we fully comprehend the complex interplay between festivals' local (site-specific) attraction and their global (cosmopolitan) appeal?

3) Programming and Identity Politics

While there has been substantial attention for film festivals in relation to processes of self-identification and community building (in particular for queer festivals), the relation between programming and identity politics remains one of the key fields in film festival research that needs to be further refined. Studies have not yet been synthesised in an overarching theory, and more case studies need to be conducted, especially on festivals in Africa and South-America. Moreover, work on programming – a field that, for cinema studies, has long been neglected and is only approached in museum studies – might bring new insights for spectatorship and reception studies, especially at a time when cinemas are losing their audiences to television and games sets at home.

4) Festivals as/and Creative Industries

Contemporary film festivals are professional institutions run by entrepreneurial managers and smart lobbyists as much as by passionate cinephiles. Cooperation with the industries has become commonplace at large events, and festival markets rival festival competitions as major attractions. Following this trend of professionalisation is a need for research examining the organisational logics of the festival institution in relation to the larger creative (media) industries. Further research needs to be done on the impact the blurring of boundaries has for film festivals, filmmakers, (public) funding structures, and the film industry. Finally, closer interdisciplinary cooperation between cinema departments, business schools, technical universities and copyright experts is necessary to tackle new research questions.

Notes

1. We have included academic as well as journalistic work that has already contributed or is likely to contribute to the study of film festivals. The academic work ranges from articles and book chapters to monographs and anthologies on the topic. Although we are aware of the existence of several interesting MA theses or unpublished conference papers, we opted to leave them out for two practical reasons: limited accessibility and space.
2. The annotated version of this themed bibliography on film festival research has been available online since December 2008:
<http://www1.uni-hamburg.de/Medien/berichte/arbeiten/0091_08.html>.
This article is a reworked and expanded version of the digital publication.
3. All references are listed in the bibliography which is included as chapter three of the article. The section numbers following author and year point to the subchapters of the annotated bibliography.

Chapter Fourteen

The Festival Syndrome: Report on the International Film Festival Workshop, University of St Andrews, 4 April 2009

William Brown

As signalled elsewhere in this volume by Marijke de Valck and Skadi Loist, there is a growing interest in film festivals within academia, an interest that is arguably substantial enough to beg the question: is there need for a new discipline, film festival studies?

It is this question that dominated the first session of the International Film Festival Workshop, hosted by the Centre for Film Studies at the University of St Andrews as part of its *Dynamics of World Cinema* project. With some 35 participants from a range of backgrounds and representing various interests (academia, journalism, film festival organisers, programmers), debate was lively and fast-moving, but for the most part it avoided the circularity and the tendency toward anecdote that are often the inevitable result of roundtable discussions.[1]

Although the consensus seemed to emerge that 'film festival studies' does not require its own discipline, it was felt that it should be recognised as an area of study in its own right; that is, film festivals should receive more academic attention, even if scholars of film festivals do not need to decamp into new a new department.

Such a conclusion may seem merely logical, perhaps even facile, but to discuss whether or not a new discipline ought to be created, or at the very least recognised, is to demand certain pertinent questions, which also formed the core subject of the first session: what *is* film festival studies? what *are* film festivals? In answering these questions, we might find the desired terminology and the conceptual framework for the study of film festivals.

It may seem odd to attempt to answer the question 'what is film festival studies?' before one answers the question 'what are film festivals?', but, perhaps by dint of being a workshop the majority of whose attendants were academics, this is what happened.

Film festival studies are by definition interdisciplinary. Both de Valck and Richard Porton, editor of *Cineaste* magazine, pointed to pre-existing

Report on the International Film Festival Workshop

scholarship by Victor Turner (1975, 1995), whose anthropological / sociological analyses of festivals can serve as a base for defining specifically *film* festivals. However, as Dina Iordanova explained, in addition to anthropology (mention was also made of the work of Daniel Dayan, 2000), the study of film festivals also demands an appreciation of the following overlapping terms/fields, themselves comprising not an exhaustive list:

- cinephilia (why and how people choose to enjoy films through festivals)
- programming as cultural critique/the political economy of film festivals (the choice of films at a festival reflects a certain ideological standpoint, be that entirely coherent or otherwise)
- management and business (how festivals are run economically; what economic function they may serve; the use of concepts such as network theory, field configuration, value added chains, etc.)
- cultural planning (choosing which products and practices enter and shape the cultural landscape)
- creative industries (film festivals as part of an enormous global culture industry, even if there is no single as-yet defined 'film festival industry')
- national/regional/local cultural histories (after the work of such histories of festivals like the studies recently published on Edinburgh IFF by Matthew Lloyd (2008) and Peter Stanfield (2008), whereby film festivals are understood as playing a formative role in a place's cultural history)
- sociology (particularly the study of film festival audiences, as exemplified by the Edinburgh International Film Festival Audiences Conference: http://www.filmaudiencesconference.co.uk/PDFs/programme_2009.pdf
- city planning/tourism (how festivals affect the geography and economy of the location in which they take place)
- cultural diplomacy and cultural policy, as exemplified by the work of scholars like Toby Miller and George Yúdice (2002)
- international relations and political science (film festivals as playing a role in these areas)
- human resources/human rights (Loist in particular raised the issue of the 'precarious' nature of film festival work).

Given this variety of approaches that may help us to understand the perhaps unique range of discourses that the study of film festivals requires (hence de Valck and Loist's provocative call for the recognition of such a field), there does follow the need to define what film festivals themselves are, as Lucy Mazdon pointed out.

Chapter Fourteen

Film festivals are multiple in nature: there are various types of film festival, of various sizes, with various commercial ambitions or otherwise, and aimed at various audiences (see Iordanova in this volume). Stuart Cunningham explained that it is because film festivals are growing in number, that they are dynamic and becoming ever more diverse, that there is a rationale for us to study them. Janet Harbord pointed out, however, that one might make an initial and easy split between film festivals aimed at (certain members of) the public (i.e. anyone can go, even if the festival is marketed, say, as a queer festival) and those 'private' festivals that are only open to accredited individuals/industry members.

Furthermore, in spite of both the diversity of festivals and this inherent split between 'public' and 'private' events, it was felt that certain properties make a film festival unique (that is, make a film festival a film festival).

Nick Roddick, of *Sight & Sound*, felt that film festivals must serve an economic function, and even though he felt that this applied more to the larger, higher profile festivals ('small festivals have no function economically'), this remains as true (except across vastly different scales) for smaller festivals too: every festival, even one that shows films for free, requires funding and expects returns, even if only corollary returns (a council pays a cinema to show films for free but hopes that money will be spent locally to improve trade; it also hopes that some cultural capital is accrued/disbursed).

Roddick also said that film festivals are defined by spectacle, and while this may too often mean the red carpet (i.e. 'grand' spectacle), it perhaps also remains true across all festivals but on vastly different scales, especially if, after Harbord, we conceptualise spectacle through the notion of the event: that is, film festivals as events that are centred around a unique place or space (even if the festival takes place across a city, or in what Marc Augé [1995] might term a 'non-place'), and over a unique time period. By involving, or at least encouraging, this intensification of experience in a limited time and space (be it at Cannes or at Barrow-in-Furness), by demanding a spectator (as Guy Debord [2002: 12] says, a spectator is essential for spectacle), a film festival can be understood as a spectacular event – even if Barrow will never match Cannes for scale of spectacle.

I shall return to the question of time and space shortly, but it is worth lingering on spectacle an instant, for spectacle, as well as relating to discourses of the event, is also based upon myth, as Michael Gubbins of *Screen International* pointed out. That is to say, by demanding a spectator, each film festival tries, after Roland Barthes (1993), to mythologise itself, to connote something more (typically glamour, leisure, prosperity, community or any number of other things) than it actually denotes (a few strips of celluloid receiving light in parallel and/or in succession). Or rather, film festivals, in order to establish themselves as spectacular events, must hide the gap between the supposedly 'natural' image that they seek to create for themselves as spectacular events, and their reality as *manufactured* events

Report on the International Film Festival Workshop

(i.e. the product of labour, including exploitative labour, and thus not 'natural' – if natural things there can be – at all).

With regard to the study of film festivals, this myth factor poses problems: festivals will not divulge, or at least will seek to control, information about themselves (data about festivals is unavailable or at best misleading). This is not simply the revelation of the possible banality of film festivals (being at Cannes and not actually seeing any films), for even these (well-known) aspects of certain, perhaps all, film festivals are always already part of the mythology surrounding them. Rather, this is one of the demands of film festival scholarship: to expose, in the manner of anthropological studies, the very fabricated nature of these mythological and spectacular events, expositions that the events themselves will always resist or at the very least try to influence.

This notion of festivals as mythological is a question of meaning: what are the mechanisms employed by film festivals in order that their 'meaning' appears 'natural' or self-evident? Furthermore, this is, as Saër Maty Bâ and David Slocum noted, a question of ideology and of politics. Film festivals always (seek to) represent something or someone (consciously or not, they reflect an ideology), and they always serve political (and economic) interests, especially for the place in which they take place. This is reflected especially by the tourist aspect of film festivals (Slocum mentioned the Zanzibar International Film Festival as being part of Tanzanian tour packages). Even if, as Irene Bignardi of Filmitalia stated, London and Rome do not need any more tourists than they already have, their film festivals are not independent from politics either, as Gubbins argued, since both the London and Rome International Film Festivals are trying to put these cities on the map of World Cinema (that is their 'meaning'). As Ruby Cheung noted of the Hong Kong International Film Festival, even if a government removes support for a festival (as happened following the handover of Hong Kong from the UK to China in 1997), it still has stakeholders who use it for certain ends. The wrangles and contradictions between stakeholders are what a festival will try to smooth over and present as non-existent (the festival appears to happen spontaneously and 'naturally'). It is these wrangles and contradictions that the scholar of film festivals should try to perceive and understand.

Returning to the notion of the time and space of film festivals, the second session of the workshop was dominated by discussions of the concept of liveness. Harbord (this volume) has theorised that, even if open to the public, film festivals are dictated by the delimitation of time and space (which helps us to differentiate festivals from repertory cinemas, cinema clubs, film seasons on television, film archives, etc). Harbord explains that they are not just manufactured spectacles themselves, but that they also feature spectacular moments (e.g. Sharon Stone making a gaffe about the Chinese earthquake). These suggest 'liveness' via the interruption of 'reality', via contingency or the accident. Paradoxically, this 'liveness' (the fact that these spectacular moments are happening in 'real' time) is dependent upon mediation: it is only because such events, be they the festival as a whole or fragments of the festival, are seen and recorded (i.e. mediated) that they are believed to be 'live'. There is, then, a positive feedback loop of mediation: Stone's 'gaffe' can be either intended or accidental, but even if it had not taken place, *something* happening at the festival would have been mythologised via mediation, not least because the media want (and will have budgeted for) column inches and screen time dedicated to these spectacular event-festivals in the first place. In other words, the festival demands media coverage and the media demand news/stories, so a spectacle will be manufactured regardless of whether or not Stone is canny or dumb enough to grab (some of) the attention for herself in the process.

Borrowing (but hopefully without misappropriating) Paul Virilio's concept of dromology (1997) might also be useful here to help us to conceptualise film festivals. If one thinks of the velodrome or the hippodrome, then we can understand the organisation of spaces into places where events, especially spectacular events, are held. The velodrome and the hippodrome are predicated of course upon movement ('drome' coming from the Greek equivalent of 'to run'). But where perhaps once there was the potential for free movement (bicycles and horses could take us anywhere) within the dromosphere (that area where bicycles and horses are run), we now observe horses and bicycles going round in circles. Movement has been contained and turned into spectacle. Similarly, might we not say that the film festival turns the potentially free-wheeling aspect of the circulation of films into a cine-drome – a confined space where films are 'run' intensely (and sometimes in competition), and over a short and defined period of time? When films are brought together in the way that happens in festivals, might we not call this a *syndrome* (things, events, actions are grouped together) – syndrome also being an apt term for the pattern of symptoms that reveals a particular condition? The festival syndrome, to paraphrase Zimmermann and Hess (1999), sees public performance counteract the loneliness of the long distance cinema goer. Inevitably, I put forward the 'festival cindrome' as a term that perhaps evokes the manufactured spectacle/liveness (the performance of liveness) that lies at the heart of the concentrated space and time of the film festival.

To continue on this theoretical bent, in a bid further to refine what a festival is or might be, we might compare the controlled spectacle of the festival, this cin-/syndrome, to the carnival as theorised by Mikhail Bakhtin (1968). In brief: a festival is a feast of consumption, which lends itself to the seemingly common culinary metaphors that accompany film festivals. However, feasts/festivals are carefully prepared – they are manufactured spectacles. A carnival, meanwhile, is based on the flesh (carne) of the participants and it involves the reversal of established hierarchies. Even if only mock-revolutionary (in that it is only for a day that the poor play rich and vice versa, thereby reaffirming the established hierarchy for the remaining 364 days of the year), carnivals suggest, at least etymologically, more 'liveness' (live flesh), more chaos, more 'raw' reality (crudeness), and more

Report on the International Film Festival Workshop

possibility for genuine rather than manufactured accidents than does the notion of the festival (festival as syndrome).

At the workshop, Núria Triana Toribio pointed out the community feeling that many or all film festivals might evoke, which does suggest both liveness ('we are here together'), and maybe even the carnival nature of the festival dromosphere (people go to the cinema for a short and intensive burst, justifying not going to the cinema at other times). But the way in which this state of 'carnival'/liveness is induced at the film festival does suggest that a 'manufactured' festival is not quite a carnival, not least because the film festival demands a mediating spectator. By which I mean: written into the very phrase 'I was there', this phrase that we pursue ('I will be able to say that I was there'), suggests the paradoxical, if not infuriating, nature of liveness: it is always in the past ('was') or the future ('will be able'), or it is always elsewhere ('there'). 'I am here ...' may be the words that TV reporters can pronounce from the red carpet, but we only hear these words when mediated by the TV news programme. 'Liveness' and community may be central to film festivals (although not exclusive to them; could this not be part of the cinema experience as a whole?), but to define them as 'real' or 'more real' than the rest of life (which seems to be the implication) is problematic: at festivals, we are always in the prefabricated. Only at carnivals might there be the (vain) possibility for the accident that brings about true change (revolution).

In addition to the 'live' time of festivals, Mazdon suggested the need to historicise film festivals if we are to understand them: what initially may have inspired the creation of the Cannes Film Festival is not necessarily what governs its existence today, and we must take this into account when studying festivals.

This second session also took in the related question of whether film festivals function as a distribution or exhibition network, prompting Bignardi to say that few festivals require new films, but that those festivals that do also enter into fierce competition with each other, since there are not enough good new films each year to fill each festival with a full programme. This then led to the suggestion that there are too many festivals for the number of films available (see also Cousins, this volume). This argument, however, does not necessarily take into account the possibility that, while films might be seen by a few people on the 'festival circuit', it is only through the proliferation of non-circuit film festivals, through the festival becoming syndrome in the sense of reflecting a wider social 'condition', that well-known (if not brand new) films, as well as retrospectives, can come to other, more diverse places and find other, more diverse audiences. Furthermore, these audiences will see these films *in a cinema*, a point implicitly raised by Slocum in his theorisation of festivals in Africa as a form of 'temporary archive' of African films that otherwise do not get theatrical exhibition. Nor does the notion of 'too many festivals' take into account the possibility that this will foster more film production, which will in turn foster the possibility of more 'good' films, since competition and diversity are surely to be encouraged in favour of the instigation of a minority of monopolistic 'major' festivals. As much was reflected in John Orr's optimistic invocation of James Gleick's (2000) 'acceleration of everything' as being potentially beneficial to cinema/film festivals.

While film festivals generally do not (yet) distribute films, even if they lend their names via awards to the commercial distribution of certain films, and even if travelling film festivals suggest the potential for festivals-as-distributors (and thus no longer festivals proper?), they do exhibit films (although there is a risk/problem, as Porton made clear, that adventurous films become ghettoised within film festivals/the festival 'circuit', not making it into wider distribution). However, one might contend that, beyond the distribution/exhibition binarism, in an age when most films are watched not at the cinema but on DVD, and when even a wide theatrical release is conceptualised as the extended trailer for the DVD of a film, festivals are themselves also (not so extended) trailers for DVDs (and other ancillary markets, which are especially important for certain kinds of films, such as documentaries, as Leshu Torchin pointed out). The festival then, by being 'live' and a communal experience (not just sitting at home watching DVDs, even if in intense 'marathons'), one that is more intense (many films in a certain space and over a short period of time) than perhaps 'regular' cinema-going, both advertises the DVD and stands as an alternative to it and to regular cinema. The festival is a combination of community, 'liveness' *and* intensity, both in terms of time (short period, lots of films) and space (in the same cinema or cinemas in a certain location). All of these characteristics are characteristics of the festival as syndrome, of the festival syndrome.

Roddick raised the issue of a top-down as opposed to a bottom-up understanding of film festivals in the second session, and this perhaps influenced the discussions of the third session, which dealt with the methodologies of studying film festivals. Mazdon proposed that film festival studies, like film studies itself, should emerge from the bottom up, in the same way that the definition(s) of film festivals should emerge through particular case studies. However, it was felt that perhaps something of an overview (top-down because 'over' view) might help to solidify the boundaries of film festival studies. This process might in itself, through the very event that was this workshop, involve a spectacularisation or mythologisation ('I was there') of film festival studies as arriving 'naturally' and already 'whole'. As the bibliography (or taxonomy?) provided by de Valck and Loist makes clear, however, film festival studies, if it is worthy of the name, has emerged from a multiplicity of sources.

Cunningham called for the need to build lateral as well as vertical research agendas: 'bringing in' people from urban planning, cultural politics, anthropology, management, etc., as well as simply carrying out further studies of film festivals. This push for growth was further recognised by the need perhaps to collaborate with journalists (represented here by Gubbins, Porton and Roddick), with filmmakers, and with film festivals themselves (the 'friendlier' film festivals, at any rate). Furthermore, Loist suggested that there must be an ethical dimension to the study of film festivals: that is, to recognise the need not to compromise one's independence through the intrusion into the field of other, vested interests or 'stakeholders', stakeholders who may compromise the scholar's ability thoroughly to discuss certain practices, e.g. the unpaid labour at the heart of many film festivals. Lindiwe Dovey added to this by mentioning the political-ethical dimension of film festivals themselves: in Africa, festivals represent perhaps the last opportunity for a cinema of diversity in the face of the behemoth that is Nollywood. Toribio pointed to the role that festivals might play in film production, as well as to the need for looking at festivals in Latin America and, by extension, other under-studied regions featuring film festivals (Iordanova mentioned the idiosyncratic political agendas of the Tashkent and Havana festivals). Harbord mentioned the need to look at 'low end' and amateur festivals, and Mazdon mentioned the possibility of including awards ceremonies within the field of film festival studies. Gubbins, meanwhile, mentioned the potential for digital technologies to influence cinema.

It is with the digital in mind that I shall close this summary of the International Film Festival Workshop. Gubbins posited that digital has the potential to be a new 'punk' movement, and on the level of production he is correct (even if the size and power of distributors and exhibitors makes the *cinematic* (i.e. theatrical) life of such films hard to imagine, except in a few, exceptional cases). What does digital technology mean for film festivals, though? Or rather, can there be a digital film festival, one that is not simply the celebration of digitally made films via digital projection, but the consumption of films in a digital/online environment? Can a film festival in *Second Life* lay claim to the apparent 'liveness' of a 'real' festival, even if it is as 'intense' and communal an experience? Can a website offering a range of films for a certain period of time similarly still be called a 'festival'? Would this, paradoxically, be too revolutionary (carnivalesque?) a festival to be worthy of the name? As a workshop designed not to answer questions, but rather to raise the questions in order to point out future directions for work on film festivals, the International Film Festival Workshop was a great success. What seems obvious in hindsight, however, was that more events like it need to be arranged so that we can try to answer (and ask) more questions, such as questions about the digital, about this phenomenon, film festivals, that all who attended, journalists and academics alike, felt is too significant a phenomenon to continue to be ignored.

Note

[1] Attendees at the International Film Festival Workshop, University of St Andrews, 4 April 2009, included: David Archibald (University of Glasgow), Saër Maty Bâ (University of St Andrews), Irene Bignardi (Filmitalia),

William Brown (University of St Andrews), Felicia Chan (University of Manchester), Yun-hua Chen (University of St Andrews), Ruby Cheung (University of St Andrews), Stuart Cunningham (Queensland University of Technology), Marijke de Valck (University of Amsterdam), Lindiwe Dovey (SOAS, University of London), Robert Duffin (University of Glasgow), Thomas Gerstenmeyer (University of St Andrews), Michael Gubbins (*Screen International*), Janet Harbord (Goldsmiths College, University of London), Yun Mi Hwang (University of St Andrews), Dina Iordanova (University of St Andrews), Tina Lee (University of St Andrews), Matthew Lloyd (independent), Skadi Loist (Universität Hamburg), Lucy Mazdon (University of Southampton), Emily Munro (Glasgow Film Theatre), John Orr (University of Edinburgh), Dorota Ostrowska (Birkbeck College, University of London), Serazer Pekerman (University of St Andrews), Richard Porton (*Cineaste*), Nick Roddick (*Sight & Sound*), Melanie Selfe (University of Glasgow), David Slocum (Berlin School of Creative Leadership, Steinbeis University), Victoria Thomas (Napier University), Leshu Torchin (University of St Andrews), Núria Triana Toribio (University of Manchester), Spela Zajec (University of St Andrews), Apple Zhang (independent).

Works Cited

Augé, Marc (1995) *Non-places: Introduction to an Anthropology of Supermodernity*, trans. John Howe. London: Verso.

Bakhtin, Mikhail (1968) *Rabelais and His World*, trans. Hélène Iswolsky. Cambridge, Mass.: MIT Press.

Barthes, Roland (1993) *Mythologies*, trans. Annette Lavers. London: Vintage.

Dayan, Daniel (2000) 'Looking for Sundance: The Social Construction of a Film Festival, in Ib Bondebjerg (ed.) *Moving Images, Culture and the Mind*. Luton: University of Luton Press, 43-52.

Debord, Guy (2002) *Society of the Spectacle*, trans. Donald Nicholson-Smith. New York: Zone Books.

Gleick, James (2000) *Faster: The Acceleration of Just About Everything*. London: Vintage.

John Hess and Patricia R Zimmermann (1999) 'Transnational Digital Imaginaries', *Wide Angle*, 21, 149-67.

Lloyd, Matthew (2008) *How the Movie Brats Took Over Edinburgh: The Impact of Cinephilia on Edinburgh International Film Festival, 1968-1980*, unpublished MSc dissertation, University of Edinburgh.

Miller, Toby and George Yúdice (2002) *Cultural Policy*. London: Sage Publications.

Stanfield, Peter (2008) 'Notes Toward a History of the Edinburgh International Film Festival 1969-1977', *Film International*, 6, 4, 62-71.

Turner, Victor (ed.) (1975) *Drama, Fields, and Metaphors: Symbolic Action in Human Society*. Ithaca/London: Cornell University Press.

___ (1995) *The Ritual Process: Structure and Anti-structure*. New York: Aldine de Gruyter.

Virilio, Paul (1997) *Open Sky*, trans. Julie Rose. London: Verso.